Further Praise for *The Handbook of Market Intelligence*

"In an interconnected world where boundaries between markets, industries and consumers evolve with increasing speed, this book provides a very useful and practical framework to guide the development of a Market Intelligence function that serves as a tool for competitive advantage. The use of multiple and diverse business cases helps readers to understand the implementation of key concepts and provides a set of practical lessons to facilitate this important journey for any organization."

**—Carlos Jose Fonseca, Senior Business Leader
International Markets Strategy, MasterCard**

"Forward looking market understanding is what any CEO needs for securing successful business today and into the future. But how does one manage that in a global organization with thousands of employees? This book neatly lays out the steps to turn systematic Market Intelligence from an ideal to everyday reality. I particularly liked the numerous case examples that demonstrate how different and, at the same time, similar to the Market Intelligence challenges are for companies around the world, regardless of their industry."

—Harri Kerminen, Former President and CEO, Kemira

"We've used GIA's Key Success Factors (KSFs) framework as we've analyzed our own Intelligence function. It is a very easy way to allow your function to become self-aware, identify your gaps and then build your capabilities in an on-purpose fashion. The KSFs language of 'Firefighters to Futurists' makes sense to people outside of an Intelligence function as well, helping your Intelligence function paint a picture of your impact to the organization."

**—Phil Britton, Market Intelligence Lead,
Competitive Strategies Group, Best Buy**

"The authors have presented a diverse look at Market Intelligence based on their experiences garnered from consulting projects with many firms around the globe. The book combines theoretical issues underlying Market Intelligence with proven real-life case examples. Many specific applications of Market Intelligence are addressed, including strategic planning, marketing and sales, product life cycle management, supply chain management and the multifaceted social media. The book's projected trends in Market Intelligence towards 2015 give lots of food for thought. This professional book would be a good addition to the library of any Market Intelligence practitioner and those who are involved in strategic planning."

**—Dr David Blenkhorn, Ph.D., Wilfrid Laurier University,
Waterloo, Ontario, Canada**

"In my experience, there's no shortage of books that advise the reader on analysis techniques and the correct phases of a solid intelligence process – all relevant for Market Intelligence development, however on a rather detailed level. What I've been missing so far is an umbrella view that addresses all elements of Market Intelligence development in a structured and approachable fashion. This book provides that."

—Henning Heinrich, Vice President Market Intelligence,
T-Systems International

"Comprehensive, practical, to the point; a must-read for any strategy, marketing and intelligence director!"

—Anders Marvik, Vice President, Corporate Strategy, Statoil

The Handbook of Market Intelligence

Second Edition

Understand, Compete and Grow in Global Markets

**Hans Hedin,
Irmeli Hirvensalo,
Markko Vaarnas**

WILEY

This edition first published 2014
Copyright © 2014 Hans Hedin, Irmeli Hirvensalo and Markko Vaarnas
First edition published 2011 by John Wiley & Sons, Ltd.

Registered office
John Wiley and Sons Ltd, The Atrium, Southern Gate, Chichester, West Sussex, PO19 8SQ, United Kingdom

For details of our global editorial offices, for customer services and for information about how to apply for permission to reuse the copyright material in this book please see our website at www.wiley.com.

Library of Congress Cataloging-in-Publication Data
Hedin, Hans.
    The handbook of market intelligence : understand, compete and grow in global markets / Hans Hedin, Irmeli Hirvensalo, Markko Vaarnas.—2nd Edition.
        pages   cm
    Includes bibliographical references and index.
    ISBN 978-1-118-92362-7 (cloth : alk. paper)   1. Business intelligence.   2. Marketing research.   3. Business intelligence—Case studies.   4. Marketing research—Case studies.   I. Hirvensalo, Irmeli.   II. Vaarnas, Markko.   III. Title.
HD38.7.H44   2014
658.8'3—dc23   2014013528

A catalogue record for this book is available from the British Library.

ISBN 978-1-118-92362-7 (hardback)   ISBN 978-1-118-92361-0 (ebk)
ISBN 978-1-118-92360-3 (ebk)

Set in 9.5/13pt GillSansStd-Light by MPS Limited, Chennai, India
Printed in Great Britain by CPI Group (UK) Ltd, Croydon, CR0 4YY

Contents

Preface to the Second Edition vii

About the Authors ix

About Global Intelligence Alliance xi

PART I
Market Intelligence in Global Organizations   1

  I   Market Intelligence: Drivers and Benefits 3

  2   Market Intelligence in Global Organizations:
       Survey Findings in 2013 21

PART 2
Roadmap to World Class Market Intelligence   51

  3   Key Success Factors of World Class Market Intelligence 53

  4   Intelligence Scope – Determining the Purpose, Target Groups,
       and Focus Areas of an Intelligence Program 63

  5   Intelligence Process – Turning Random Data
       into Meaningful Insight 77

  6   Intelligence Deliverables – Building a High-Impact
       Market Intelligence Product Portfolio 87

  7   Intelligence Tools – Collecting, Storing, and Disseminating
       Intelligence 101

  8   Intelligence Organization – The People and Resources
       that Generate the Impact 115

  9   Intelligence Culture – Engaging the Organization
       in Market Intelligence 131

PART 3
Market Intelligence for Key User Groups   141

  10   Market Intelligence for Current Awareness Across
       the Organization 143

  11   Market Intelligence for Strategic Planning 157

12   Market Intelligence for Marketing, Sales,
     and Account Management... 175

13   Market Intelligence for Innovation and Product Life Cycle
     Management 189

14   Market Intelligence for Supply Chain Management 203

PART 4
Developing World Class Market Intelligence Programs   215

15   Implementing Market Intelligence Programs.................... 217

16   How to Develop an Existing Market Intelligence Program
     for Greater Impact 227

17   Demonstrating the Impact of Market Intelligence 241

18   Trends in Market Intelligence 253

Index 267

Preface to the Second Edition

The Handbook of Market Intelligence — Understand, Compete and Grow in Global Markets summarizes almost 20 years' worth of our experience in working together with global companies to build world class MI programs. The Handbook has grown from the consultative thinking that we first started marketing as GIA's thought-leading White Papers at around year 2000. Subsequently, we have also built the lessons learned over the course of the years into the GIA World Class Market Intelligence Roadmap that has been adopted by numerous global companies as a tool for both strategic and operative MI development.

It's almost exactly three years since the first edition of *The Handbook of Market Intelligence* was published in June 2011. Its reception has been enthusiastic among executives, seasoned MI professionals, and freshmen alike, and it has been thanked for both its MI development frameworks and the pragmatic, hands-on case examples.

A lot of the content in *The Handbook of Market Intelligence* is not particularly time-sensitive. Developing world class corporate MI programs is largely about influencing human behavior, establishing new practices and nurturing an intelligence culture. These things don't change overnight, and many of the book's chapters are as current today as they were in 2011.

At the same time, MI programs and priorities in global companies do evolve, and new best practices emerge. We have therefore updated the second chapter in this book with the latest, 2013 research results from GIA's Global Market Intelligence Survey. The survey yielded a record number of 1,207 responses globally, and it provides an unparalleled overview of how MI is being implemented today in global companies across industries. The updated chapter two also compares the 2013 Global MI Survey results to those in 2011, highlighting differences and essential developments in how global companies conduct MI activities.

Out of the many components that make up world class MI programs, IT tools are currently evolving as fastest. Microsoft's SharePoint has become a de facto standard platform in global organizations for the corporate intranet, and SharePoint also offers many of the features and functionalities that traditional MI software applications do. Because many IT departments in global companies today are keen to achieve cost efficiencies and to reduce the number of different software applications in use in the company, MI tools are emerging that have been built directly on SharePoint. Chapter seven about Intelligence Tools has been updated to discuss these developments in more detail.

How the value and benefits of systematic MI efforts can be demonstrated is an enduring topic among MI professionals and budget holders. Much like marketing or other corporate support functions, MI can be measured with different sets of Key Performance Indicators. However, the eventual impact of MI efforts on the company's performance usually blends in with the impact of many other influencing factors, and it's often hard to point out afterwards exactly how much MI contributed. We have added an entirely new chapter seventeen on demonstrating the impact of MI that discusses this interesting topic. Specifically, we have approached the topic from the perspectives of i) the readiness of decision-makers to adopt and direct MI efforts, ii) the financial ROI calculations for MI efforts, and iii) the long term, "soft" benefits of MI that cannot be quantified in exact terms.

In addition to the above described updates, we have updated minor parts of the content throughout the book to ensure the continued full relevancy of the content in this new edition.

The material for this book has been developed over years through hands-on work with GIA's clients and in the back office. Hence, we are extremely grateful to all our clients for their genuine interest in working together with us, searching for excellence in MI. Our clients have had a key role in developing the content of this book through openly sharing their own best practices, challenging them, and being open-minded towards developing and adopting new ones. What's more, we have had the pleasure of working with countless individuals that are both respected professionals and great persons, which has been both fun and very rewarding.

Of our colleagues at GIA we want to first thank the entire GIA Group – so many current and past GIA employees have contributed to the ideas that we're presenting that it would be impossible to list out all of them. For direct contribution to the book's content we thank Hans Kjellberg, Aleksi Grym, Rahul Dhingra, Victor Knip and Jouko Virtanen in particular, and also extend our specific thank you to Pete Read for first establishing the "Understand, Compete and Grow" concept.

Finally, this book would be much less interesting without its practical case studies, for which we are most grateful to Michel Bernaiche from Dunkin' Brands, Philip Britton from Best Buy, Daniel Pascheles from Merck & Co., Terry Thiele from Lubrizol, Jan Brooijmans from Randstad Nederland, Joost Drieman from Cisco Systems, Andrew Beurschgens from Everything Everywhere, Troy Pfeffer from Cintas, Robin Kirkby from Nycomed, René Loozen from Royal Vopak, Fredrik Vejgarden from Luvata, Anders Marvik from Statoil, Julian Stocks from Rettig, Luis Madureira from Sociedade Central de Cervejas e Bebidas (SCC) – Group Heineken, Ubald Kragten from DSM and Daniel Niederer from ABB, with whom it has been a great pleasure to work on this book project.

Hans Hedin

Irmeli Hirvensalo

Markko Vaarnas

Helsinki, June 2014

About the Authors

Hans Hedin is an expert and consultant in the field of Market and Competitive Intelligence. He has conducted hundreds of Market Intelligence (MI) development and implementation projects for international organizations in Europe, the Middle East, USA, South America, and Asia. Examples include MI product development, organizing and optimizing the MI function, Early Warning Systems, strategic workshops such as war/future games, and scenario analysis. Hedin is also a recognized speaker at international intelligence conferences such as SCIP and IIR, and he has chaired the most recent GIA Conferences in Europe and North America.

Hans Hedin has had a leading role in building up the Global Intelligence Alliance Network. It consists of over 100 GIA Member and GIA Research Partner companies and over 1,000 freelance consultants around the world. Through his global network, Hedin has earned a reputation as one of the most networked persons in the global intelligence industry.

Between 1992 and 1997, Hans Hedin taught and conducted Competitive Intelligence (CI) research at Lund University together with professor Stevan Dedijer, the "grandfather" of intelligence. Hedin's area of research focused on how international companies were organizing their intelligence activities. He is still a popular guest lecturer at academic institutions such as The Royal School of Engineers Executive School, Stockholm School of Economics, Lund University, as well as Stockholm University at undergraduate, MBA and executive education levels.

Early on in his career Hans Hedin worked for Nordea, one of the largest Scandinavian banks, where he developed software for conducting industry and company analysis. He has also been a partner at Docere Intelligence, another intelligence consulting firm.

Hans Hedin was the SCIP Sweden Chapter Coordinator between 1999 and 2003 and is now a Management Board Member of the newly started Journal of Intelligence Studies in Business. He has authored *Corporate Intelligence* (in Swedish, 2006) and *Intelligence in Sweden 1638–2006* (*Journal of Competitive Intelligence*, SCIP 2006), and co-authored the GIA White Paper Series (2003–2011).

Hans Hedin earned his Master's degree from the University of Lund in 1993, having also studied Information Management at the University of St. Gallen. Hedin is married and has three children.

Irmeli Hirvensalo worked for GIA Group during the years 2001–2012, gaining exposure to best practices in MI in a variety of roles: Conducting strategic analysis assignments, leading MI workshops and consulting projects, managing client relationships, speaking at seminars and webinars, as well as working on strategic MI concepts and the related marketing messages. In 2012, Hirvensalo joined Ahlstrom Corporation, a fiber-based materials company, as Market Insights Manager, and is now putting MI concepts and approaches into practice by herself.

From early on, Irmeli Hirvensalo was involved in producing GIA Group's thought-leading White Papers that are very much at the core of the company's consultative approach to Strategic Market Intelligence. As most of the GIA White Papers created over the years have been a team effort by Markko Vaarnas, Hans Hedin and Hirvensalo herself, writing *The Handbook of Market Intelligence* together was a natural continuum of that work. In addition to this book, Hirvensalo is a co-author of the book *Market Information in the Internationalization of Companies*, published by the Finnish Institute for International Trade (FINTRA) in 2005.

Irmeli Hirvensalo earned her Master's degree (Financial Economics) in 2000 from the Helsinki School of Economics. She is married and has two children.

Markko Vaarnas is one of the founders of Global Intelligence Alliance Group (GIA), a company founded in 1995 specializing in customized MI solutions. Vaarnas has been the CEO of GIA Group since the beginning, leading the development and global expansion of the company into an organization with offices around the world.

The expansion of GIA Group's global footprint grows from the vision that Vaarnas and his colleagues had when establishing the company in 1995: Global companies need a reliable, highly insightful and large enough partner for organizing and operating their daily intelligence activities, an increasingly crucial and demanding task in today's turbulent market environment. Executing on the strategy to reach this vision, Vaarnas has worked with countless business leaders around the world to map out their intelligence needs, establish the teams and processes required to address those needs, and leverage the resulting MI program for impact on decision-making.

A SCIP (Society of Competitive Intelligence Professionals) member since 1998, Markko Vaarnas has presented in numerous international seminars and training events, while leading consulting projects in Europe, USA and Asia. In addition to this book, he is a co-author of the book *Market Information in the Internationalization of Companies*, published by the Finnish Institute for International Trade (FINTRA) in 2005.

Prior to co-founding GIA Group, Vaarnas did academic research in the field of MI and earned his Master's degree (International Business) from the Helsinki School of Economics in 1998.

Markko Vaarnas is married and has three children. During his leisure time, he coaches junior soccer teams and reads business literature.

About Global Intelligence Alliance

Global Intelligence Alliance (GIA) helps companies set up and develop world class market intelligence (MI) programs. In addition to consulting and software tools, we provide strategic research, analysis and advisory for decision making. With the proprietary knowledge GIA has developed over time, we serve our clients using world class intelligence best practices and a strong client mindset.

GIA was established in 1995 by a team of MI specialists, management consultants, industry analysts and technology experts. Since the beginning, we have differentiated ourselves with our Intelligence PartnershipTM approach. Our service offering covers the entire range of MI requirements, and today we are the preferred partner for organizations seeking to understand, compete and grow in international markets. Our industry expertise and coverage of over 100 countries enables our customers to make better informed decisions worldwide.

To learn more about GIA's global clients or career opportunities, or to sign up for events and to subscribe to the thought-leading GIA White Papers and Bulletins, visit **www.globalintelligence.com**.

PART I

Market Intelligence in Global Organizations

I **Market Intelligence: Drivers and Benefits** 3
Understand, Compete and Grow – The Decision-Maker's
    Challenge 3
Market Intelligence: Turning Data into Insight 8
About This Book 17

2 **Market Intelligence in Global Organizations:**
   Survey Findings in 2013 21
Introduction 21
How the Survey Was Conducted 22
State of Market Intelligence in Global Companies in 2013 24
Industry Comparison 36
Companies with World Class MI Functions 38
Market Intelligence in B2B and B2C Companies 43
Summary 47

Market Intelligence: Drivers and Benefits

UNDERSTAND, COMPETE AND GROW – THE DECISION-MAKER'S CHALLENGE

ANOTHER DECISION AHEAD

On another busy morning in a large international apparel company, two executives are sitting in a meeting room, having agreed on a planning session in preparation for the upcoming strategic planning workshop. Their challenge is to come up with a preliminary market entry strategy to Brazil that seems to provide lucrative business opportunities among the growing middle class population. Indeed some of the company's competitors have already established a presence in Latin American countries, with varying degrees of success.

Knowing the complications of the task ahead, the executives have decided to first compile a list of questions that they will need an answer to before they can formulate a market entry strategy. Who are the potential customers; what are the demographics, and how does the local culture shape the habits and preferences of people with regards to clothing? Where does the competition come from, and are the competitors making money? What about the local legislation and interest groups; who are the local players that should be taken into account? What are the primary trends affecting local consumer behavior, and how vulnerable is the market to economic or political disruptions? How differentiated should the market entry strategies be for different countries in Latin America? And the list goes on.

The questions to strategic decision-makers are hardly new, yet the executives find themselves putting their best effort into trying to make sense of the unknown territory that they have set their eyes on. The company's executive team and indeed the shareholders would expect to see a winning strategy that will help the company enter a new market, compete successfully in it, and grow its revenue, profits, and brand value as a result.

THE MARKETPLACE IS GETTING INCREASINGLY COMPLEX

Companies operating in the global marketplace derive their revenue from an increasingly complex set of local markets, and the executives in our example above are not alone with their challenge: to be able to compete and grow, there's a lot to build an understanding about. In the Global Market Intelligence Surveys conducted by GIA, executive and professional respondents have listed out opportunities and threats that frequently top the agendas of executive decision-makers:

Opportunities

- Mergers & Acquisitions

- Winning market share from competition

- Expanding into new markets geographically or product-wise

- Finding innovative business models

- Spotting new demand for products and services

- Generating new partnerships

Threats

- Price erosion

- New competitors entering the market

- Emerging business models

- Consolidation or fragmentation of the value chain

- Limited understanding of the current trends

- Changing customer behavior

Looking at the list of remarkably broad and strategic topics, it is easy to see why competitiveness and growth can only be driven by an understanding of the business environment: every single opportunity and threat that the survey respondents brought up involves a number of market players, industries and trends, and a number of complicated interdependencies between them.

While the operating environment of any global organization nowadays is complex and multidimensional, it can be analyzed in a structured fashion. In Figure 1.1, we present a model to map out the operating environment of an organization in a straightforward, yet comprehensive way. Although the model is simplistic, or even because of that, it has proved its usefulness in companies across different industries.

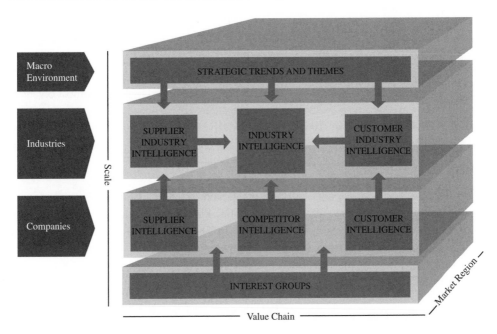

Figure 1.1   The operating environment of global organizations is complex and multidimensional

Every organization is part of a value chain within which it has customers, potentially customers' customers, different types of competitors, and suppliers. In a typical scenario, the organization also needs to work with a number of interest groups, such as legislators, government bodies, and trade unions.

The individual market players alone will make up a complex operating environment: some of the players are old and well established, others are emerging either with new business models or services, or they are simply entering the market as newcomers. In addition to providing different business models and substituting products and services, some of the market players may also be seeking growth by forming partnerships or integrating forwards or backwards along the value chain. Finally, the interest groups also bring about changes and developments in the marketplace that the organization needs to stay aware of.

The individual suppliers, competitors, and customers along the value chain make up clusters and *industries*, the dynamics of which the company will also need to understand (going up the vertical axis in Figure 1.1). To be able to maintain a forward-looking strategy, understanding the current and future developments, especially in the customer segments and industries, will be necessary for any organization. Technologies and business models in one industry easily also transfer over to the neighboring one, generating trends.

Trends and megatrends, in turn will expand the scale further still, as they will be the drivers of business opportunities and threats beyond the immediate future. Again, trends add to the complexity of the operating environment, as organizations should understand not only the obvious high level developments currently surrounding them but also those, potentially distant-looking, trends and megatrends that may cause surprises and/or generate threats and opportunities in the more far-reaching future.

Finally, while some of the players and trends in the marketplace are truly global, for most organizations, each geographical area in which they have operations will introduce a distinct group of local suppliers, competitors, customers, and interest groups that will need to be understood both in the local business units and to some extent in the headquarters. Some trends of course may be local as well, further adding to the list of topics to be kept under radar.

In sum, the operating environment of a global organization is indeed complex; however, the elements in it can be arranged into a structured set of market players, industries, trends, and geographical areas. The list of topics may become very long though, and, to capitalize on the many opportunities for growth that the marketplace provides, the organization will need to put considerable effort into managing the information that will enable future-oriented decision-making.

Change is the Only Constant

The elements in a global organization's operating environment are multidimensional enough without the aspect of time; however, in a dynamic world changes will naturally occur in all areas of the operating environment. Change, too, can come from different directions: competitive moves in the industry, changes in customer preferences, changes in technology, and evolving megatrends.

The recent years have provided numerous practical examples of change in the operating environment to which organizations have needed to react. Some have been able to capitalize on growth opportunities, gain market share, or form new partnerships, while for others being once caught in an unpleasant surprise may even have marked the start of a new era in managing business information in a systematic manner.

Figure 1.2 highlights examples of recent developments and events that have had an impact on organizations across industries and geographies. These topics have presented themselves to organizations as either opportunities or threats, depending largely on how well the facts have been understood and turned into successful decisions.

- **The rise of China and the Chinese companies** has been under the radar of most global companies and public organizations for years already. However, what many Western organizations still do not have much knowledge of is the impact of Chinese companies entering their traditional home turf, either through mergers and acquisitions or other forms of business. Some may think of this as a threat, but the phenomenon will also generate tremendous opportunities for many. Whichever the case, and indeed to find out what it might be, the first thing for organizations outside of China to do is to build insight about the topic and turn it into successful decisions.

- The **growing middle class in emerging economies** will present tremendous growth opportunities for countless companies in different industries, as these

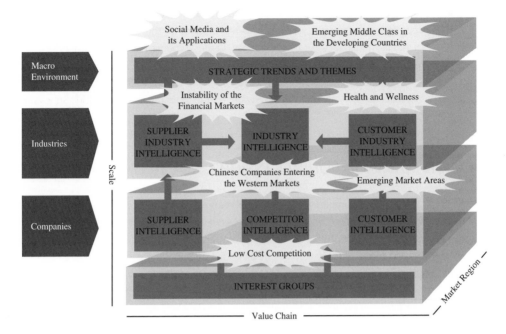

Figure 1.2 Changes are constantly happening in different parts of the operating environment

consumers adopt the habits of traditional Western consumers: they will fly and drive, they will need household appliances, computers and mobile phones, they will go to gyms and restaurants, and they will use services ranging from laundry to interior design. As a group of customers, the emerging middle class is new to most potential suppliers, hence lots of effort to understand their preferences and behavior is in order.

- The **financial crisis** took full effect in late 2008 and has since been discussed and analyzed immensely; however, it is still a very good example of how developments in the marketplace can surprise companies and cause remarkable damage. Even though most companies were not in a position to prevent the crisis or even influence it in any way (rather, the crisis uncontrollably influenced them either through direct actions of other market players or perhaps through shifting trends), some companies emerged from the subsequent recession stronger than others. For many of the "winners", having already included the financial crisis in the possible future scenarios likely provided a competitive edge at least after the initial market shakeout, as they had already made action plans for such a scenario.

- **Health and wellness** is a megatrend that is now expanding from being "luxurious fun" of a limited segment of consumers to being even a prerequisite for employment or at least career advancement in some parts of the business world. What this means for the business, not only for the health and wellness sector but also for the recruitment services industry, food industry, or, for instance, media and publishing should be on the radar of companies in these industries.

- By now, **social media applications** are familiar to most in the business world, yet countless companies still struggle to make sense of the opportunities and threats of social media to their own business. Understanding topics that range from the features of certain technical applications to psychology of the masses would present sizable business opportunities for not only consumer businesses, but also, for instance, hi-tech companies that want to tap into their organization's innovation capability.

DECISION-MAKING REQUIRES INSIGHT, NOT JUST INFORMATION

In parallel with the growing complexity of the global marketplace, the amount – and the range of quality – of available market information has also increased enormously over recent decades. Many decision-makers feel the symptoms of an "information paralysis": any additional piece of information will only make it more difficult to digest it all and distinguish the relevant parts to utilize in decision-making.

Managing business information, that is, finding the relevant data and processing it into insights that will aid growth-oriented decision-making has become a distinct area of professional competence. Most decision-makers do not possess such competence, and it would not make much sense for them to do, as they should indeed concentrate their efforts on drawing conclusions based on information rather than spend time on learning about information sources and tools. Hence executives will need experts to handle the information retrieval and processing that is inevitably associated with high quality decision-making in today's complex business environment.

Another bottleneck to dealing with masses of information, along with the lack of specific skills, is of course the lack of time. Even if executives did possess in-depth knowledge about the information sources that are relevant for their company, it would be hugely unproductive to have them spend their time on going through data and processing them into insight, when someone else can do it for them and become a valuable expert in the company's business while doing so.

Yet another addition to the challenge of managing the growing mass of business information are the insights that already exist in the organization, that is, the knowledge, views, and experiences of colleagues at many levels of the organization. Decision-makers would do well to tap into this pool of insight when preparing for important decisions, but how to do it in an organized fashion?

MARKET INTELLIGENCE: TURNING DATA INTO INSIGHT

We have discussed the challenge decision-makers face of having the right business information at their fingertips when decisions are due; decisions that should lead the organization towards a future that the customers, employees, and shareholders alike will be happy with. We concluded that, at the end of the day, the decision-makers' task is not very complicated: to understand the operating environment, to compete in it, and to grow the organization profitably. At the same time, we acknowledged that the operating environment is getting increasingly complex, as is managing the information concerning it.

This book is about supporting the goal of companies to "Understand, Compete, and Grow" through organized Market Intelligence (MI). In the following, we will introduce the concept of MI and its critical role in generating market insight, promoting competitiveness, and achieving growth.

WHAT IS MARKET INTELLIGENCE?

MI[1] helps organizations understand their business environment, compete successfully in it, and grow as a result. As a program, MI collects information about market players and strategically relevant topics, and processes it into insights that support decision-making. Organizationally, MI is typically placed under strategic planning, business development, or marketing.

Summarizing what has been discussed already, MI is business critical for two reasons above others:

1. The operating environment of organizations is getting increasingly complex and dynamic, and, as a reflection of this complexity, accurate business information is needed not just by the headquarters but virtually all levels of the organization.

2. At the same time, decision-makers are challenged by "information disconnect" that is not caused by lack of information as such, but by lack of time to digest it and to distinguish and process what is truly relevant for decision-making purposes.

MI as a discipline is both old and new. All organizations operating in a competitive environment have always needed intelligence to learn about what the market wants from their products and services, and what is being offered to customers by the competition. Traditionally, the intelligence activity has often been narrowly perceived as "keeping an eye on the competition", which has sometimes even earned it a shady reputation. Whatever the focus, the intelligence activity has often been performed rather randomly by small teams or individuals in different parts of the organization.

Yet more recently – as dictated by the global economy and the complex requirements set for modern strategic planning, sales, marketing, and innovation management – MI has reached a position in the organization that compares to other professional support functions such as risk management,

---

[1] *Market Intelligence (MI) is sometimes used interchangeably with Business Intelligence (BI) or Competitive Intelligence (CI). Whereas CI typically refers to the same concrete activity as MI, BI in most cases rather refers to computer-based techniques used in processing numerical business data.*

PR, or sourcing. To be successful, an increasingly knowledge-intensive enterprise simply cannot do without an organized intelligence program as one of its support groups.

Indeed, the Global Market Intelligence surveys conducted by GIA have demonstrated that, in organizations where MI has been systematically organized, decision-making is more efficient compared to organizations without an MI program: four out of five respondents with an MI program in place typically believe that information necessary to support decision-making is available immediately or after a short delay, while only half of the respondents without an MI program feel the same. The GIA surveys have also reported decision-making in organizations without MI slowing down because of the time consumed by executives on wading through large volumes of data, and executives fearing to make poor decisions due to inaccurate or faulty information.

MARKET INTELLIGENCE AS A PROGRAM

Fundamentals

Processing business information into actionable insights that help organizations understand, compete, and grow in their market is a cyclical process. Within the cycle, a needs analysis always drives the process where data are collected and processed into analyses that will be utilized in decision-making.

Decision-makers need MI both in the format of ad hoc projects and on a continuous basis. Ad hoc projects usually relate to very specific decision-making situations such as entering certain geographical market areas, as in our example in the beginning of this chapter. Continuous market monitoring, in turn, is necessary for the organizations to maintain awareness about the current developments in the marketplace, for example, in the newly entered market area.

In a world class MI program, information from external and internal sources is combined into a systematic intelligence process that serves decision-making with timely and accurate MI that helps them capitalize on opportunities and avoid threats.

The existing literature on MI and Competitive Intelligence (CI) largely addresses specific aspects of the MI activities, ranging from information collection techniques and analysis methods to discussing the ethics of the entire intelligence activity. However, based on the consulting experience of the authors with companies in different parts of the world, the most important questions that companies face when considering the options for organizing their intelligence activity are rather more strategic and organizational than tactical and focused on methods and techniques:

- How do we go about organizing and resourcing a program that enables us to systematically make well-informed decisions?

- How are other companies doing it and how do we compare?

- What are the expected benefits and the required investments?

- How can we measure progress once we have started something?

Program Benefits

MI programs have by now been established in most large companies around the world. However, heads of MI still often find it challenging to clearly communicate the hard and soft benefits that the investment in a corporate MI program is expected to yield, especially at times when budgets are under scrutiny. The benefits of systematically organizing an MI program can be grouped under three categories as has been illustrated in Figure 1.3.

Impact: Better and Faster Decision-Making

What the corporate MI program yields as a result should be demonstrated by the organization's competitive success in its operating environment. The intelligence activity should be able to continuously produce deliverables that respond to true information needs and provide such valuable business support that timely and educated decisions are being made as a result.

In its eventual impact on decision-making, the financial worth of a well-organized MI program may be enormous, yet it is hard if not impossible to point out and quantify exactly which MI efforts contributed to which successful decisions and by how much. These benefits are therefore considered qualitative in nature.

Even though it is often hard to put a finger on exactly how big an impact MI efforts have had on the quality of a single decision, it is safe to say that an organized MI program improves the average quality of decisions made. When decision topics regularly go through a systematic process of research

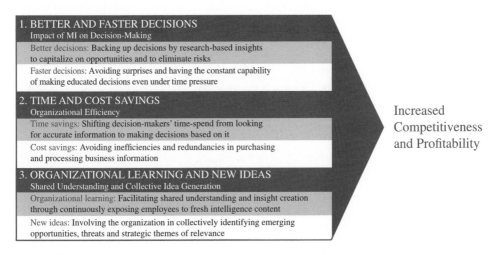

Figure 1.3   Benefits of a systematic MI program

and analysis, the resulting decisions will be based on solidly grounded insights into aspects covering anything from the anticipated competitive response to compliance with the governing laws. Over time, this tradition makes an intelligent organization, and business literature continuously brings us success stories of how such organizations have survived even critical periods of transition.

However insightful and well grounded the decisions in an organization are, sometimes they are just made too late. One of the characteristics of an organization where the intelligence program is deeply rooted is the capability to react fast, that is, an ability to reach decisions quickly while its slower peers may still only be digesting the original surprise. The speedy process of course should not compromise the quality of the related analysis; again a reason to have an intelligence infrastructure in place that can handle rapidly emerging topics for research and analysis.

Case: Intelligence Input to Strategy at ABB

ABB is a leader in power and automation technologies that enable utility and industry customers to improve their performance while lowering environmental impact. Interviewed for this case article was Daniel Niederer, Assistant Vice President, Head of Strategy Controlling and Operations.

Background on ABB

Intelligence activities at ABB weren't always in such a visionary shape. In 2004, ABB was in the process of recovering from a lengthy crisis that had resulted from poor financial performance. The cost-cutting exercises had slashed most non-business critical activities in the short term, and Business Intelligence (BI) had been one of the sufferers.

Niederer describes the situation: "New executives were hired who obviously had an urgent need for accurate business information, based on which they could make decisions on both strategic and operational level. Back then, we came to the somewhat embarrassing conclusion that investment banks and consultants knew more about ABB's competitive situation than we did ourselves."

Virtually no-one was equipped to provide answers to the management's questions in-house, and Niederer with his team in the Corporate Strategy department made it their mission to change this.

Because of the dramatic downsizing that had taken place earlier, Daniel Niederer says the company still had a relatively poor intelligence capability back in 2004. They were faced with several challenges:

- BI work was mostly an insular activity.

- BI was poorly coordinated, and different types of BI products existed in the organization that were completely unknown to each other.

- There was no-one clearly responsible for corporate BI.

- No BI recognition or awareness existed from top management.

- As a result, no commonly shared understanding existed about the competitive landscape.

Structured MI for ABB's Strategy Process – Framework

Getting to work to improve ABB's BI operation, Niederer and his team developed a BI model that was based on three different frameworks. These frameworks serve to ensure that ABB has a continuous process in place to cater to the BI needs of different end users, while at the same time maintaining an umbrella view of the business environment of the entire organization.

- The first framework is the standard intelligence cycle that helps ABB get the structure in place for an on-going BI capacity.

- The second framework presents the different BI areas where ABB is active: BI as a whole has been divided into CI, MI, and macro intelligence.

- In the third BI framework, described in the table in this case study, ABB has made the distinction between strategic and operational intelligence.

Strategic intelligence	Scope of ABB BI network
o Long-term strategy of competitors o Outspoken long-term goals and targets o Mergers, acquisitions, and divestments o Portfolio analysis, touching point analysis o Market share, regional competitive position o Footprint: manufacturing, engineering, R&D o Financial benchmarking	o Focus on most common denominator between ABB's very diverse businesses to reduce complexity o Strategic intelligence enables management decisions, but may not have the highest relevance for front line sales
Operational intelligence	**Scope of front end sales, marketing, and R&D**
o Product level comparisons o Detailed analysis of product features o Analysis of competitors' go-to-market tactics o How to beat competitor X with product Y?	o Operational intelligence has the highest importance within its respective organizational silo, but would be too complex for group level

Focusing specifically on strategic intelligence, Niederer lists out the primary issues under ABB's radar screen:

- Long-term strategy of competitors.

- Articulated long-term goals and targets.

(Continued)

- Mergers, acquisitions, and investments in the industry.

- Portfolio analysis and touching point analysis.

- Market share development and regional competitive position.

- Footprints: manufacturing, engineering, R&D.

- Financial benchmarking.

"From the long list above, we generally need to put specific focus on the common denominators between ABB's very diverse businesses in order to reduce complexity", Niederer says.

Results of the Strategic Intelligence Capability

"We have developed a portfolio of different Business Intelligence products in order to respond to different end users' needs in different situations", Niederer describes. "It is very important to standardize the Business Intelligence products in order to reduce complexity through operationalized Business Intelligence and high recognition value with all Business Intelligence stakeholders."

The output is delivered through several media: presentations, face-to-face discussions, seminars, and workshops. Each Friday, a report is sent to the ABB Group's CEO, CFO, and other members of the executive committee. The purpose of the Friday briefing is not to provide rocket science, but rather to recap the most important issues from that week.

ABB's intelligence team also produces quarterly reports for management that cover the macro environment, vertical industries, markets, and competitors. The quarterly report is a thorough research package with extensive analysis included.

"We also give intelligence presentations to ABB's Head of Corporate Development, who is a member of the ABB executive committee who in turn makes presentations in the executive committee or to the Board of Directors on a regular basis", Daniel Niederer says. "However, most intelligence products end up being delivered through our dedicated Business Intelligence Portal, so that everyone with an access to the tool can retrieve the information for their personal needs."

Case: To Divest or Not to Divest

Niederer describes a specific decision-making situation where strategic intelligence was needed to back up the decision: "The management was evaluating the potential divestment of a certain part of a business. The perception was that the business did not seem to have a sound outlook for the future since the market growth was limited."

"We did our analysis and came to the conclusion that the future capital expenditures of the particular vertical industry where this business was active in, were in fact likely to increase quite dramatically. Based on this intelligence, the divestment plans were stopped. It seems now that our analysis was indeed right, the industry sector picked up and ABB is making good business in that field."

Lessons Learned

When asked about the key success factors in developing effective strategic intelligence, Daniel Niederer raises three different points:

- Become a preferred business partner to management by delivering customized and dedicated intelligence services. "We should be the preferred speaking partners to management. We do this in-house by adding the kind of value to the output that no external source could achieve."

- Deliver professional intelligence – go beyond the facts. "It is essential to deliver intelligence rather than just data. In order to be able to do this, resources will be needed in the form of both time and money. Integrating Business Intelligence with especially the strategy process is vital."

- Communication and customer awareness. "Business Intelligence output has little impact if it's not marketed internally. Business Intelligence products should be discussed in management meetings, sales events, and marketing meetings alike. End users of intelligence output should be aware of the intelligence efforts in order to be able to learn from each other and share best practices in Business Intelligence. One thing, for instance, that we could have done better from the beginning is to have focused more on the intelligence needs of BU marketing managers."

EFFICIENCY: TIME AND COST SAVINGS

The impact of an MI program on decision-making is of course the primary justification for its existence. However, regardless of what its eventual impact is, in today's corporate world it is safe to assume that almost every organization gathers and disseminates business information somehow, which brings us to the efficiency perspective: if time and resources will be put into collecting and analyzing information in any case, it makes a big difference whether this process is organized and cost-efficient or not. While the impact of MI on the quality of decision-making is hard to quantify, the efficiency of an intelligence program can be quite accurately measured in both time and money.

Accurate information is needed to back up decisions, and without a systematically organized intelligence program, decision-makers repeatedly find themselves in situations where they have to dig for missing pieces of information. Over time, this collective search by executives becomes very expensive for the company, and organizing the MI program therefore yields measurable benefits in the form of liberating decision-makers from searching for to actually using information. The related cost savings can be derived from the amount of expensive hours that executives save by always having the information they need at their fingertips when they need it.

Another form of very measurable benefits of MI is cost savings through optimizing the purchases and processing of information. A large organization easily spends millions of euros or dollars annually on different forms of business information, and several people may be analyzing the same topics internally without knowing of each other's efforts. If this activity is not centrally coordinated, overlaps are hard to avoid, and it may be that no one knows exactly how many budgets are being tapped into at different levels of the organization. Coordinating the purchases and processing of information therefore helps the organization to control the overall MI budget, to negotiate better deals with consultants and information vendors, and to eliminate redundancies.

Case: Creating Business Impact through Market Insights at a Global IT Company

The best MI programs exist to create true impact on business and help companies generate revenue. The degree of business impact greatly depends on how well MI is embedded into the decision-making processes and what the level of collaboration is with key stakeholders.

Our case company has organized their MI program around a set of fundamental principles.

Aligning MI to Business Priorities

Seeking for growth is the one over-arching business priority that drives the activities in the company, especially after the recession in 2008–2009. MI is no exception. Everyone involved in it will have to align their daily work to support the company's growth.

Running a Business within a Business

The MI team is essentially run like a business inside the company; the team wants to continue to thrive and be viable, therefore using its services needs to make business sense for the company. To stay tuned to the business priorities the MI team regularly meets with experts such as business unit CFOs, chief economists, or external speakers.

Partnering with Business Leaders

Without partnership with business leaders, there's no impact on business: and without an understanding of business priorities, there's no partnership with leaders. The true power of an MI organization is reached at the nexus of understanding the business context and matching it with the MI-specific skills and capabilities that the rest of the organization does not possess.

Organizing the Team to Drive Impact

In our case company the large MI team has been organized around skills and expertise, as experience suggests that specialization typically drives the heaviest business impact. Hence they have analysts that partner with business leaders, supported by research specialists of various topic areas.

Contributing to the Bottom Line

The MI team strives to impact the bottom line by focusing their efforts around four types of engagement:

- Proactively identifying pockets of growth

- Uncovering inhibitors to growth

- Providing foundation to key growth initiatives

- Supporting the sales team in revenue growth

Based on their work on the above topics, the MI team delivers to the organization by recommending how to expand beyond core base of clients, alter current strategies, capitalize on trends in the market, or take out competition.

ORGANIZATIONAL LEARNING AND NEW IDEAS

Finally, the third category of MI benefits highlights the role of MI in facilitating the development of a shared understanding in the organization about its operating environment and in that way involving a large part of the organization in generating valuable new ideas.

Organizational learning and collective idea generation contribute to the eventual impact of MI on decision-making, but refer more to the process of constantly having potentially relevant topics for decision-making on the radar than to the actual decision-making itself. Having many years experience on the ground also contributes to the company's ability to implement decisions rapidly, as the organization, being collectively aware of the developments in its business environment, is prepared for and even expects swift reactions from the decision-makers.

ABOUT THIS BOOK

FULL-BLOWN INTELLIGENCE PROGRAMS ARE MOSTLY FOR LARGE COMPANIES

As much as MI is necessary for any size of organization in any industry in order for them to target their customers in an educated manner and maintain an understanding about their competitive environment, we don't suggest that any company should develop a formal intelligence program like the ones discussed and showcased in this book. We are describing a structured and process-oriented way of systematically building up an intelligence program that will have the capacity to respond to the intelligence needs of a large and often globally operating organization. What exactly is "large" varies between industries; however, in our experience, annual revenue of €100 million is a signpost below which developing a full-blown systematic intelligence program would in many cases be exaggerated. There are exceptions to this rule: even some smaller companies may be investing very heavily on rapid growth at a global scale, and to support it, they will need to invest in a robust MI program as well to develop the necessary understanding about the various market areas in which they intend to do successful business.

INTELLIGENCE PROGRAMS ARE BEST SUITED TO STRUCTURED MANAGEMENT SCHEMES

Besides the size of the organization, its management style will also often determine whether the approaches presented in this book will be fully applicable. We are presenting a structured and process-oriented approach to developing world class intelligence programs, and this is typically best suited to organizations that are run with a relatively structured management scheme. We realize that not all organizations have a set of recurring processes such as an annual strategy process in use; however, the frameworks and approaches discussed in this book will find their most natural context in the existing corporate business processes.

PEOPLE GENERATE THE IMPACT

Everything said about the process-oriented approach of this book, we want to emphasize the critical role of humans in bringing any world class intelligence program to life. Processes, templates, tools, and organizations alone will not perform the intelligence work, nor will they have the power of influencing the future of the company. Rather, behind every "needs analysis", "process phase", "template", "market signal", and "analysis" there's an individual or a group of people who will need to use their personal skills and character to produce anything ranging from smart information retrieval to insightful consulting about where the company's business may be heading. Of course the same individuals will not necessarily have to possess the same set of skills (rather, it makes sense to divide the responsibilities among the intelligence team if there are several people involved), but all the same the eventual impact of the intelligence program will always be attributed to people, not structures and processes as such.

STRUCTURE OF THE BOOK

After introducing the drivers for MI in global organizations, we will move on to providing the most recent global facts and figures related to corporate MI programs in large organizations in Chapter 2.

Part 2 of the book, that is, Chapters 3–9, will discuss the GIA Roadmap for developing world class MI. The Roadmap contains six Key Success Factors, each of which will be introduced and show-cased in a dedicated chapter.

Part 3 of the book, that is, Chapters 10–14, will discuss how MI is best leveraged for successful decisions in different decision-making contexts: strategic planning, marketing, sales and account management, innovation and product management, and supply chain management. We will also present MI as the facilitator of continuous current awareness in the organization about the impor-tant developments in its operating environment.

In Part 4, that is, Chapters 15–18, we will first address the "How to" questions in introducing Mark, the head of MI in a logistics company who initiates an MI program and subsequently works to take it towards world class levels in a coordinated fashion. Chapter 17 is entirely new in this second edition of the book and concentrates on a burning topic for intelligence professionals and executive decision-makers alike: how to demonstrate the value and benefits of the MI investment. Finally, in Chapter 18 we will discuss the trends and anticipated future developments in MI in global organizations.

Throughout the book, we will present case examples showing how large and mid-sized global companies have organized their MI programs and are leveraging them for well-informed decision-making.

2 Market Intelligence in Global Organizations: Survey Findings in 2013

INTRODUCTION

Following the explosive growth over the last 15–20 years of both the need of decision-makers for accurate business information and the available amount of it, Market Intelligence (MI) has become a profession of its own. Subsequently, MI itself has also become a topic for professional research. Many companies are putting a lot of resources into the activity and are interested in how their investments compare with those of other companies, and what kinds of benefits can realistically be expected.

In February–April 2013, GIA conducted its Global MI Survey for the sixth time since 2005. With 1,207 unique responses in total[1] (see Figure 2.1) from 880 companies in 21 separate industries and 64 different countries, the survey is the most extensive in its field to date. Many of the survey questions have evolved over the years, reflecting the increasing maturity of the MI profession.

The survey questions were kept largely identical to those in the 2011 edition of the survey, to allow for comparisons between the two data sets. As shown in the analysis, the results in 2013 were notably similar to the 2011 results, thus further validating the data presented in this chapter.

While the 2011 survey was groundbreaking in being the first large study to measure the level of sophistication of MI in global companies, the new study takes the analysis one step further. It analyzes not only the level of sophistication, but also the different focus of MI in different types of organizations: business-to-business (B2B) and business-to-consumers (B2C). The survey also accentuated how those companies with the most sophisticated MI programs (world class MI) have evolved since 2011 in order for them to stay ahead. Furthermore, it also highlights cross-industry comparisons.

---

[1] As the survey was anonymous by default, GIA was only able to distinguish between unique companies if the respondent submitted his/her company's name. The data most likely represent more than 1,000 different companies and no single company had more than 12 respondents.

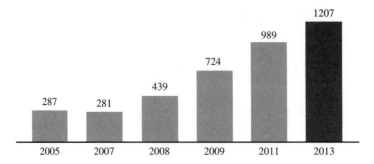

Figure 2.1   The number of respondents to the Global MI Survey
Source: 2005–2013 Global Market Intelligence Surveys, GIA.

HOW THE SURVEY WAS CONDUCTED

The survey was conducted online in February–April 2013, using both direct invitations and open invitations through social media groups related to MI.

All responses were validated by GIA and data that seemed implausible were removed before the analysis. The 1,207 unique responses were used for the analysis, representing at least 880 different companies and 21 industries.

The structure of the survey grouped responses into three topics related to MI: i) efficiency of decision-making, ii) structure and resources for MI, and iii) maturity of MI function (level of sophistication), which is based on GIA's framework for world class MI.

The study also segmented the responses: i) by industry, ii) by geography, iii) by annual revenues, and iv) by type of business (B2B, B2C, or both B2B and B2C).

RESPONDENT DATA

All in all, 68% of respondents indicated that their organization had a formal MI function in place (as shown in Figure 2.2). This represents a slightly smaller share than in the 2011 survey, where 76% of the respondents had a formal MI function in place. However, in terms of actual figures, there were still significantly more companies with an MI function (820 in 2013 compared to 750 in 2011).

Respondents to the survey were also asked to indicate whether they were MI professionals or MI users (decision-makers) (see Figure 2.3). Out of the 1,207 respondents, 58% identified themselves as MI professionals, which is a smaller proportion than in previous surveys. However, the larger share of MI users most likely provides a more balanced result on the state of MI in companies, as MI users are likely to be more objective about the topic.

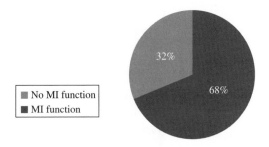

Figure 2.2   Formal MI function in place?
Source: 2013 Global Market Intelligence Survey, GIA.

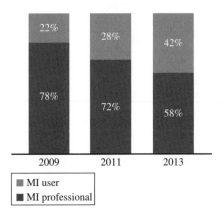

Figure 2.3   Role of respondents
Source: 2009–2013 Global Market Intelligence Surveys, GIA.

Executives from 64 different countries participated in the survey and a strong majority of respondents represented global companies, making the study truly global in nature. By geographical distribution, respondents based in Europe accounted for over 50% of the responses (see Figure 2.4).

Two additional factors that impact how MI operations in companies are organized are the size of the company (by annual revenues) and which industry the companies operate in.

The manufacturing and industrial sectors were most well-represented in the study with 179 responses (15%), followed by professional and financial services (including insurance). Overall, 21 different industries were represented in the survey but the top ten industries accounted for 71% of the total number of replies.

In terms of company size, there were a larger proportion of companies in the smallest revenue band in the 2013 study compared to that of 2011 (see Figure 2.5). Of the organizations represented in the survey, 30% had annual revenues of less than €100 million or $130 million, whereas the equivalent proportion in 2011 was 21%.

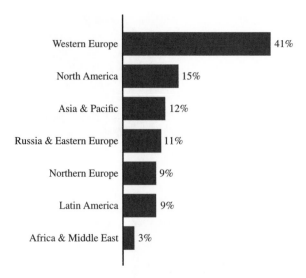

Figure 2.4   Respondents by region
Source: 2013 Global Market Intelligence Survey, GIA.

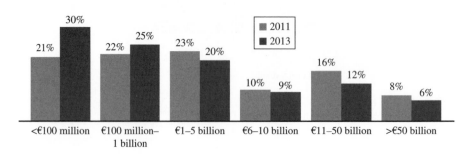

Figure 2.5   Respondents by company size
Source: 2011–2013 Global Market Intelligence Surveys, GIA.

When comparing figures to 2011, the higher proportion of smaller companies in the 2013 data should be taken into account. Many of the average figures would have been slightly higher with a lower proportion of companies in the smallest revenue band. However, even when excluding the data from the companies in the smallest revenue bracket, the patterns and trends discovered in the 2013 survey are still valid. The large proportion of smaller companies in the study has been shown to have relatively negligible impact.

STATE OF MARKET INTELLIGENCE IN GLOBAL COMPANIES IN 2013

Overall, the results from the 2011 and 2013 Global MI Surveys were very similar. This validates GIA's findings on the state of MI in global companies and strengthens the conclusions drawn from the data.

When comparing the state of MI in 2013 to 2011, the average number for all respondents in the survey is used under the term global average. For some indicators, such as budgets and the size of the MI team, it is also important to look at the distribution of responses as the global average can be misleading when the mean and the median figure differ significantly.

BENEFITS AND RETURN ON INVESTMENT OF MARKET INTELLIGENCE

The study shows that companies with a formal MI function see clear benefits from it (Figure 2.6) and that the program pays off (Figure 2.7).

In 2013, 92% of all respondents agreed that their organization has benefited from MI, compared to 93% in 2011. Only 3% of respondents disagreed with the statement that MI has benefited their organization and 6% neither agreed nor disagreed.

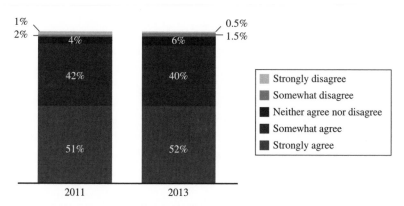

Figure 2.6   Our company has benefited from MI
Source: 2011–2013 Global Market Intelligence Surveys, GIA.

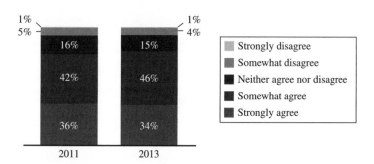

Figure 2.7   Our organization's investments in MI have paid off
Source: 2011–2013 Global Market Intelligence Surveys, GIA.

Furthermore, segmenting the answers in relation to MI (not shown in the graph in Figure 2.6), it is also clear that MI users see as much benefits as MI professionals (92% agree in both cases).

In terms of returns on investments for MI, the proportion of people who agree is slightly smaller, but still represent a convincing majority (Figure 2.7).

The proportion of respondents who considered MI to have paid off in 2013 (80%) was very similar to the proportion in 2011 (78%). Notably, only 5% of respondents think that investments have not paid off, as many as in 2011.

In relation to MI, MI professionals are slightly more optimistic about the return on investment (ROI) for market intelligence (82% agree) compared to decision-makers (not shown in the graph in Figure 2.7). However, 77% of decision-makers still agree that investments have paid off and only 5% disagree with the statement, indicating that budget-holders also see clear benefits of MI.

EFFICIENCY OF DECISION-MAKING

As an internal support function, the key purpose of MI is to enable people in the organization to make better informed decisions. It is therefore important not only to investigate whether people consider MI to be beneficial or not, but also whether it actually improves decision-making in organizations.

Respondents were asked to answer six questions related to the efficiency of decision-making in their respective companies. By comparing the answers from organizations that have a formal MI function with those that do not, an indication as to whether MI supports decision-making positively or not is uncovered (Figure 2.8).

In 2013, the results clearly show that companies that have a formal MI function in place are consistently more efficient than companies that do not. This validates the findings from 2011 and adds to the evidence that having a formal MI function in place supports decision-making positively.

In companies with formal MI in place, decision-making is rated significantly more efficient than in companies without a formal function in place. The most noticeable difference in companies that have MI is that information, to a much greater extent, is readily available when needed.

Inaccurate or incomplete information appears to be a sizable problem for all companies, including those with a formal MI function. This indicates that the level of analytical capabilities in companies remains somewhat basic and that provision of the right type of intelligence is something many companies are struggling with.

There are a few potential reasons why inaccuracy or incomplete information causes problems, even in companies that have formal MI in place.

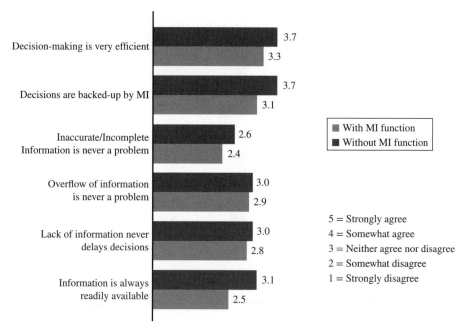

Figure 2.8   Efficiency of decision-making in companies with or without formal MI programs
Source: 2013 Global Market Intelligence Survey, GIA.

First and foremost, not all relevant information is publically available and thus becomes more difficult to collect. However, another plausible explanation is that intelligence teams often do not know the exact intelligence needs of their internal customers, and decision-makers' needs in particular. This often results in the MI function providing intelligence which is either inaccurate or incomplete with regards to the needs of the decision-makers.

MARKET INTELLIGENCE SET-UP AND RESOURCES

As confirmed in previous Global MI Surveys by GIA, MI is most often positioned under the strategic planning/business development or sales and marketing functions in organizations (77%). Only in 12% of the cases is MI placed under R&D/product development, which represents a 2% drop since 2011 (Figure 2.9).

The hierarchical position of the MI function has improved slightly over the last two years, although the results are almost identical on the surface. The head of MI is currently, on average, 1.9 steps away from the CEO, compared to 2.0 steps in 2011 (Figure 2.10).

A clear majority of MI work continues to be conducted in a centralized fashion (57%) as opposed to decentralized across different units or regions or being outsourced (Figure 2.11). One key difference

Figure 2.9 Placement of MI function
Source: 2011–2013 Global Market Intelligence Surveys, GIA.

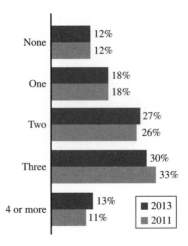

Figure 2.10 How many organizational layers between head of MI and the CEO?
Source: 2011–2013 Global Market Intelligence Surveys, GIA.

compared to 2011 is that MI teams, to a greater extent, are serving their top management, who now constitute 36% of the internal client base (Figure 2.12).

On average, in 2013, companies reported employing 12 people working on MI as their primary job, which is one person less than in 2011. However, when considering the distribution, 63% of all companies have MI teams of one to five people and only 10% of companies have large teams with over 25 people.

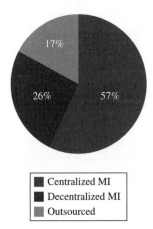

Figure 2.11 Distribution of MI work
Source: 2011–2013 Global Market Intelligence Surveys, GIA.

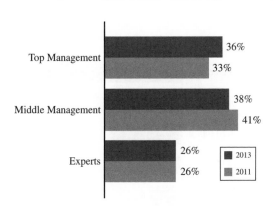

Figure 2.12 Internal clients for MI
Source: 2011–2013 Global Market Intelligence Surveys, GIA.

The average size of the MI team also depends on the size of the company. Larger companies, by revenue, have more people employed in MI than smaller companies (Figures 2.13 and 2.14).

By industry, there are notable differences between the average number of people with MI as their primary job.

In the chemicals, defense and aerospace, and financial services industries, there are on average 20 people or more working in MI. In the media, private equity, and construction industries, however, there are only four people on average (Figure 2.15).

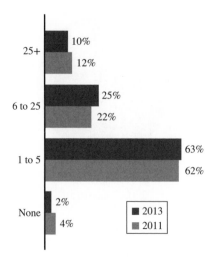

Figure 2.13   Number of people in the MI team
Source: 2011–2013 Global Market Intelligence Surveys, GIA.

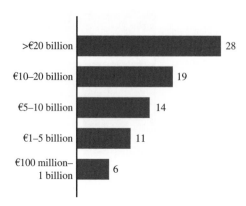

Figure 2.14   Average number of people in the MI team (x axis) by company size (y axis)
Source: 2013 Global Market Intelligence Survey, GIA.

The industries with MI teams that are larger than the global general average (12 people) are primarily B2B in nature. B2C companies tend to employ fewer than 12 people, compared to B2B companies.

In the average company, the MI team spends only 47% of their working time on regular deliverables, as opposed to ad hoc projects and deliverables (Figure 2.16). The figure remains largely similar to 2011, but is to be considered fairly low as a higher proportion of regular deliverables is known to increase efficiency.

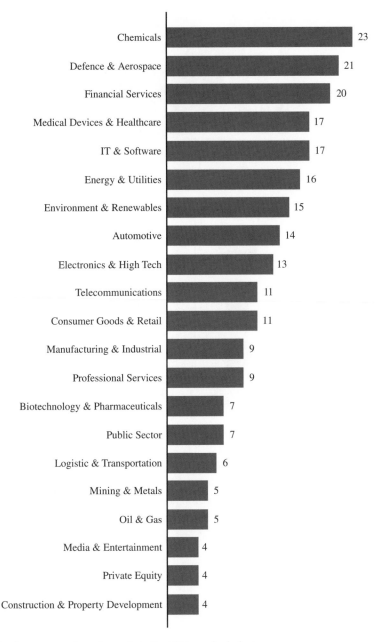

Figure 2.15   Average number of people in the MI team by industry
Source: 2013 Global Market Intelligence Survey, GIA.

For the first time, GIA investigated the most common scope of MI professionals' job roles in terms of geography and the number of business topics covered. The results show that almost half of all MI professionals (49%) have global responsibilities, and that 29% of all MI professionals have a global role with a corporate-wide scope.

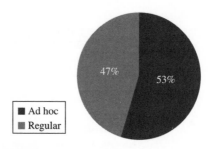

Figure 2.16   Regularity of MI work
Source: 2013 Global Market Intelligence Survey, GIA.

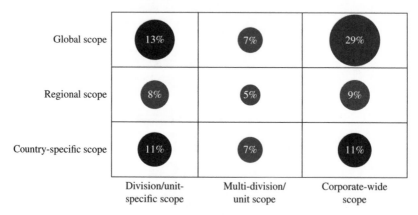

Figure 2.17   Scope of MI professionals' job roles
Source: 2013 Global Market Intelligence Survey, GIA.

The results, furthermore, indicate that it is uncommon for MI professionals to have roles that cover a few geographies or a few business units. The scopes of the roles are more often concentrated on either one unit and a specific geography, or all units (corporate-wide) and all geographies (global) (Figure 2.17).

MI budgets vary significantly depending on the size of the company and the industry the company operates in. Therefore, the average MI budget does not necessarily serve as a good benchmark for all companies.

Respondents were asked to provide their total MI budgets (including salaries and other HR costs) as well as their budgets for MI projects and services (excluding salaries and HR costs). The latter serves as a better figure for comparison as it disregards the number of MI employees in that particular company.

The average MI budget (excluding HR costs) in 2013 was €1.6 million or $2.1 million (Figure 2.18), which would indicate a 53% increase since the average in 2011. However, the median budget

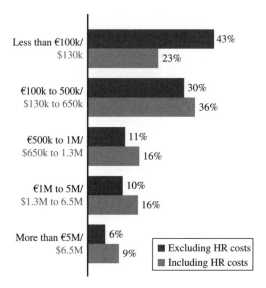

Figure 2.18   MI budgets
Source: 2013 Global Market Intelligence Survey, GIA.

(excluding HR costs) was €150,000 or $195,000, which is a 25% drop since 2011. Including salaries, the average MI budget was €2.8 million or $3.6 million, while the median was €346,000 or $450,000, similar to the median in 2011.

Of the companies in the survey, 73% reported spending no more than €500,000 or $650,000 every year on projects and services related to MI. Including salaries, 59% of companies spend no more than €500,000 or $650,000.

However, as explained already, these figures vary significantly and therefore it is more valuable to look at the distribution of budgets by company size and industry, something GIA offers through its MI benchmarking services.

Looking at average budgets by company size (Figure 2.19), it is important to keep in mind that the budgets represent average figures in a fixed revenue group, and do not indicate a correlation between company size and MI budgets.

Companies with less than €100 million or $130 million in annual revenues, spend on average €368,000 or $478,000 per year on MI projects and services, while companies with over €20 billion or $26 billion in revenue spend an average of €5.1 million or $6.7 million a year. It is evident that larger companies have larger MI budgets on average.

Companies with annual revenues of over €10 billion or $13 billion spend significantly more on MI than companies in the revenue band of €5–10 billion or $6.5–13 billion. The sharp increase is

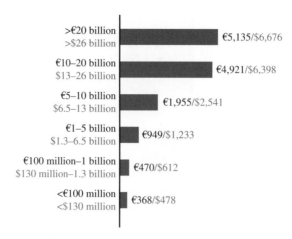

Figure 2.19   Average annual MI budgets (excluding HR, thousands) by company size
Source: 2013 Global Market Intelligence Survey, GIA.

potentially explained by companies centralizing MI purchases to a greater extent when reaching a certain size, whereas purchases are kept on regional or country-level budgets in smaller companies.

Looking at the spending on MI compared to revenues, smaller companies spend proportionately more on MI than larger companies, although exact figures cannot be derived from the revenue bands.

Figure 2.20 displays average MI budgets (excluding HR costs) in different industries. The order of industries is similar also when including salaries, with the exception of biotechnology and pharmaceuticals being the industry with the largest MI budgets (including HR costs).

In Figure 2.20 we can see that Medical devices and healthcare companies spend almost €6 million a year on MI projects and services. This is almost twice the amount spent in the consumer goods and retail industry, which has the second largest budget by industry.

The wide range of MI budgets in different industries is explained by the different characteristics of specific industries and the availability of specific data in these industries. In some industries, the supply and availability of consumer data, for example, is substantially higher than in others, and such industries tend to spend more on data, licenses, and reports.

By region, companies in Western Europe have the largest MI budgets for projects and services and spend an average of €2.3 million or $2.9 million every year. The differences in budgets between regions are large and have changed significantly since 2011.

In 2011, North American companies had the largest average MI budgets, spending €1.6 million or $2.1 million a year, followed by Western Europe, Asia Pacific, and Africa and Middle East where

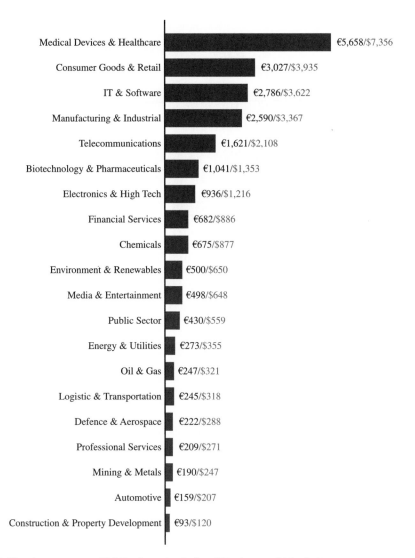

Figure 2.20   Average annual MI budgets (excluding HR, thousands) by industry
Source: 2013 Global Market Intelligence Survey, GIA.

average annual budgets were approximately €1.0 million or $1.3 million (Figure 2.21). However, MI budgets in North America have decreased slightly over the last two years, while they have increased significantly in Western Europe and Asia Pacific.

In Western Europe, one potential reason for the increase in budgets is probably related to the economic crisis. Companies might be willing to spend more on MI in uncertain times, in order to gain market share. In Asia Pacific, however, the increase is likely related to the growing trend of MI in companies overall. Compared to North America and Europe, MI is a relatively new phenomenon for many Asia Pacific companies, but is growing steadily.

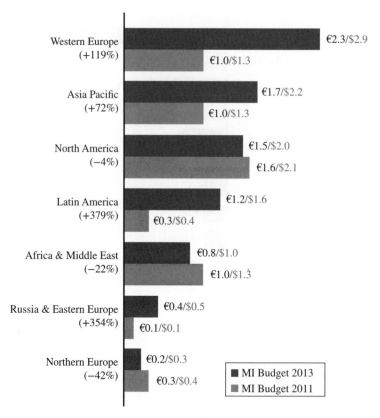

Figure 2.21 Average MI budgets (excluding HR, millions) by geographical region compared to 2011
Source: 2011–2013 Global Market Intelligence Surveys, GIA.

INDUSTRY COMPARISON

Figure 2.22 illustrates the average MI maturity* score in ten different industries against perceived ROI of MI, as well as the average MI budget in each industry. The industries in Figure 2.22 represent the highest scoring industries in GIA's world class MI framework (additional industries in Figure 2.23).

Interestingly, MI is most advanced in media and entertainment companies but that is also where the perceived ROI is the lowest. The highest perceived ROI for MI is instead in the environment and renewables industry, where budgets are also slightly higher.

Looking at MI in the IT and software and biotechnology and pharmaceuticals industries, it is clear that a large MI budget is no guarantee for an advanced MI function.

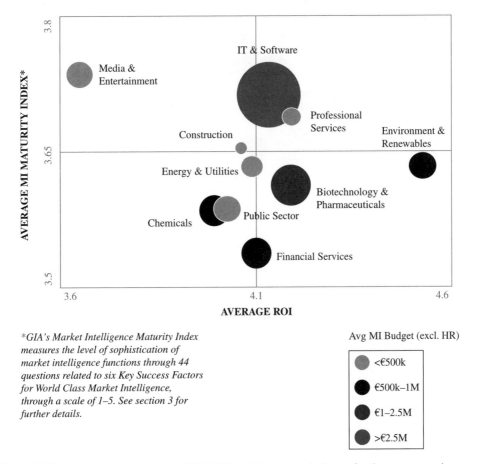

Figure 2.22   Level of sophistication of MI, ROI, and budgets by industry for the top ten scoring industries
Source: 2013 Global Market Intelligence Survey, GIA.

When looking at the industries scoring 11–20 on the MI Maturity Index*, it becomes even more evident that there is no correlation between a large MI budget and an advanced MI unit. There are more industries with large average MI budgets represented among the bottom ten, than in the top.

Medical devices and healthcare companies reportedly spend significantly more on MI every year than companies in other industries, yet their MI programs are the fourth least advanced of all industries and ROI is perceived to be rather low.

On average, MI is least developed in the defense and aerospace industries, followed by oil and gas and electronics and high tech. Perceived ROI is also among the lowest in these industries.

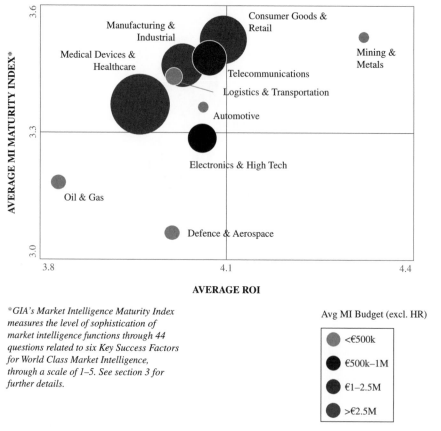

Figure 2.23   Level of sophistication of MI, ROI, and budgets by industry for the bottom ten scoring industries (please note that the scale in the graph is different from that in Figure 2.22)
Source: 2013 Global Market Intelligence Survey, GIA.

COMPANIES WITH WORLD CLASS MI FUNCTIONS

GIA's framework for world class MI is based on six Key Success Factors (KSFs) that MI programs need to address in order to reach world class status. The framework is comprised of 44 questions in total, grouped into the six different KSFs:

- Intelligence Scope

- Intelligence Process

- Intelligence Deliverables

- Intelligence Tools

- Intelligence Organization

- Intelligence Culture

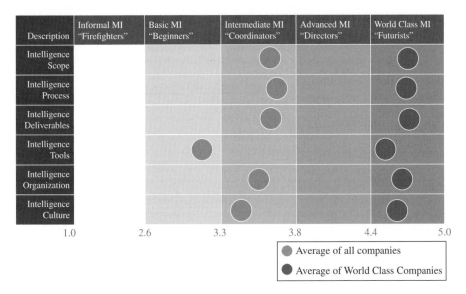

Figure 2.24   MI maturity scores of companies in the survey
Source: The Handbook of Market Intelligence; 2011, Hedin, Hirvensalo, Vaarnas (GIA).

The 44 questions are measured on a 5-point Likert scale, ranging from a minimum value of 1 to a maximum value of 5. Companies that have an overall average score of 4.4 or above, are considered to have a world class MI program. The level of sophistication for each of the six KSFs can be visualized in an MI Maturity Index, which ranges from "Informal MI" to "World Class MI" (Figure 2.24). In the 2013 survey, 11% of the companies had world class MI programs.

ATTRIBUTES OF WORLD CLASS MARKET INTELLIGENCE FUNCTIONS

It was evident from the 2011 Global MI Survey that companies with world class MI operations share certain traits, in that their MI functions are more developed than in other companies. For example, world class MI functions have, on average, larger MI teams and more internal customers. However, it is not necessarily these factors that determine world class MI functions. Rather, it is the scope and processes set in place for MI that distinguish world class functions (Figure 2.25).

World class MI functions centralize their MI work more, serve their top management to a greater extent, and spend most of their time on producing regular deliverables (as opposed to ad hoc). These factors lead to higher efficiency in the function, which in turn relates to the organizational set-up of world class MI programs (Figure 2.26).

The higher efficiency of world class MI programs also leads to higher efficiency of decision-making overall. Comparing companies with world class MI to other companies, it is evident that companies

- 64% of all market Intelligence work is conducted centrally in World Class Market Intelligence functions, compared to 57% in the average company.
- 58% of all MI work goes into regular deliverables in World Class MI functions, compared to only 47% in the average company.
- 46% of all MI deliverables in companies with World Class MI are directed towards the top management in the company, compared to 36% in the average company.

Figure 2.25   MI processes in world class MI functions
Source: 2013 Global Market Intelligence Survey, GIA.

- The Head of Market Intelligence in companies with World Class Market Intelligence is on average 1.4 steps away from the CEO, compared to 1.9 steps in the average company.
- World Class Market Intelligence functions have an average market intelligence team of 18 people, compared to 12 people in other companies.
- World Class Market Intelligence functions serve on average 862 internal customers, compared to 579 in the average company.

Figure 2.26   Set-up in world class MI functions
Source: 2013 Global Market Intelligence Survey, GIA.

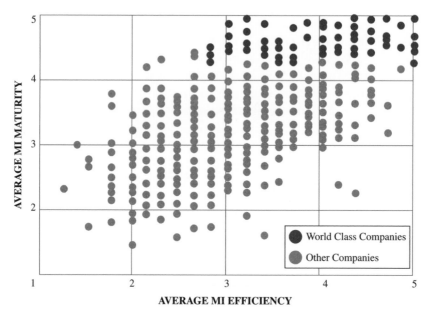

Figure 2.27   MI maturity index score versus average efficiency scores
Source: 2013 Global Market Intelligence Survey, GIA.

with a high score in the MI Maturity Index usually also score high on the efficiency-related questions (see Figure 2.27).

Companies with world class MI functions are found across all industries and in companies of all sizes and there is no correlation between MI budgets and the Maturity Index score (Figure 2.28).

Figure 2.28   MI maturity index score versus MI budgets (excluding HR, EUR)
Source: 2013 Global Market Intelligence Survey, GIA.

TRENDS IN COMPANIES WITH WORLD CLASS MARKET INTELLIGENCE

One of the key findings of the 2013 Global MI Survey was that companies with world class MI appear to have taken their MI function in an almost opposite direction compared to those companies with less sophisticated MI functions.

While the average company has reduced the size of its MI team (from 13 to 12 people) and increased its number of MI contributors[2] from 86 to 109 people, the average company with world class MI has expanded its MI team (from 13 to 18 people) and reduced its dependency on MI contributors (from 151 to 86 people).

A brief analysis of the findings in Figure 2.29 would conclude that companies with world class MI are centralizing their MI operations even further today, whereas the average company is attempting a decentralized approach. This hypothesis, however, is inconclusive. As seen in Figure 2.30, companies with world class MI do centralize MI work to a greater extent than the average company, but they actually centralize less today than in 2011.

---

[2] *MI contributors are defined as internal employees or stakeholders who do not have MI as their primary job function, but who systematically assist the MI team with information and intelligence related to their particular field of expertise.*

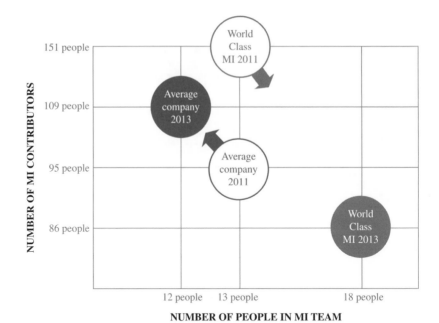

Figure 2.29   Summary of MI human resources
Source: 2013 Global Market Intelligence Survey, GIA.

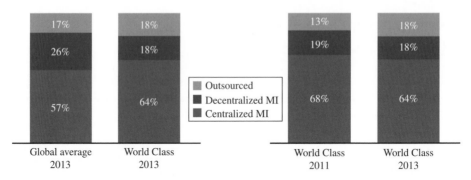

Figure 2.30   Centralization of MI work in world class companies in 2013 compared to the global average and 2011
Source: 2011–2013 Global Market Intelligence Surveys, GIA.

As illustrated in Figure 2.30, companies with world class MI have increased the proportion of MI work that is outsourced to 18% in 2013, while the share of work conducted by the central MI team has dropped from 68% to 64%.

Therefore, rather than just centralizing their MI further, companies with world class MI appear to have adopted a two-pronged approach towards their key internal stakeholders. On the one hand, they have enlarged their MI teams to be able to serve their top management better (Figure 2.31).

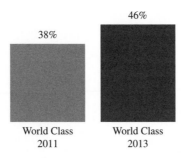

Figure 2.31   Proportion of MI deliverables to top management
Source: 2011–2013 Global Market Intelligence Surveys, GIA.

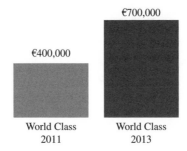

Figure 2.32   MI budget (excluding HR costs) in companies with world class MI
Source: 2011–2013 Global Market Intelligence Surveys, GIA.

On the other hand they have increased their budgets for MI projects and services (Figure 2.32) that are less strategic in nature, such as off-the-shelf reports or industry news monitoring.

Serving top management typically requires a deeper level of customization and strategic insight than that which is available from third parties. Hence, companies with world class MI require larger MI teams to meet the needs of their top management. However, since MI functions must still provide basic insights to the rest of their internal customer base, MI work that needs less customization and is less strategic in nature is likely to be outsourced.

MARKET INTELLIGENCE IN B2B AND B2C COMPANIES

Respondents to the survey were asked whether they considered the nature of their business to be primarily B2B, B2C, or both B2B and B2C.

The data on B2B and B2C companies (Figure 2.33) show that there are quite clear organizational differences in the set-up of MI functions between the two types of businesses. Most likely, the dissimilarities possibly point to the fact that MI has a different scope and purpose in a B2B company when compared to a B2C company.

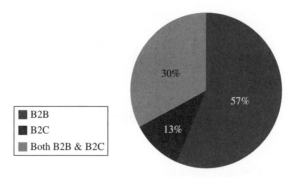

Figure 2.33   Survey responses by nature of business
Source: 2013 Global Market Intelligence Survey, GIA.

In terms of the level of sophistication or efficiency, however, there are no distinguishable differences between the two business types. Overall, 16% of responding B2C companies are considered to have world class MI, versus only 10% of responding B2B companies. However, there is no statistical evidence of a correlation.

ORGANIZATIONAL SET-UP OF MARKET INTELLIGENCE IN B2B AND B2C COMPANIES

The most noticeable difference between B2B and B2C companies, in terms of the average organizational set-up of the MI function, is that MI teams in B2C companies serve significantly more internal clients while at the same time having smaller MI teams.

As displayed in Figure 2.34, MI functions in B2C companies have on average two people less in their MI teams compared to B2B companies, but serve on average 630 more internal clients.

The large number of clients in B2C companies suggests that their key internal stakeholders are more likely to be experts, sales people, or middle managers in their companies, rather than top managers. This would also explain why MI functions in B2C companies are positioned further away from the CEO.

In B2B companies, MI teams instead serve their top management to a greater extent and thus need more people to be able to meet the intelligence needs of top management, which is more difficult to outsource.

The suggestion that MI teams in B2B companies spend more time serving their top management than MI teams in B2C companies is confirmed in Figure 2.35. Additionally, MI professionals in B2B companies also spend a larger proportion of their time on ad hoc intelligence requests, which typically come from top managers in organizations (Figure 2.36).

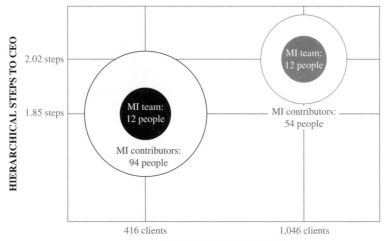

Figure 2.34 Position of MI in B2B and B2C companies
Note: black = B2B, grey = B2C
Source: 2013 Global Market Intelligence Survey, GIA.

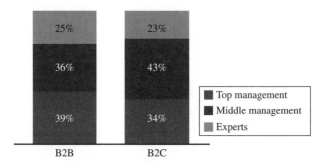

Figure 2.35 Proportion of time spent on intelligence deliverables to different internal customer groups
Source: 2013 Global Market Intelligence Survey, GIA.

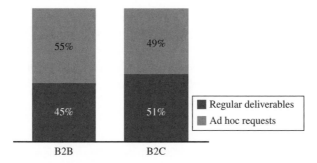

Figure 2.36 Time spent on regular MI deliverables
Source: 2013 Global Market Intelligence Survey, GIA.

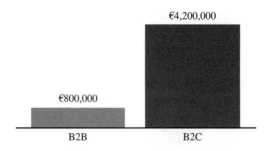

Figure 2.37   MI budgets in B2B and B2C companies (excluding HR)
Source: 2013 Global Market Intelligence Survey, GIA.

Surprisingly, MI work in B2C companies is outsourced only slightly more than in B2B companies (20% versus 16%) despite having more than twice as many internal customers to MI. In fact, MI professionals in B2C companies even centralize their MI work to a greater extent than in B2B companies (60% versus 57%).

However, budgets for MI projects and services in B2C companies are significantly higher than in B2B companies (Figure 2.37). A likely explanation for this is that in many B2C industries, there is substantially more data available on markets, competitors, and trends from third party providers than in many B2B industries. In B2B industries, there might simply not be any data available and thus the MI team needs to focus on in-house analysis.

CASE FOR DIFFERENCES IN B2B AND B2C COMPANIES

Market intelligence programs in B2B companies differ from those in B2C companies in that they tend to be placed closer to top management (Figure 2.38, strategic function), have more people involved in MI work, and have significantly smaller budgets for MI projects and services. However, despite these distinctions, there is no indication that MI is more developed in B2B companies than B2C ones. This indicates that the two different models serve their purposes equally well, but through different means.

Typically, the greater the focus is on serving the top management in companies, the more resources are required in the centralized MI team. The reason for this is that top management has more strategic and future-oriented needs, than other internal customers. Furthermore, the required deliverables by top management are often complex in nature and require a high level of customization, which makes outsourcing or purchasing reports from third parties a less attractive option. Thus, in order to meet those needs, the MI function needs to dedicate more effort to in-house strategic analysis, which requires additional resources.

Conversely, more standardized MI deliverables often suffice more for sales people and experts than for top management. MI functions in B2C companies are therefore able to serve a larger number of people through the purchase of more reports from external providers. They can also

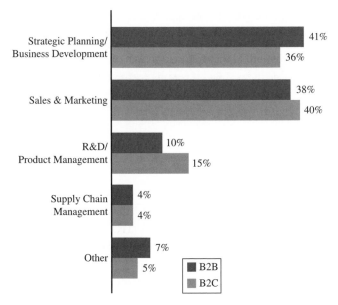

Figure 2.38 Placement of MI function in B2B and B2C companies
Source: 2013 Global Market Intelligence Survey, GIA.

spend more of their time on regular deliverables, which requires fewer people. The set-up does, however, require larger MI budgets.

In conclusion, when there is high availability of intelligence on the market, MI functions will try to serve as many people in their organization as possible. However, in industries where availability of intelligence from external providers is scarce (mainly B2B), MI programs aim to serve primarily their top management.

SUMMARY

The 2013 Global MI Survey measures the state of MI in over 880 companies from 21 separate industries and 64 different countries. Over 1,200 decision-makers and MI managers responded to the survey, making it the largest study on MI to date.

KEY FINDINGS: MI IS CONDUCTED MORE EFFICIENTLY IN GLOBAL COMPANIES COMPARED TO 2011

- In relative terms, decision-making is 15% more efficient in companies that have an MI function in place, compared to those without.

- ROI from MI is becoming more apparent; 80% of all companies say that investments in MI have paid off, an increase of 2% since 2011.

- The average size of MI teams has been reduced by one person to 12 people since 2011. However, the number of contributors to MI has risen by 15% to 109 people.

- The average MI budget for projects and services has increased 53% to €1.6 million or $2.1 million since 2011. However, 50% of all companies spend only €150,000 or $195,000 or less.

KEY FINDINGS: COMPANIES WITH WORLD CLASS MARKET INTELLIGENCE FUNCTIONS ARE EXPANDING THEIR TEAMS AND OPERATE WITH BOTH CENTRALIZED (IN-HOUSE) AND OUTSOURCED SERVICES TO BETTER SERVE NEEDS THROUGHOUT THEIR ORGANIZATIONS

- Companies with world class MI functions are adopting a two-pronged approach to MI, where a larger central MI team serves top management, while the rest of the organization is served through a greater use of outsourced MI services.

- Companies with world class MI operations have enlarged their central MI teams by five people to 18 people on average.

- Companies with world class MI have increased their use of outsourcing for MI deliverables from 13% to 18% since 2011.

- The proportion of MI deliverables directed towards top management has grown from 38% to 46% in companies with world class MI.

KEY FINDINGS: MARKET INTELLIGENCE TEAMS IN B2B COMPANIES ARE CLOSER TO THEIR TOP MANAGEMENT, AND OPERATE WITH 20% OF THE BUDGETS THAT B2C COMPANIES ENJOY

- The average B2B company employs 12 people in MI, two people more than the average B2C company.

- B2B companies serve their top management 5% more often than B2C companies and spend 6% more of their time on ad hoc MI requests.

- The average B2C company outsources more MI work and operates with four times the MI budget of a typical B2B company (€4.2 million versus €0.8 million).

KEY FINDINGS: INDUSTRY COMPARISONS SHOW THAT LARGE BUDGETS ARE NO GUARANTEE FOR MORE ADVANCED MI FUNCTIONS OR HIGHER ROI

- MI is most advanced in media and entertainment companies but, interestingly, that is also where the perceived ROI is the lowest.

- The highest perceived ROI for MI is instead in the environment and renewables industry, where budgets are slightly higher.

- Large budgets, however, are no guarantee for advanced MI functions. For example, medical devices and healthcare companies spend significantly more on MI every year than companies in other industries, yet their MI programs are the fourth least advanced of all industries in the study.

PART 2

Roadmap to World Class Market Intelligence

3   **Key Success Factors of World Class Market Intelligence**.............. 53

The World Class Market Intelligence Roadmap.................................. 53

Summary 62

4   **Intelligence Scope – Determining the Purpose, Target Groups, and Focus Areas of an Intelligence Program** 63

Introduction: Intelligence Scope as a Key Success Factor of Market Intelligence... 63

Getting Started: Determining the Scope of the Intelligence Program.. 66

Continuous Development: Towards World Class Levels in Intelligence Scope.. 72

Summary 75

5   **Intelligence Process – Turning Random Data into Meaningful Insight** 77

Introduction: The Intelligence Cycle.. 77

Getting Started: Developing the Intelligence Process 79

Continuous Development: Towards World Class Levels in Intelligence Process 83

Summary 85

6   **Intelligence Deliverables – Building a High-Impact Market Intelligence Product Portfolio**.. 87

Introduction: Market Intelligence Deliverables as a Key Success Factor of Market Intelligence 87

Getting Started: Developing an Optimized Market Intelligence
   Delivery Capability 88
Continuous Development: Towards World Class Levels
   in Intelligence Deliverables 94
Summary 98

**7   Intelligence Tools – Collecting, Storing, and Disseminating
       Intelligence** 101
Introduction: Intelligence Tools as a Key Success Factor
   of World Class Market Intelligence 101
Getting Started: Planning and Implementing
   an Intelligence Portal 103
Continuous Development: Towards World Class Levels
   in Intelligence Tools... 111
Summary 113

**8   Intelligence Organization – The People and Resources
       that Generate the Impact**.. 115
Introduction: Intelligence Organization as a Key Success Factor
   of World Class Market Intelligence 115
Getting Started: Planning for an Optimized Intelligence
   Organization... 117
Continuous Development: Towards World Class Levels
   in Intelligence Organization... 127
Summary 129

**9   Intelligence Culture – Engaging the Organization
       in Market Intelligence**.. 131
Introduction: Business Impact through an Intelligence Culture......... 131
Getting Started: Planning for an Optimized Intelligence Culture 133
Continuous Development: Towards World Class Levels
   in Intelligence Culture.. 137
Summary 139

3 Key Success Factors of World Class Market Intelligence

THE WORLD CLASS MARKET INTELLIGENCE ROADMAP

In Chapter 1, we concluded that organizations should invest in generating such collective understanding about their operating environment that can be leveraged for competitiveness and growth. Market Intelligence (MI) as a program contributes to this goal through enabling:

- Better and faster decisions

- Time and cost savings

- Organizational learning and new ideas

A properly designed and implemented MI program yields benefits that far exceed the cost of developing and maintaining the activity. Yet many companies have found it troublesome to orchestrate their efforts around MI once the decision has been made to invest in the activity. Lack of structure, in turn results in many challenges over time: how to demonstrate value right from the start, how to prioritize the development efforts, how to move to the next level once the basic MI setup has been implemented, how to measure success, and, ultimately, how to win the continued support by top management to the investments in MI?

As a response to the need of companies to structure their MI development efforts, we have designed a World Class MI Development Roadmap that captures the essential elements of MI development:

- Defining why the program exists and whom it will serve.

- Addressing the various "how?" questions:

  o How to design and implement the process of collecting, refining and delivering information

  o How to assist the process technically

  o How to organize the human resources around MI

  o How to root the intelligence program in the organization, blending it in as part of its culture

Responding to the challenges laid out here, the World Class MI Roadmap divides the MI development effort into six Key Success Factors (KSFs), on one hand, and the levels of maturity that organizations typically go through with regards to each KSF on the other. The World Class MI Roadmap has been adopted by a significant number of large organizations to guide their MI development efforts and to provide a concrete yardstick for measuring progress.

In Part 2 we will first introduce the World Class MI Roadmap and its dimensions, dedicating thereafter a separate chapter to each of the six KSFs and their related sub-frameworks. The stages of maturity that organizations typically go through with regards to each KSF will then be introduced and discussed.

The World Class MI Roadmap is static in that it describes stages of MI development at a given point in time. It is best suited for assessing the current state of an existing MI program and for planning the incremental steps required for taking it from one stage to the next and towards the best-in-class standards. In contrast, Chapters 15 and 16 will address the hands-on "How to get started" question by presenting a more dynamic development approach for setting up an intelligence program based on a needs analysis that will direct and sequence the efforts around each of the KSFs.

The World Class MI Roadmap, illustrated in Table 3.1 and later on, simply referred to as the "MI Roadmap", draws on the extensive consultative experience of the authors with hundreds of companies around the world, and also relies on several extensive research studies on how large companies conduct intelligence activities on a global scale.

SIX KEY SUCCESS FACTORS OF MARKET INTELLIGENCE DEVELOPMENT

Before going into detail in discussing the KSFs presented in the World Class MI Framework, definitions will be given in Table 3.2 for each one. Also, the five levels of evolution for each KSF in the matrix will be explained. Overall, any MI development efforts need to be seen as parts of a systematic initiative to build and maintain an intelligence program, as opposed to addressing the KSFs in isolation from each other.

FIVE STAGES OF MARKET INTELLIGENCE MATURITY

The World Class MI Roadmap divides each six KSFs of MI development into five levels of maturity, where the levels range from "Firefighters", the beginners, to "Futurists", the ideal and the most advanced organizations with regards to the level and maturity of their intelligence activity.

Reviewing the current status of their MI development, organizations typically find themselves at different levels with regards to different KSFs. Ideally, all success factors would be developed hand in hand since they are highly inter-dependent. However, in reality the more "technical" a success factor is by nature, the easier it tends to be to bring it towards world class levels.

Table 3.1 The World Class MI Roadmap

Description	Informal MI "Firefighters"	Basic MI "Beginners"	Intermediate MI "Coordinators"	Advanced MI "Directors"	World Class MI "Futurists"
Intelligence Scope	No Specific focus has been determined. Ad hoc needs drive the scope.	Limited scope, seeking quick wins. Focus typically on competitors or customers only.	Wide scope with the attempt to cover the current operating environment comprehensively.	Analytical deep dives about specific topics complement the comprehensive monitoring of the operating environment.	Broad, deep and future-oriented scope that also covers topics outside of the immediately relevant operating environment.
Intelligence Process	Reactive ad hoc process puts out fires as they emerge. Uncoordinated purchases of information.	Needs analysis made. Establishing info collection from secondary external sources. Little or no analysis involved in the process.	Secondary info sourcing complemented by well established primary info collection and analysis.	Advanced market monitoring and analysis processes established. Targeted communication of output to specific business processes and decision points.	Intelligence process deeply rooted in both global and local levels of the organization. MI fully integrated with key business processes; two-way communication.
Intelligence Deliverables	Ad hoc deliverables quickly put together from scratch.	Regular newsletters and profiles complement ad hoc deliverables.	Systematic market monitoring and analysis reports emerge as new, structured MI output.	Two-way communication is increased in both production and utilization of MI output. Highly analytical deliverables.	High degree of future orientation and collaborative insight creation in producing and delivering the MI output.
Intelligence Tools	Email and shared folders as the primary means for sharing and archiving information.	Corporate intranet is emerging as a central storage for intelligence output.	Web-based MI portal established that provides access to structured MI output. Users receive email alerts about new info in the system.	Sophisticated channeling of both internally and externally produced MI content to the MI portal. Multiple access interfaces to the portal in use.	Seamless integration of the MI portal to other relevant IT tools. Lively collaboration of users through the MI portal.
Intelligence Organization	No resources specifically dedicated to MI. Individuals conducting MI activities on a non-structured basis.	One person appointed as responsible for MI. Increasing coordination of MI work in the company. Loose relationships with external info providers.	A fully dedicated person manages MI and coordinates activities. Centralized, internally or externally resourced info collection and analysis capabilities exist.	Advanced analytical and consultative skills in the intelligence team. MI network with dedicated resources in business units for collecting local market info. Non-core MI activities outsourced.	MI team has reached the status of trusted advisors to management. Internal MI network collaborating actively. Internal MI organization smoothly integrated with the outsourced resources.
Intelligence Culture	No shared understanding exists of the role and benefits of systematic MI operations.	Some awareness exists of MI, but the organizational culture overall is still neutral towards MI.	MI awareness in a moderate level. Sharing of info is encouraged through internal training and marketing of MI.	MI awareness is high and people participate actively in producing MI content. Top management voices its continuous support to MI efforts.	A strong MI mindset is reflected in the way people are curious towards the operating environment and co-create insights about it.

Source: Global Intelligence Alliance.

Table 3.2   Key Success Factor definitions

Key Success Factor	Definition
Intelligence Scope	"Intelligence Scope" refers to defining the very purpose of the intelligence program, the user groups, and timeframe (past – present – future) of the intelligence activities, and the specific topics of which the user groups will need information on a regular basis. Topics under the intelligence scope typically include, e.g. customers, competitors, suppliers, trends, and geographical market areas.
Intelligence Process	"Intelligence Process" refers to the gathering, analysis, and reporting of information to its user groups. The intelligence process should always be anchored to the existing corporate processes, such as strategic planning, marketing and sales, innovation and product management, as well as supply chain management.
Intelligence Deliverables	"Intelligence Deliverables" are the concrete output of the intelligence process. Deliverables may be tangible content products such as analysis reports, profiles, or market signals monitoring, or they can be interactive workshops and briefings. Deliverables may also include software tools designed to enable "self service" usage of MI.
Intelligence Tools	By "Intelligence Tools" we refer mainly to dedicated intelligence software tools that help keep the intelligence process together by serving as a searchable database of structured and relevant information. Also, intelligence tools help to automate routines of processing data into intelligence and regularly delivering the intelligence output to its users. Intelligence tools may also include templates and analysis techniques.
Intelligence Organization	"Intelligence Organization" refers to the resources that combined make the intelligence process happen. Appointing someone as the owner of the corporate intelligence activity typically is the starting point of forming an intelligence organization, but the person needs both internal and external networks to support their work: internal network of intelligence users and contributors from different parts of the organization, as well as an external network of information sources that may include outsourcing partners, databases, industry consultants, research report providers, and so forth.
Intelligence Culture	"Intelligence Culture" keeps the entire intelligence program alive, and it obviously cannot be sourced externally. The most important element in building an intelligence culture is senior management's genuine support of the activity. Other important building blocks are demonstrated benefits of the activity as well as internal training and marketing efforts.

Similarly, the softer success factors such as MI culture tend to lag behind, as quick wins are seldom associated with developing such abstract and indistinct topics, and progress is not very simply measured, either.

Then what does each of the five different levels of maturity stand for? Our generic descriptions for the maturity of the MI program as a whole have been presented in Table 3.3.

Reaching the intermediate, "MI Coordinator", level is relatively straightforward with regards to any of the KSFs, provided that sufficient resources are available. However, the rate of progress tends to slow down towards the higher end of the scale, as the challenges lie increasingly in changing human behavior and customary ways of doing things rather than just technically implementing new processes, tools, and deliverables.

In the following chapters, we will discuss each of the KSFs individually, addressing their specific characteristics and the related challenges in bringing them closer to the world class level. Case examples will be presented in conjunction with each KSF to further showcase ways to take the corporate intelligence program forward and towards the ideal state of affairs.

Table 3.3 Descriptions for the maturity of the MI program

Level of maturity	Description
1. Informal MI "Firefighters"	Intelligence activities are mainly conducted on an ad hoc basis with little coordination. Few resources for MI exist, and no scope or process has been defined for MI activities.
2. Basic MI "Beginners"	"Beginners" are taking the first steps towards a structured intelligence program. Based on an intelligence needs analysis, some fundamental elements of the organization's business environment are being monitored, still mainly in an ad hoc fashion.
3. Intermediate MI "Coordinators"	A structured MI process has been adopted in the organization. Narrow as its scope may still be, the level of analysis has reached a reasonable level. However, the intelligence program is only loosely integrated to business processes, if at all. A software tool for MI is typically implemented at this stage.
4. Advanced MI "Directors"	The intelligence program is already on a very sophisticated level, and involves an internal organization and connectivity to business processes. A solid external network of information sources and vendors has also been established. The deliverables of the MI process match the needs articulated by decision-makers and generate true impact.
5. World Class MI "Futurists"	MI plays a vital role in both formulating and implementing the company strategy, enhancing the quality of work and future orientation of the entire organization. MI is an integral part of most business processes.

Case: Building a Sophisticated Intelligence Program at Royal Vopak Using the World Class MI Roadmap

Background

Interviewed for this case was Mr. Rene Loozen, Business Intelligence Manager in the Commercial Excellence Department at Royal Vopak, a Dutch company and the world's largest provider of conditioned storage facilities for bulk liquids.

Having been with the company since 2001 in various business analysis and project management related positions, Mr. Loozen joined Vopak's Commercial Excellence program in spring 2007, with the task to start executing new strategic initiatives of which Business Intelligence (BI) was one. The "BI network" was kicked off in September 2007, and, in the same conjunction, an intelligence software tool was set up to serve as the centre point of the BI program from the beginning.

The BI Network at Vopak consists of members from each of the company's six divisions, and the network has one or two workshops each year in addition to a teleconference held on a monthly basis. Each member in the BI network has 20% of their time allocated to intelligence work, and they report to their respective supervisors. Rene Loozen's supervisor reports to the CEO.

(Continued)

Developing Intelligence Activities at Vopak with the Help of the World Class MI Roadmap

Vopak started using the World Class MI Roadmap right from the beginning in 2007 to set milestones and yardsticks for progress measurement in the intelligence initiative. In October 2007, Rene Loozen considers that they had largely reached Level 2 with regards to all KSFs in the Framework, while the status in February 2009 was approaching Level 4 already. In the following we will look into what has happened in between.

Level 1 – The Inauguration of Intelligence Work at Vopak in Mid-2007

"We started the journey towards more systematized intelligence operations in 2007", says Loozen, who describes the starting situation as follows:

- Market information was scattered over the different Vopak divisions and business units
- No policy existed on how to share this information/knowledge
- The perception prevailed that the effectiveness of the intelligence process within Vopak had to improve in order for the company to become more competitive

At the same time, a number of market developments suggested that bringing the intelligence activity to the next level was in order:

- The pace of change in the market is accelerating every year > increasing market dynamics
- The oil and chemical industry is increasingly globalized > linkages between different regions are essential
- Emerging economies play an increasingly important role in Vopak's business
- The number of competitors is growing
- Vopak seeks strong organic growth, for which an effective intelligence process is needed
- Vopak's Board of Directors had identified 17 strategic improvement initiatives of which BI was one

"As a result, we understood that we needed to take an approach to intelligence development where different aspects were developed in parallel", Loozen says. "GIA's World Class MI Framework seemed to fit the purpose well", he continues.

Level 2 – End-2007

Having completed the very first tasks such as intelligence status analysis and the formulation of BI objectives and working principles, Vopak had an initial idea of how the intelligence activity should be developed, going forward. A "BI mission statement" was articulated in order "to increase our competitiveness through a better decision-making process, which is based on better analysis of and maximum insight in our business environment". Also, at Vopak, "We don't want to be surprised" gained support as a tagline for the intelligence activity.

The main goals for BI were identified as:

- To ensure efficient communication mechanism for sharing knowledge

- To coordinate and improve BI at Vopak in order to take more proactive and better informed decisions and to become more competitive

- To become a serious business partner for customers, both internal and external

"One obvious step in the initial phase was of course to structure the use of external business information sources", Loozen says. "We had a number of information sources in use throughout the company, and we tried to identify the best ones that could be used throughout the company."

The BI network described in the beginning was also set up in the same conjunction, and since it was soon understood that an intelligence platform was also needed to support the intelligence process, a software tool was selected and implemented to serve the purpose. "We definitely didn't want to start developing something from scratch in-house, simply to save time and effort for more important things. That's why purchasing a software product was an obvious choice for us", Loozen comments.

Level 3 – An Expanded Intelligence Scope Yields an Increasingly Comprehensive Understanding of Market Dynamics

Rene Loozen describes the evolution of the Intelligence Scope at Vopak: "We understood that the scope of the intelligence activities must be rather broad if we were to really understand change and to identify emerging business opportunities. Naturally the scope also needed to link to the expertise areas of the members in the Vopak BI Network."

BI efforts were subsequently organized around the following topics:

- Competitor Intelligence

- Product Flow Intelligence

- Market Intelligence

- Customer Intelligence

- Major Trends in the Business Environment

(Continued)

The portfolio for intelligence deliverables has also come a long way since mid-2007:

1.   In early 2008, a competitor and market database was launched that includes information about market definitions, size, share, and growth. Vopak also had to identify which terminals would be viewed as competitors and which ones would not.

2.   Based on the above database, competitor profiles were developed. This was also the start of strategic competitor benchmarking on a regular basis.

3.   Product Flow Intelligence was developed to provide analysis of the global market dynamics for different products like benzene, methanol, or biofuels.

4.   Quarterly market share presentation was set up for the executive Stratcom committee that consists of Vopak's Board and divisional presidents.

5.   Global market reports provide insight into customers' market dynamics and strategies.

6.   Trends in the business environment describe major macro- and micro-level trends that may have an impact on Vopak's business.

7.   A global customer survey is now being conducted in which 2,600 customers and 1,400 third parties (service providers for customers, agencies, trucking companies, shipping companies) are surveyed for their perception of Vopak's services.

Level 4 – Continuous Development

"I believe now that we are on level 4 on GIA's World Class MI Framework", Rene Loozen says in February 2009. "We have all the fundamental elements in place, and have now shifted the focus on raising the level of analysis of our deliverables, and on developing the 'soft' issues such as the culture of knowledge sharing within the organization."

One particular current initiative is to survey all intelligence users at Vopak for their perceptions about the quality of the BI function. In addition, tighter integration of the BI output into various business processes is very much on the agenda at this stage. An increasingly collaborative approach has been taken here, with arranging BI workshops and regular meetings and teleconferences among BI representatives and the end users within the different business units.

"To conclude, it is my feeling that we now have a broad scope but also analytical depth in what we produce", Rene Loozen says. "We are future oriented in our approach and frequently use scenario analysis in combination with forecasting as methods to understand the future dynamics of our industry. One example is that we have a project focusing on as far as the year 2035", Loozen continues. "We have an intelligence network in place and are producing deliverables that have been tied into our strategic and operational business processes. We also have an intelligence platform to collect, store, and share our business information and intelligence reports."

Areas for Improvement

Intelligence culture: "People are sharing more and more knowledge, and we also enjoy the strong support of our Board to the intelligence operation", Loozen says, "but I still think we could do even better. I guess the challenge is that people are on different levels of experience with regards to intelligence, which does influence their willingness to share market information."

Marketing of the intelligence activities: "One of the tools to enhance the intelligence culture is definitely marketing, which in our case is a quarterly newsletter that our Commercial Excellence department publishes. BI plays a big role in the publication already, but we still need more concrete examples of success stories", Loozen explains.

Lessons Learned at Vopak

Step by step development process: it is important to focus on one step at a time, and to do it according to a proper intelligence implementation plan of which the World Class MI Framework is a useful example in our experience. Good contacts with management in order to prioritize the work are of course also essential.

Well defined Intelligence deliverables: delivering valuable intelligence output is the key to the success of the entire intelligence program. "We started with the intelligence software tool as the first 'deliverable' in the sense that it made intelligence something tangible that could be used by many different groups within the company", Loozen says.

Proper BI network management and personal contacts: expectations need to be managed in a BI network where people participate on a part time basis and always have their own division as their first priority. Training is also required to bring the BI network members to the same level. At the same time, it helps tremendously to have an extensive network of people in the company that goes far beyond those that actually have intelligence included in their job description.

Support from the Board: it is of course vital to have the top management's support, and as few layers between management and the intelligence operation as is meaningful.

SUMMARY

- The World Class MI Development Roadmap has been designed in response to the need of companies:

  o   to structure their efforts around the many aspects of MI development

  o   to have a yardstick with which to measure progress with the development efforts

  o   to benchmark their MI programs against other companies and the world class standards

- In the World Class MI Roadmap, the MI development efforts have been divided into six KSFs:

  o   Intelligence Scope: the purpose, user groups, breadth, depth, and time horizon of the intelligence program

  o   Intelligence Process: the phased processing of an intelligence assignment from a needs analysis to the information collection, analysis, and delivery phases, and finally, utilization and feedback

  o   Intelligence Deliverables: the output that the intelligence program produces for the MI users

  o   Intelligence Tools: techniques, templates, and, most notably, intelligence software tools for storing and disseminating the intelligence output

  o   Intelligence Organization: the resources required to run the intelligence program

  o   Intelligence Culture: the shared interest in the organization towards knowledge sharing about the important topics in the operating environment

- The World Class MI Roadmap further divides each of the KSFs into five stages of maturity, ranging from "Beginners" at level I to "Futurists" at level 5.

4 Intelligence Scope – Determining the Purpose, Target Groups, and Focus Areas of an Intelligence Program

INTRODUCTION: INTELLIGENCE SCOPE AS A KEY SUCCESS FACTOR OF MARKET INTELLIGENCE

Case: Launching a Business Intelligence Function in the Additives Division of the Lubrizol Corporation

The Lubrizol Corporation (NYSE: LZ) is an innovative specialty chemical company that produces and supplies technologies to customers in the global transportation, industrial, and consumer markets. The Additives Division (LZA) focuses on lubricant additives.

Prior to the recent economic recession, changes affecting LZA's markets generally were gradual and incremental. Consequently, business planning responsibilities frequently were stovepiped within the individual business segments. However, the abrupt disruptions brought about by the recession prompted senior management to commission the development of a pan-segment function to provide broader and deeper intelligence support to business segment planning activities.

The challenges included:

1. Developing an intelligence program to serve a broad array of additive business segments (passenger car, heavy duty vehicle (on-road and off-road), driveline, fuels, marine engines, small engines, hydraulics, greases, metalworking fluids).

2. Overcoming internal cultural barriers to pan-segment cooperation.

(Continued)

3.   Delivering a work product of material value to business segment planning activities.

4.   Doing all of the preceding with extremely limited resources.

LZA took a phased approach to developing the intelligence function: the 1.0 deliverable was due in June 2010, to be followed by "2.0"; incremental improvement in 2011, and "3.0"; future perfect, in 2012. The development effort is headed by Terry Thiele, Director of Sustainable Product Strategies.

In our case example about Lubrizol Corporation, the intelligence function was initiated as a response to the need of improving the quality of strategic planning in the company's Additives Division. Indeed, strategy should be the primary driver for setting up and developing intelligence activities: high quality MI will help the company to implement strategies, but also to formulate new ones. When derived from strategy, not only the purpose of the intelligence program but also its user groups, topics to be covered, and time horizon will be inherently meaningful and valuable for the organization.

Considering the above from a more technical perspective, the questions to be addressed at the stage of setting up and scoping an intelligence program include:

- User groups

    o   What are the corporate activities and target user groups that the intelligence program should serve?

- Breadth of scope

    o   What are the topics on which the above target groups will need information, and how will they be prioritized?

- Depth of scope

    o   What requirements will the above needs set to the intelligence team's analytical and consultative capabilities?

- Time horizon

    o   What will be the time horizon and, in particular, the future orientation of the intelligence program?

Defining the scope of the intelligence program translates into conducting a needs analysis for the entire intelligence program: identifying the corporate functions that will be using the intelligence deliverables, and topics and themes that will be most relevant for each of them. Additionally, the degree of future orientation needs to be addressed; looking into the rearview mirror is a good starting point. However, in a mature MI program, a great deal of time is spent on outlining possible future scenarios about the anticipated developments in the operating environment.

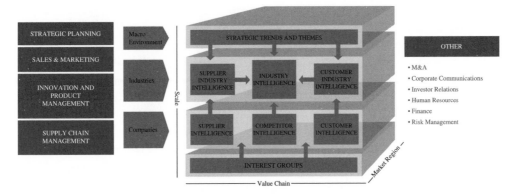

Figure 4.1   The scope of the MI program covers the target groups of the activity, and their primary information requirements. Topics of importance will vary between target groups, as will the ideal deliverables of MI.
Source: Global Intelligence Alliance.

Figure 4.1 highlights some of the most common user groups to intelligence, and the intelligence topics of interest. In a typical scenario, the first target group to the intelligence activity is the corporate function (and the adjacent ones) under which the intelligence program has been placed. Since the strategic planning, business development, or marketing functions quite often initiate the intelligence program, the primary target groups of the activity are typically made up of people working in client-facing positions, or in those that involve strategic planning or corporate development.

Establishing and operating an intelligence program is an investment in internal "process infrastructure"; it would be a waste of resources not to at least consider expanding its reach beyond the initial target groups that have intelligence needs. Innovation and product management, supply chain management, M&A or investor relations are examples of activities that are highly dependent on accurate business information and may benefit from the existing intelligence activity, if only its scope will be extended to cover their specific needs. Indeed what is typical of rather immature intelligence programs is that information to cater to the needs of different user groups is being collected and processed in silos, which easily results in cost redundancies and missed synergies.

Case: The Purpose Statement of MI at Merck & Co.

"Global Competitive Intelligence (GCI) is the recognized Center of Excellence that provides MSD with actionable intelligence, insight, and recommendations essential for strategy development, execution and decision-making."

While it is many times beneficial to leverage an existing intelligence infrastructure to serve additional organizational functions and units, there may also be situations where synergies

(Continued)

will not be achieved or they would be so minimal that they will not justify the engagement of several different functions or units into one intelligence program. This may be the case in, for instance, large organizations that run very different businesses that have entirely different intelligence needs. Or an intelligence program may have been set up to serve marketing and sales in a company, but to extend the scope of the intelligence program to also cover the needs of innovation management could require an entirely separate set of skills, information sources, and tools from the intelligence team. Hence it may make sense to readily separate the intelligence development approaches and either define a separate scope for the intelligence work that serves innovation management, or run a separate intelligence program altogether.

Still another potential case for separate intelligence programs is a company whose business is so complex that an attempt to list out all relevant factors in its operating environment would end up in a list of several hundreds of topics. Conducting, for instance, daily market monitoring on such a complex set of topics would typically have to be handled by several analysts anyway, so defining the scope for each one would readily suggest that a centralized approach to serving all intelligence needs in the organization may not be the most meaningful one.

GETTING STARTED: DETERMINING THE SCOPE OF THE INTELLIGENCE PROGRAM

START SMALL AND EXPAND THE SCOPE ALONG THE WAY

Developing an intelligence program from the ground up may seem like a daunting task, considering all the aspects that should be covered with very limited resources, especially at the start. Getting just the intelligence *scope* right will require considerable efforts if one aims at going both wide and deep in the topics of interest, serving numerous corporate functions, and delivering highly future-oriented intelligence output.

In practice, the intelligence scoping effort is best started small and expanded gradually as the intelligence program matures and resources are made available for those activities that are seen as valuable for the business.

The first step is to reach a stage where there's at least some sort of focus in the intelligence activity rather than only putting out fires as they emerge. Most companies concentrate on first understanding their customers and competitors better, and this immediate focus may often carry over as the most important focus area throughout the intelligence development effort.

Also, at first the intelligence program may only be serving one group of users in the organization instead of several. Indeed with limited resources it is wise to rather first concentrate the efforts on narrow areas where good results can realistically be expected than trying to serve too many user groups for any of them to see any true impact from the activity.

Many companies call the immediate priorities "KITs", Key Intelligence Topics, of which there may be only ten or even fewer, depending on the company and its line(s) of business. Working on the immediately relevant, strategic topics first is also wise from the return on investment (ROI) perspective: with success stories, it is possible to rapidly prove the value of the intelligence activity and legitimate further investments in the area. Gradually with added resources, companies tend to widen their intelligence scope by expanding the information architecture, i.e. the organized list of topics that are deemed relevant for the company's business.

To determine the primary purpose of the intelligence program and to make up the list of the most immediate KITs, a needs analysis will have to be conducted among the users of the first intelligence deliverables. Different methods exist for mapping out their requirements:

- Deriving the needs directly from the **existing corporate strategy.**

- **One-on-one interviews** will consume a lot of time and effort; however, they are the best way of developing an in-depth understanding about the different drivers that each user group of the intelligence program will have for involving themselves in the activity at all.

- **Surveys** are an efficient needs analysis method, yet they may only yield superficial results that reflect the relatively little amount of time and effort that is required from the respondents.

- Conducting **workshops** will again require considerably more time and preparation; however, if one wants to reach a solid consensus about the focus areas of the intelligence program, time to discuss the topics face to face will almost inevitably be required.

- **Combining all of the above methods** is the recommended way of defining the ultimate purpose of the intelligence program: conducting a survey, or several, and complementing it with selected interviews will serve as valuable preparation for sharing thoughts and making conclusions in an eventual workshop among a group of key people.

Over time, the scope of an average intelligence program tends to deepen, i.e. the analytical and consultative delivery capability of the intelligence program increases, and so will the usefulness of the deliverables for strategic decision-making purposes. Finally, an increasing emphasis will be placed on future-orientation, i.e. in addition to producing highly analytical output on a wide range of topics – and probably for a wide user base – the intelligence program will be able to drive discussions about the future strategic choices that the organization has, going forward.

BREADTH OF SCOPE: DETERMINING THE KEY INTELLIGENCE TOPICS AND INFORMATION ARCHITECTURE

Once the primary user groups of the intelligence program have been defined, their intelligence needs should be addressed. These needs will fall under two categories: the *topics* on which information is needed, and the *format* in which the output should be delivered. Figure 4.2 highlights

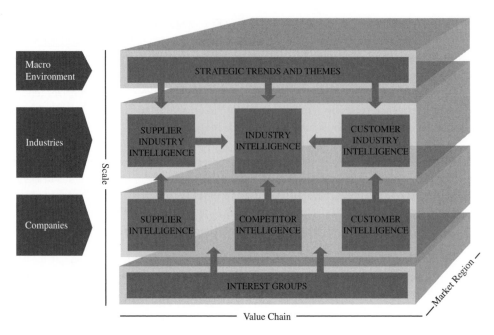

Figure 4.2   Dimensions of the intelligence topics
Source: Global Intelligence Alliance.

the topics on which most organizations need information through their intelligence program and
organizes them into a three-dimensional framework.

- **The value chain dimension** is illustrated as the horizontal axis in Figure 4.2: understanding customers is important for any company, as is understanding what the
  competitors are doing. With the tendency of many companies moving up the value
  chain to reach for the end customer in their search for higher value-add and higher
  margins, it has also become commonplace to add "customers' customers" to the
  list of intelligence topics on the value chain. As the activity of moving up the value
  chain may also be taking place at the back end on the supplier side, increasingly
  many companies have added suppliers to their list of intelligence topics even though
  the suppliers may have traditionally been something that "the company already
  knows enough of". Finally, there may also be parties around a company that are not
  directly part of the same value chain but may still have an impact on the company's
  business (for instance authorities or industry associations). We call these parties
  "interest groups".

- **The scale of topics** is illustrated as the vertical axis in Figure 4.2: many market developments that are relevant for a company are taking place at the level of individual
  companies, i.e. suppliers, competitors, customers, and customers' customers that
  are therefore included under the company's radar. Grouped together, the individual
  companies make up industries, the dynamics of which a company also needs to

understand to be able to assess the developments that may be affecting their business and other companies on the value chain. Still beyond the industry level there are trends and drivers that may be forces completely outside of one's own immediate business focus. However, a social or political trend that is happening today might well impact one's business environment several years from the current moment, and the company should therefore also keep trends and megatrends under their radar.

- **The geographical dimension** is illustrated as the third axis in Figure 4.2: the companies, interest groups, industries, and trends that make up a company's external operating environment are typically not identical for each geographical area that the company operates in, and the geographical dimension therefore presents yet another set of priorities to the topics that the company should focus on. Where does the company's money come from today? What are the emerging growth areas? Which markets can perhaps be left with little attention?

Taking the intelligence scope towards increasing sophistication often starts with addressing the breadth of the intelligence activity, i.e. the topics: a taxonomy – an organized list of topics and subtopics of interest to the company will be developed that maps out the business environment as in Figure 4.2: the company's relevant competitors, customers, customers' customers, and suppliers will be included, as will the respective industries, and the trends and interest groups that will likely have an impact on the company's business. Finally, the geographical areas from which the company needs information may also be added to the topics of relevance that now forms the skeleton around which the information content will be organized.

The length of the eventual information architecture is not a value in itself even though the list of topics tends to become longer with the growing maturity of the intelligence program. An alternative way of addressing the breadth of the intelligence program is to first only focus on the KITs of one or just a few target groups instead of the entire company, and the focus areas may subsequently only cover, for instance, customers and competitors, and further topics are added to the list as the intelligence needs evolve. At some point the direction of the development in the information architecture may also bounce back: it may not make sense to deliberately lengthen the list of focus areas with new companies or trends if very little is happening around certain topics on an annual basis, or the impact of those happenings to the own company would be minimal anyway.

The length of the list of priorities is also a result of a cost–benefit analysis: once the company starts conducting regular intelligence efforts on the selected topics of interest, it soon becomes apparent just how pricey it may be to include anything and everything under one's radar (if, for instance, relevant information is not available from public sources in the English language). Also important is people's ability to digest information: massive amounts of data, even if relevant, as opposed to carefully digested and strategically meaningful messages may make all the difference in how well the entire intelligence program is received in the organization.

Once the initial breadth of the intelligence program has been determined, it depends on the company and the target group(s) of the intelligence deliverables, whether the first development efforts will center around setting up regular market screening for daily business signals about the selected topics, or whether it makes more sense to first concentrate on conducting strategic analyses on certain key topics. Continuously collecting news and business signals about the developments in the business environment does make sense as it serves as a pool of readily validated information that feeds into the more analytical output. However, individual business signals alone, even if carefully selected and processed, will not lead to any strategic decisions, and many companies may want to first conduct careful analysis on a narrow list of topics before determining which of them are relevant enough to be put under continuous screening.

DEPTH OF SCOPE: INCREASING THE ANALYTICAL AND CONSULTATIVE CAPABILITY OF THE INTELLIGENCE PROGRAM

Along with the meaningful breadth of scope for the intelligence program, the depth should be worked on, in other words, ensuring that the intelligence program can deliver actionable insights that will have an impact on business rather than just gathering and further disseminating information.

Business needs of the primary target groups of the intelligence program will drive the analytical and consultative efforts towards topic areas where insightful intelligence output should serve as decision-making support. On the other hand, if in conjunction with the intelligence topics set up a continuous market screening system has already been established to monitor the entire operating environment of the company, the system may also raise topics to the agenda that call for further analytical processing: opportunities and threats may arise from the business environment that would go unnoticed without systematic market screening. As a result, companies start adding depth to their intelligence output. Profiles, analysis reports, briefings, and workshops will emerge as intelligence deliverables on selected topics of interest.

Adding depth to the scope of the intelligence program may also happen in parallel with adding breadth, i.e. expanding its user base: for example, the corporate communications function, having seen that the current services do not fully match their information needs, may start to require media monitoring and peer group reviews, and people working in R&D might feel that they would benefit from the existing analysis reports with a twist towards product and innovation management.

FUTURE ORIENTATION: BUILDING ON THE PAST BUT LOOKING AHEAD

Even though the scope of the intelligence program may be both wide and deep, i.e. the program serves the needs of several intelligence user groups and produces highly analytical deliverables, the organization may still be looking primarily in the rearview mirror. The natural next step in the scoping effort is therefore to shift the relative focus of the intelligence activity towards the anticipated future developments of the operating environment that may have an impact on the company's business.

Simple as it may sound, this initiative will put an entirely new set of requirements to the intelligence team producing the output: they will now have to adopt the role of a forecaster, i.e. they will need to start providing interpretations and adding their own business judgment into the analysis output that perhaps only used to concentrate on delivering facts about the past.

Forecasting and anticipating future developments is not simple, and it is hence not surprising to see entire groups of people with different backgrounds taking part in these efforts as the intelligence program matures and gains ground in the organization. Scenario analysis projects and war gaming or market simulation workshops are good examples of activities that are best conducted in groups, preferably involving senior management that is responsible for the future success of the company. The outcome of the efforts is highly future-oriented by definition: scenarios deal with alternative futures, and market simulation is all about anticipating the potential competitive movements in the marketplace and developing alternative strategies for the own company, should some of them become reality.

Case: Enhancing Future Focus in a Sales Driven Company at Randstad Netherlands

In a company that's particularly focused on sales, it is often challenging for the MI professionals to convince the organization about the necessity to also look beyond the most immediate future. Yet, even for the most sales driven organization, understanding the long-term business drivers will naturally dictate the company's future success.

In an effort to further professionalize the MI program of his company, particularly in the areas of forecasting and future focus, Jan Brooijmans concluded that producing and circulating far-reaching future forecasts alone would not fly well in his sales-driven organization. Rather, he decided to take the future focus down to earth:

1.   **Concrete time horizon**. Split the future forecasts into parts and bring them close to the current moment in order to speak the language of all stakeholders. What will this forecast mean next year? Next quarter? Next month? Next week?

2.   **Concrete meaning**. Break down the forecasts by customer industries and further by Randstad's own business lines. Where do the forecasts suggest the next sales efforts should be put and when?

3.   **Concrete language**. Partner with the finance department in order to produce forecasts in number terms, an approach that typically goes down well in a sales-oriented company.

As a result, Brooijmans says, the scope of Randstad's business forecasts has widened both in terms of market coverage and future orientation, yet without compromising the pragmatic need of sales to have something concrete to work with during the next weeks, months, and quarters.

CONTINUOUS DEVELOPMENT: TOWARDS WORLD CLASS LEVELS IN INTELLIGENCE SCOPE

When defining the scope of its intelligence activity, it is recommended that an organization always considers not only the most obvious and immediate user groups to it, but also thinks through whether process and cost efficiencies could be achieved by bringing in additional corporate groups to the user base of a centralized intelligence program. This review may of course also reveal that some functions are *not* best served by a centralized intelligence function but will rather depend on locally or functionally produced market information; however, such a conclusion should be reached through an active evaluation process.

Serving numerous corporate functions with a centralized intelligence program naturally means that the information architecture will be expanded accordingly. A comprehensive list of topics to be covered is not a value in itself (rather, prioritization is); however, the list of topics tends to be longer in an organization where the scope of the intelligence program is mature and approaches world class levels as opposed to an organization in the early stages of its scoping exercise.

In any case, the evolution of the list of KITs and the longer information architecture should never stop: strategies and business environments change, and in alignment with them will change the intelligence priorities of a company that conducts world class MI activities. Trends emerge, companies are acquired and sold, and industries expand and disappear. The scope of an intelligence program is never "ready", but will continue responding to the requirements that the changes both outside and inside of the company will set on it.

The more mature the intelligence program of an organization is, the more time is typically spent on analysis work as opposed to just collecting information: the level of analysis is first raised in intelligence deliverables looking into the rearview mirror, but the relative focus should also be shifted towards analyzing different possible futures. Therefore reaching world class levels in intelligence scope is characterized by a high degree of future orientation in the entire intelligence program. In practice this means that the intelligence program is capable of producing deliverables such as:

- Sales leads reports that directly help generate new business in the future

- Strategic reports that include analytical conclusions and suggested interpretations in the company's context

- Scenario analyses and workshops

- War gaming and market simulation exercises

One of the key things to bear in mind when initiating and further adjusting the scope of an intelligence program is that the intelligence requirements of the different target groups vary, and so should the topics and deliverables with which the groups are being serviced. Few companies are uniform in their intelligence needs, and while the marketing function may be happy with a couple of analytical brand development reports annually, the sales team, for example, might require detailed, daily signals about new local business opportunities. The strategic planning function may require still different intelligence output to support its operations. This takes us back to square one: determining the scope of the intelligence program is about discovering the areas where the corporate intelligence activity will be of most value for the entire company's business.

**Case: Creating Strategic Foresight by Using Megatrends
in Market Intelligence at Cisco Systems**

Future orientation as a facilitator of growth

Future orientation is one of the key characteristics of an intelligence program's SCOPE taken to world class levels. Joost Drieman, Director, Market and Business Intelligence European Markets at Cisco Systems, explains how the company is using megatrends in MI to create strategic foresight.

At Cisco, the MI program has been built around four pillars:

- **Environment intelligence** (economic predictions, market characteristics, social sustainability, opportunities in the addressable and adjacent markets)

- **Customer intelligence** (customers' buying behavior, segmentation, profiling, demographics, upselling and cross-selling opportunities, customer satisfaction and loyalty)

- **Competitive intelligence** (the competitive landscape and power lines, strategies, presence in different markets, co-opetition)

- **Channel intelligence** (the channel landscape and dynamics)

Understanding megatrends is seen as important in all of the intelligence areas above, but what is a megatrend? Joost Drieman gives an example: over the next few years, 30 million Chinese will move over to Europe on business. A chain analysis quickly reveals that this trend will drive significant business opportunities in several industries: more aircrafts and airports will be needed – in the middle of the growing pressures of reducing air pollution – more hotels, restaurants, entertainment, and various professional services will be needed, and all of the above will eventually set new requirements for communication infrastructure, which is of particular interest to Cisco.

Why then is understanding megatrends so vital for a company's success? One naturally does not want to miss a trend so as to avoid losing market share, but for Cisco, understanding megatrends still represents more of an opportunity: one of the company's objectives is to grow faster than the IT market on average, and understanding megatrends is seen as a means to facilitate such growth.

(Continued)

How to identify and prioritize megatrends?

Joost Drieman explains how Cisco has gone about mapping out megatrends that may have an impact on its business over the coming years:

1. Invite a group of internal experts from different parts of the organization.

2. Gather insights from research providers such as academia, research institutions, and consulting houses.

3. Conduct own surveys (Cisco conducted one on LinkedIn).

4. Brainstorm based on the input on the potential upcoming megatrends, and list them out.

In the end, Cisco had compiled a list of as many as 200 trends, and a critical assessment was in order: was each one really impactful and enduring enough to be a megatrend, or were some of the observations rather just phenomena that would possibly fade away? As a result of the re-evaluation, Cisco ended up with a list of 50 megatrends that were put under surveillance to see if future signals would continue to reinforce the identified trends, or if further developments were already in process.

How to assess the impact of megatrends and derive opportunities from them?

In a complex world, not all trends happen at the same time, nor do they have an identical impact on the company's business. Acknowledging this, Drieman and his colleagues at Cisco developed an Impact Grouping map where the identified trends were grouped under six categories based on their anticipated impact on business, and the timeline:

1. Missed the train

2. Are we taking action?

3. Are we preparing?

4. Nice to know

5. Interesting

6. Keep an eye on

The trends were then further mapped into a framework that connects potentially interesting trends together. As an example, maybe the trend of public sector indebtedness combined with the trend of sustainability will lead to a business opportunity for those who can produce green IT solutions for the public sector?

How to communicate the results of a megatrends analysis?

The results of a megatrends analysis are necessarily strategic in nature, but the analysis effort may be wasted if the messages are buried in a pile of PowerPoint slides that is thick enough to exhaust any busy decision-maker up front. Knowing this, Drieman with his team paid specific attention to building fact sheets that were as crisp and digestible as possible:

- What is the trend?

- Facts and figures

- Impact on Cisco

- Assessment of disruptiveness

For most of the trends, more information was available in the notes. Also, the reports were available in both ppt and pdf format.

Finally, Joost Drieman points out that there's ample evidence about global megatrends also provoking subsequent anti-trends, which is something for the trend analysts to bear in mind. Another thing to bear in mind is that, eventually, all trends are driven by the end customers', i.e. the consumers', wants and needs. Hence, even though many companies operate in a B2B environment, consumer behavior may have a significant impact on their business, too. Whatever the most impactful trends are for each company, a genuinely future-oriented corporate intelligence program should be equipped to systematically detect, monitor, and communicate them.

SUMMARY

- The Scope of an intelligence program refers to the purpose, user groups, breadth, depth, and time horizon of the intelligence program.

    o Purpose

        ♦ What will be the primary drivers for the entire intelligence program? Some companies have developed mission and vision statements to address the questions, however the most important thing is that the purpose is clear.

    o User groups

        ♦ What are the corporate activities and target user groups that the intelligence program should serve?

    o   Breadth of scope

        ◆   What are the topics on which the above target groups will need information, and how will they be prioritized?

    o   Depth of scope

        ◆   What requirements will the above needs set to the intelligence team's analytical and consultative capabilities?

    o   Time horizon

        ◆   What will be the time horizon and, in particular, the future orientation of the intelligence program?

- Being at world class with regards to intelligence scope

    o   A clear target group exists that covers a defined set of functions and/or processes and the related key decision-makers.

    o   The breadth and depth of intelligence activities are aligned with business strategy and the decision-making needs of the target groups.

    o   The intelligence program is highly future oriented.

        ◆   Megatrends, trend spotting, and scenarios.

        ◆   Early warning and opportunity tracking.

        ◆   War gaming.

        ◆   Forecasting.

5 Intelligence Process – Turning Random Data into Meaningful Insight

INTRODUCTION: THE INTELLIGENCE CYCLE

"Intelligence process" refers to the continuous, cyclical process that runs from defining decision-makers' information demands to eventually delivering content that responds to those demands. Here, we want to make the distinction up front between intelligence scope and intelligence process in that the scoping effort will determine the purpose and content needs for the entire intelligence program, whereas the intelligence process starts with determining the needs for a single intelligence deliverable, however small.

The intelligence process should always be anchored to the existing corporate processes, such as strategic planning, sales, marketing, or product management, within which information will be used. In practice, the utilization of the intelligence output should either link directly to decision-making situations, or the intelligence output should help facilitate awareness in the organization about topics in the operating environment that have relevance to the various business processes.

Figure 5.1 illustrates the phases in the cyclical intelligence process, explained below in more detail. The concrete output of the intelligence process, in turn is illustrated on the right hand side of the

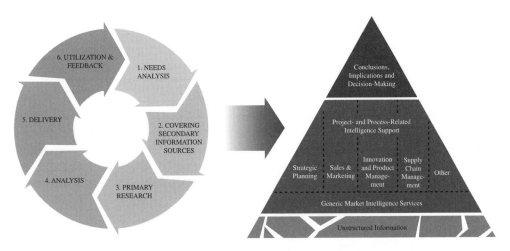

Figure 5.1   Intelligence process and the role of its output as part of business processes
Source: Global Intelligence Alliance.

graph, where decision-making is backed up by generic MI services, and intelligence output that is specifically related to different business processes and projects.

The intelligence cycle divides into six phases that we explain in more detail in the following.

1.   **Needs analysis**. A careful needs analysis sets the purpose and scope of an intelligence assignment. Even when the ones conducting the assignment would be gathering the information for their own use, it pays to crystallize the very drivers for the task so that resources will be focused on the most relevant areas. More typically, however, those who are conducting the research will not be the end users of the results, so they will need to have an in-depth understanding of what the eventual deliverables will be required for in order to avoid collecting and analyzing pieces of information that in the end will be irrelevant for the users. Various templates and questionnaires have been developed to aid the needs analysis phase and to ensure that the assignment will be kicked off in a high quality manner.

Most importantly, however, the intelligence needs in the organization must be thoroughly understood and internalized in order for the intelligence program to be of any value, and no templates and questionnaires alone will achieve this. They may be helpful, yet excellent needs analyses have also been conducted through informal conversations with executives. This, in turn requires a consultative approach from the intelligence team or at the very least the ability to lead an educated business discussion with decision-makers.

2.   **Covering secondary information sources**. In the intelligence cycle, we have separated the collection of information from secondary and primary sources. There are several reasons for this. First, collecting information from public sources is cheaper than going directly after primary sources. Second, it is easier – given of course that those who are working on the task have sufficient expertise in tapping into the secondary sources available. Indeed source management and the related cost optimization is an expertise area of its own. Third, having covered secondary information sources before conducting interview research will provide the ones conducting the research with valuable background information that they can further validate and also use for giving some information in return to the interviewees. Also, having some of the questions already answered through secondary research will reduce the cost of the primary research phase – or even sometimes make it unnecessary.

3.   **Primary research**. However huge the pool of publicly available information is today, not all information can be accessed through secondary research. Once the secondary sources have been covered, gaps in the research can be addressed by interviewing experts that are knowledgeable about the topics under research. This phase may be relatively expensive compared to the secondary research, depending naturally on the coverage of the assignment and also on the resourcing – frequently, companies involve outsourced resources to take part in the primary research phase.

4.   **Analysis**. Once the pieces of information have been collected from the variety of sources, it is time to make sense of them in the context of the original needs analysis of the assignment. Again, depending on the scope of the assignment, this may be a

relatively expensive phase in the research, involving at least time consumption by internal and sometimes also external resources, and perhaps some additional validation of the analyses through further interviews.

5. **Delivery**. The delivery format of the results of an intelligence assignment is not at all insignificant for the eventual users. As a rule, decision-makers are busy and will not have time to search through a data dump for the key results of an analysis, but the core content will need to be catered to them in an easy to digest format. At the same time, the supporting background facts should also be easily accessible for those who are interested in digging deeper into them. These ground rules apply regardless of the delivery format, whether a software database, a newsletter, a PowerPoint presentation, or a face to face briefing or workshop. This is also the reason why we are separating the delivery phase from the eventual utilization and feedback of the intelligence content. Sometimes decisions will be made in the same conjunction as the intelligence content is delivered, but more frequently, background material will be delivered prior to the actual decision-making situation, and the delivery format, channel, and style do have an impact on how the messages get across.

6. **Utilization and feedback**. The utilization stage serves as the acid test of an intelligence assignment – do the results respond to the needs identified at the setout of the intelligence process? Regardless of whether all the answers were obtained that were initially looked for, the utilization phase typically raises new questions and puts forward a new needs analysis, especially when the intelligence need is of continuous nature. Also, in the spirit of co-creating intelligence content among end users and intelligence professionals, the end users of intelligence may have already contributed to the eventual deliverables by the time the utilization stage has been reached, and, on the other hand, those who have produced most of the analysis may be heavily involved in providing the conclusions and interpretations based on which the eventual decisions will be made. Ideally, thoughtful feedback at the utilization phase already serves the purpose of needs analysis for the next intelligence assignment in line, and the intelligence process has made a full cycle.

GETTING STARTED: DEVELOPING THE INTELLIGENCE PROCESS

MAPPING OUT DECISION POINTS IN THE BUSINESS PROCESSES THAT REQUIRE MARKET INTELLIGENCE SUPPORT

The term "decision point intelligence" has gained in popularity, as companies that already have an existing intelligence program have started looking into ways to still better integrate the program with decision-making processes. Just how abstract or concrete the exercise of "improving the linkage between intelligence deliverables and business processes" is will largely depend on whether the business processes have been formally defined, and whether the intelligence team has visibility to the specific information needs that are associated with the decision points in those processes.

As we mentioned in Chapter 1, the methods and approaches discussed in this book are optimally suited for companies that do have structured business processes in place such as the process of formulating strategy. Companies that are managed in a more loosely structured fashion may have to use some creativity in applying the approaches of the World Class MI Roadmap to their management schemes, yet the main principles that we are presenting will hold for any company.

INTELLIGENCE NEEDS ANALYSIS – WHY IS IT SO IMPORTANT?

Considering that understanding the key intelligence requirements in the beginning of the intelligence process has a heavier impact on the quality of the eventual deliverables than any of the other stages in the intelligence process, the needs analysis phase is surprisingly often left with too little attention. Despite the potential limitations of resources in the other phases of the process, an increased emphasis on the needs analysis alone would often significantly improve the value and usefulness of the end results of the intelligence process, that way also ensuring that the time and resources invested in an intelligence assignment will be justified. In the following we will therefore look into ways of perfecting the quality of the needs analysis specifically.

Often it is automatically assumed that the management of a company knows what information the company will need. In reality, however, senior management typically only recognizes a fraction of all the information needs that their organization has, and even then they may not be best positioned to determine exactly what information is needed, let alone where it could be found.

As a result, intelligence assignments may be regularly kicked off with only a vaguely formulated idea of a problem and its business context. Those who are best familiar with the information sources and analysis methods may be spending their time on processing data in an apparently random manner, while missing the big picture and the approaches that would matter most for the company. This easily results in decision-makers receiving much more information than they need, which is generally counterproductive, as they will soon begin to ignore the relevant information along with the irrelevant noise. What decision-makers need is not more information, but better and more accurate information.

At the same time, the decision-makers may have unrealistic expectations about the availability and accuracy of information, having not consulted the intelligence professionals before assigning the task. Hence the intelligence professionals and the decision-makers are ideally in frequent contact with each other and work together to make sure the essential information needs will be similarly understood by both parties. The ability to manage this will require many skills from the analysts doing it:

- The analyst has to understand how to identify and elicit the information needs of decision-makers.

- The analyst has to develop effective communication, interviewing, and presentation skills.

- The analyst ideally has an eye for psychology types in order to appreciate the different orientations of decision-makers.

- The analyst has to know the organizational structure, culture, and environment as well as the key informants.

- The analyst has to remain objective.

We will discuss the ideal characteristics of the intelligence team in more detail in Chapter 8 about the intelligence organization.

WORKING THROUGH THE INTELLIGENCE CYCLE AND REMOVING BOTTLENECKS FROM THE PROCESS

In the early phases of initiating an intelligence program, the target group of the activity is typically limited, and so is the number of deliverables that the program produces. Similarly, there are often bottlenecks in processing the eventual deliverables. Simply collecting the necessary data pieces from secondary and primary sources may require expertise that the company lacks, and when the information collection is done, there may not be enough time and resources left to conduct a thorough analysis, let alone to produce insightful and polished presentations for decision-makers' use. Further still, in the early phases of intelligence program development, few companies have dedicated tools existing for storing and disseminating the intelligence output, and it typically ends up being delivered to the target groups simply as email attachments.

The challenges of an intelligence assignment that is taken through the intelligence cycle can be described with the generic Project Management Triangle, i.e. the assignment needs to be performed and delivered under three major constraints: budget, time, and scope. These three constraints often compete with each other: in a typical intelligence assignment, increased scope will require increased time and an increased budget, a tight time constraint probably means an increased budget and yet still a reduced scope, and a tight budget easily means both a limited scope and not much time available for conducting the project.

As a result of the bottlenecks in the intelligence process, there's typically considerable friction in how the research assignment flows through the intelligence cycle in the early phases of the intelligence program development. As resources are scarce, the most critical bottlenecks should be removed first. Is the intelligence team missing analysis capability and should it be trained more? Or is the problem rather that the analysts do not have enough valuable information to work on; in other words is information collection the most critical bottleneck? Or, does the intelligence team simply lack time, i.e. is the team incapable of responding to urgent requests in a timely manner?

The flow of the intelligence assignment in the intelligence process cycle can be improved in two dimensions: the "capacity" of the cycle, i.e. the thoroughness with which the intelligence team can process intelligence assignments at each stage, and the speed at which a question gets answered.

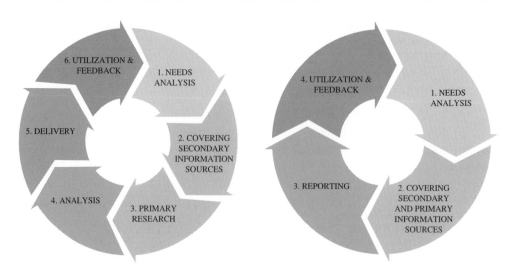

Figure 5.2   A rapid response research assignment goes through a streamlined intelligence cycle, while in a strategic analysis project the MI team will be putting more time and effort into most phases of the intelligence process
Source: Global Intelligence Alliance.

Figure 5.2 illustrates the difference between the approaches, and essentially differentiates between strategic analysis assignments and rapid response research requests. While both approaches will take the intelligence assignment through all stages in the intelligence cycle, in the rapid research assignments the intelligence team will work on secondary and primary research in parallel (sometimes a single phone call with an expert may provide the necessary answers to the research request), and the analysis and delivery are also frequently combined through, for instance, a short briefing by an analyst to the executive who requested the information.

The capacity of the intelligence process cycle can be increased by adding either internal (hired) or external (purchased) resources to where they are needed, to achieve higher quality results and to have the capability to serve increasingly many user groups in the organization.

The same applies to ensuring the speedy process flow, i.e. how smoothly an urgent research assignment can be taken through the phases of the cycle. Traditionally, companies have mainly focused on securing the stable bandwidth through long-term resourcing arrangements and training of staff. However, adding flexibility through temporary arrangements on a case by case basis is becoming increasingly common, as the intelligence profession matures and the availability of professional outsourced resources improves globally.

The two types of output of the intelligence cycle, i.e. strategic analysis and rapid response research, will also find their places in the intelligence deliverables graph in Figure 5.1. While the rapid response research assignments typically link to business processes, their level of analysis is not very high due to sheer lack of time in conducting the analysis. Strategic analysis assignments on the other hand typically involve a high level of co-creation in the analysis and delivery stage, bringing them very close to the top of the triangle where the interpretation and utilization of the information takes place.

CONTINUOUS DEVELOPMENT: TOWARDS WORLD CLASS LEVELS IN INTELLIGENCE PROCESS

The maturity of the intelligence process could be visualized in a uniform thickness of the cycle graph in Figure 5.2 in the sense that a mature intelligence process does not have "weak links", major bottlenecks in the process flow. This uniformity calls for adequate resourcing in each phase, which in turn is typically a result from having gone back and forth along the cycle over time. For instance, the initial needs analysis may have gradually improved as decision-makers, when utilizing the results, have spotted weaknesses or typical misunderstandings in the very beginning of the MI assignments. As well, the cooperation between information specialists and analysts – if the roles have been separated – may have been improved over time through the analyses typically raising previously undetected questions that would go back to the information specialists for more data collection. Over time, experience will show how each of the phases should be resourced for the best results.

What results eventually are "best" is determined by how well the intelligence output matches the needs that decision-makers have within business processes. Again, this brings us back to the uniform thickness of the intelligence cycle: a world class intelligence process in fact does not start with a needs analysis but with carefully determining where and how the eventual intelligence output should be utilized. Indeed at world class levels in the intelligence process, the communication between decision-makers and the intelligence professionals should be frequent, insightful, and go both ways.

One way to solidify the linkage between decision-making and MI is to establish Service Level Agreements (SLAs) with key stakeholders that the MI program serves. Agreeing on the desired MI service level with top executives in strategic planning, sales, marketing, and R&D should yield clearly defined MI deliverables and activities for each stakeholder group for the coming six to 12 months, including the MI budget, roles involved, milestones, and interaction along the way.

The SLA approach has several advantages:

- Requires time to sit down and discuss the overall objectives and decision points of the key business process owners = increases the MI team's insight into what the management has on their agenda and enhances personal relationships along the way.

- Reduces the risk of unanticipated ad hoc project overload by identifying areas for regular reviews, strategic intelligence topics, and so on.

- Allows time for intelligence co-creation: often, MI briefings and workshops with busy leaders will need to be scheduled months in advance.

- Brings discipline to the MI activity and raises its ambition level through clearly defined objectives and evaluation of the results.

- Overall, reduces the "silo effect" and enhances the fruitful cooperation between executives and MI professionals.

Two case examples in the end will illustrate how the intelligence team in a smoothly running intelligence process can respond to the different requirements that an intelligence assignment may have, depending on the geographical region that the assignment is focused on. In the "Western world" plenty of reliable information is available on most topics in secondary sources, and the task for the intelligence professionals is to utilize the best sources for cost-effectively collecting the information to be subsequently analyzed and delivered.

On the other hand, in the emerging markets there's often a shortage of reliable secondary sources, or the relevant data is not available in the English language. The intelligence professionals therefore will need to quickly turn to primary sources and conduct interviews, typically in the local language. Here, it is important to rely on sufficiently many sources in order to validate the research results before moving on to analyzing them.

Case: Business Cycle Study for the Chemical Industry

A company in the chemical sector needed extensive information on the historical, present, and future business cycles on several chemical industry product areas in the North American market. The information would be used to assess future growth of certain chemical product areas, and to plan future business through understanding of business cycles in the industry.

The analysis was done with statistical methods that included regression and visual analysis. Business cycles were analyzed both quantitatively and qualitatively and industry expert's views on long-term growth were added. The assignment relied entirely on secondary information sources, and statistical methods including regression and visual analysis were used to conduct the analysis. As a result, a detailed analysis report was delivered that described the length and nature of business cycles and assessed the future outlook for the company's key product areas (ethylene, polyethylene, styrene, ammonia, and butyl rubber).

Case: Assessment of Ammonium Bi-fluoride and Hydrofluoric Acid Market in Russia and CIS

One of world's biggest nuclear centers wanted to understand the market for two by-products of its production processes, namely ammonium bi-fluoride and hydrofluoric acid in Russia and CIS. In case the market for the products was too small, they would have to invest in utilization facilities for them.

Secondary research was conducted both on the Russian and CIS level and on a global level. Due to the niche nature of the market and the high in-house consumption of the by-products, the main focus was on primary research. Fifty in-depth interviews with potential customers, competitors, and industry experts were conducted in preparation for the subsequent analysis.

The final report contained an estimation of market size without the in-house consumption, an analysis of segments, an import analysis, a value chain analysis, an analysis of substitute technologies and products in each industrial segment, a market development forecast, a pricing analysis, and finally an evaluation of market potential in Russia and CIS.

SUMMARY

- The intelligence process is a cyclical flow of events that is kicked off with a needs analysis about a topic that should be looked into for decision-making purposes. Information will subsequently be collected from secondary and/or primary sources, and it will be analyzed and reported to decision-makers for them to use it and give feedback on the project.

- Intelligence professionals will process any assignment through the same phased cycle, yet roughly speaking there are two types of approach to doing it, depending on the goals set in the needs analysis:

    o Rapid response research where speed is important, hence there's little time for conducting analysis and producing comprehensive reports.

    o Strategic analysis where being thorough and producing polished and detailed reports is more important than speed.

- Being world class in intelligence process:

    o Decision points in key business processes have been identified and matched with regular intelligence deliverables.

    o A world class intelligence process starts with a world class needs analysis, i.e. anticipating and verifying the upcoming decision-making needs.

    o The information collection phase is "industrialized", allowing time and resources for conducting primary intelligence and hence adding insight to readily available secondary information.

    o The majority of time and resources is spent on analyzing information and drawing conclusions and making interpretations.

    o The delivery of the resulting intelligence content is personalized and followed up.

    o The intelligence team has adopted a mindset of continuous improvement.

6 Intelligence Deliverables – Building a High-Impact Market Intelligence Product Portfolio

INTRODUCTION: MARKET INTELLIGENCE DELIVERABLES AS A KEY SUCCESS FACTOR OF MARKET INTELLIGENCE

Intelligence deliverables are the tangible output of the corporate intelligence process: different types of MI content that decision-makers and the rest of the MI users receive as a result of the organization having an intelligence program in place. No intelligence program should exist for its own good, and the scope, process, organization, tools, and culture are merely means to an end, i.e. to producing high quality intelligence deliverables. Figure 6.1 illustrates a typical way of classifying the deliverables according to four service areas and five product types. In this chapter, we will take a closer look at how the management and production of intelligence deliverables should be organized.

SERVICE AREAS	INTELLIGENCE PRODUCT TYPES
CONTINUOUS SERVICES	
Intelligence Portal	Workshops
Market Monitoring	Briefings
PROJECT SERVICES	Analysis Reports
Rapid Response Research	Profiles
Strategic Analysis & Advisory	Market Signals

Figure 6.1 Intelligence deliverables divide into four service areas and five product types
Source: Global Intelligence Alliance.

By intelligence *deliverables* we refer to all output that the MI users will have available to them: the intelligence team's service areas, intelligence product types, and the eventual intelligence products that are unique to each organization. In other words, intelligence deliverables is an umbrella term for what we will discuss in this chapter.

Under intelligence deliverables we will present

- Intelligence *service areas*. The four different types of services that the intelligence team ideally offers to the organization: intelligence portal, market monitoring, rapid response research, and strategic analysis and advisory.

- Intelligence *product types*. The grouping of five very common types of intelligence products: market signals, profiles, analysis reports, briefings, and workshops.

- Intelligence *products*. Clearly defined pieces of intelligence output that combined will form the organization's unique intelligence product portfolio.

QUALITY OF DELIVERABLES WILL DETERMINE THE SUCCESS OF THE INTELLIGENCE PROGRAM

At the end of the day, measuring the value and impact of the eventual deliverables that the intelligence program produces is simple: if they provide decision-makers with timely and accurate insights that will help them make confident decisions, the deliverables are probably worth the investment made into them. In the long run, an intelligence program's future will depend on how well those who produce the deliverables have understood the needs of those who use them. This of course assumes that the users and producers of intelligence deliverables are two different groups of people. With the increasing maturity of the intelligence program, however, "co-creation" of intelligence deliverables typically also increases, involving the end users of the output in actually producing the insights as well.

GETTING STARTED: DEVELOPING AN OPTIMIZED MARKET INTELLIGENCE DELIVERY CAPABILITY

MARKET INTELLIGENCE PRODUCT DEVELOPMENT: WHY AND HOW?

When considering the quality standards to be set for intelligence deliverables, it is helpful to think of the entire intelligence program as an organization that produces marketable products to end users just like a company would do. Deliverables that only respond to ad hoc needs and are fully customized each time are expensive to produce and hard to manage, market, or measure systematically in any organization, and the same applies to the organization that produces intelligence deliverables. The solution is intelligence product and process development that – when properly planned and executed – will add greatly to the professionalism of the intelligence program.

An intelligence product is the outcome of a systematic intelligence process, where the users, resources, information topic areas, format, delivery channels, and schedule have been defined. The term product development refers to standardizing both the format and the production process of the intelligence deliverables. The eventual content, however, will change every time: intelligence product development really addresses the structures associated with the output, while the content will always reflect the latest insight and foresight related to developments in the business environment.

Things to address in defining each of the intelligence products include:

- Defining the user groups, i.e. segmenting the internal market for the intelligence products.

- Ensuring a thorough understanding of the intelligence needs that each intelligence product will respond to.

- Appointing an owner, "a product manager", to take responsibility for making sure that each intelligence product will fulfill its need.

- Defining a solid process for making the product and assigning sufficient resources for carrying it out:

  o Timing

  o Human resources

  o Information sources

  o Budget for off the shelf information purchases and outsourced assignments

  o Format including look and feel

  o Delivery media

  o Collaborative, "co-creation" elements in producing, delivering, and utilizing the product

- Marketing the product systematically, sometimes also beyond the immediate target group if relevant from the point of view of spreading word about the tangible output of the intelligence program.

- Staying tuned for changes in the original requirements set for the intelligence product, i.e. constantly gathering feedback from the user groups of the intelligence products and adjusting the delivery process and the end product accordingly.

As a result of the formal structures that are now associated with producing the portfolio of intelligence products, the intelligence team may eventually have more time and degrees of freedom in their work. When the process of producing regular intelligence output follows the same, predictable steps and schedule each time, those people involved in the activity will also be able to assess the time and effort required to conduct the ad hoc assignments that each intelligence program will inevitably have to take on regularly.

ORGANIZING THE INTELLIGENCE TEAM'S SERVICES

Typically, when the efforts are started to systematically develop an intelligence program, the deliverables that have been produced so far, if any, have only responded to random intelligence needs, putting out fires entirely on an ad hoc basis. With the introduction of intelligence product portfolio development, the relative share of ad hoc assignments will, in most cases, drop significantly, whereas the intelligence team will work increasingly on continuous, standardized deliverables.

However, in a mature intelligence program that continuously responds to the evolving intelligence needs of the organization, there will always be ad hoc assignments, and indeed their relative share may even increase again after the initial drop, as the organization learns about the capabilities of the intelligence team, and the team in turn has had time to perfect the processes related to conducting ad hoc assignments in an efficiently organized manner. In the Global MI Survey 2011 results, the average split between ad hoc versus continuous services in the surveyed companies was 55% and 45%, respectively.

Figure 6.2 illustrates the organization of the intelligence team's services into continuous and project (ad hoc) services.

Continuous intelligence services: "the push and pull services"

   1. **Intelligence portal.** Central storage and delivery software for MI content that stores the information in an organized manner and makes it accessible to its audience at different locations.

   The intelligence portal ideally features both "push" and "pull" functionalities: at the very least users can pull information from the portal based on their needs in a "self-service" fashion, and the users can also tailor the portal interface to match their individual interests.

Figure 6.2   Organizing the intelligence team's services
Source: Global Intelligence Alliance.

The more sophisticated intelligence portals also push information to the users, and this functionality, too, can be tailored by the users themselves in a self-service fashion. Finally, intelligence portals ideally also enable sharing of information between users by allowing them to put in information in addition to receiving it.

Intelligence portals may be software tools specifically developed to serve the corporate intelligence process, or they may be various types of other software that has been configured to also serve as a storage and delivery tool for MI content, along with their other purposes.

2. Market monitoring. Continuous, standardized deliverables produced by the intelligence team in order for the organization to stay on top of the relevant developments in the company's business environment.

Examples of continuous market monitoring deliverables are daily or weekly market signals monitoring and different types of recurring reviews and analyses that respond to continuous intelligence needs. "Continuous" in this context refers to especially the intelligence need, as the exact content of the deliverables changes each time. For example, even though there is a continuous need for the organization to receive timely MI from the emerging business areas where a presence has been established, the market signals of course are new every day. Similarly, even though the sales team needs their sales leads reports and the R&D team their technology trends reviews on a regular basis, producing the deliverables means that the intelligence team needs to conduct fresh research and analysis each time.

Project services: "the on demand services"

1. Rapid response research. Industrialized ad hoc research capability that enables delivering results reliably despite a tight schedule.

Developing the capability to rapidly conduct demanding research assignments requires a lot of background work from the intelligence team. In a rather typical scenario, rapid response research is needed when there's a management meeting coming up, and a quick briefing about the essential facts will be needed about a certain market player, say, in one of the emerging markets for the company. Ideally, the intelligence team will not be caught by surprise: through their readily accessible secondary information sources and external partner network, they will be able to deliver at least initial research results ahead of the meeting.

The quick turnaround time will not be possible, however, without a thorough knowledge of the available secondary sources that will be useful and cost-effective for the particular research. Also, primary research is often required in these types of on-demand intelligence assignments for complementing and validating the secondary research results. The intelligence team will not have time to start looking for and assessing external partners within the timeframe of a typical rapid research assignment, but they need to be able to rely on a readily established network of partners.

2. **Strategic analysis and advisory**. Capability of the intelligence team to serve as a trusted advisor to decision-makers, delivering thoroughly processed analyses in a consultative manner.

The strategic analysis assignments typically require a highly consultative approach from the intelligence team. Here, decision-makers will appreciate an equal, trusted partner to evaluate the strategic options with, based on carefully conducted research and analysis. Often, the end results of the assignment are presented and discussed in face to face briefings or workshops, where the final conclusions are reached through cooperation between the intelligence team and the decision-makers.

Again, to build up the capability of delivering valuable strategic analyses, the intelligence team needs to do a lot of background work. Naturally the team will need the right types of individuals to begin with that can lead a discussion between equals with executives, but that's only the starting point. The team's "consultants" need to have a thorough understanding of the company's business environment and its key strategic themes and business drivers. In addition, they will also need to be familiar with research approaches and analytical frameworks with which to make sense of complex business scenarios. Finally, they will need to be able to summarize the essential facts and to present them in a convincing fashion.

Exactly what portion of the eventual intelligence products in an intelligence program should be continuous and ad hoc varies between companies, and no one correct formula can be given that would serve as a guideline for every organization. An entirely standardized intelligence product portfolio will not be able to respond to the rapidly emerging intelligence needs in a constantly changing business environment, but the capability to conduct high quality ad hoc research will also be necessary. Similarly, an intelligence team that only produces ad hoc deliverables will hardly ever live up to its full potential due to inefficiencies that are necessarily associated with a fully random set of deliverables, however high their quality might be.

LEVERAGING THE INTELLIGENCE SERVICE AREAS FOR CONCRETE INTELLIGENCE PRODUCTS

Building a portfolio of different products instead of offering the same thing for everyone bears the built-in logic that there are a variety of different needs that should each be responded to with a different product. Building the portfolio of intelligence products is not an exception: the users of intelligence products have varying intelligence needs in terms of topics, level of analysis, and delivery. Hence the intelligence product portfolio design starts with identifying the users that will be served, and tailoring the intelligence output to best serve the interest of each user group. There is no one generic intelligence deliverables portfolio that could be uniformly recommended. The company-specific definition of scope, i.e. the purpose and primary user groups of the intelligence program, should drive the efforts to produce the eventual intelligence product portfolio as well.

In the following we will discuss the types of different intelligence products of which an intelligence product portfolio typically consists. Not all product types may ever be necessary in an

Figure 6.3 Intelligence product types
Source: Global Intelligence Alliance.

intelligence program, nor have the product types been introduced in any order of priority. The intelligence products can be arranged into groups according to the typical degree of insight involved as presented in Figure 6.3.

- **Market signals** are individual pieces of information that originate from either outside or inside of the organization. Market signals, both those collected centrally from news databases, social media, and other external sources and those shared spontaneously by the internal intelligence network, serve the purpose of maintaining current awareness in the organization about the developments in its operating environment. While market signals typically are the least processed deliverables in the intelligence product portfolio, adding analytical comments and interpretations to even single news pieces is becoming increasingly common. Also, what makes this content relevant for the organization is the KITs and information architecture based on which the signals are collected: the themes and market players under the company's radar screen have been specifically defined as topics that the company should keep a strategic eye on.

- **Profiles** are structured snapshots of, typically, companies, but also products, technologies, or countries, to name a few examples. A uniform structure eases the making of these products and also facilitates comparisons between profiles. Usually, profiles are part of the company's continuous intelligence deliverables.

- **Analysis reports** is a large, loosely defined group of analytical intelligence output that serves a variety of purposes, either continuous or ad hoc. Hence only a fraction of analysis reports follow an entirely standardized format and structure, but they often contain ad hoc elements that may address emerging strategic topics. Also, their level of insight may vary greatly. Further still, some analysis reports have been purchased off the shelf from information vendors, leaving it to the users to find the pieces of information they need, while other reports are entirely customized to the specific requirements of their users.

- **Briefings** are presentations of analytical findings that usually also include a questions and answers session. Briefings are typical in situations where a large amount of analyzed information needs to be presented to an audience that will subsequently discuss it and eventually make decisions on the topic. Often, a briefing follows the completion of a customized analysis report, and the ones giving the briefing will need to adopt a consultative style, being prepared to lead an educated discussion about both the strategic conclusions of the analysis and the detailed facts leading to the conclusions even though the details will not be presented in the briefing. Briefings may also be organized at a more generic level when, for instance, a large group of people needs to be updated about a specific topic of interest.

- **Workshops** are collaborative events that generate shared insight about topics of strategic relevance. Workshops bring a group of people together to work on a topic in a two-way fashion: interaction and content co-creation are the very point of conducting workshops in the first place. As preparation for workshops, analysis reports are often produced so as to facilitate high quality discussions about topics of strategic relevance. The final conclusions and interpretations are typically reached together by intelligence professionals and decision-makers.

CONTINUOUS DEVELOPMENT: TOWARDS WORLD CLASS LEVELS IN INTELLIGENCE DELIVERABLES

A fundamental characteristic of a truly valuable intelligence product is that it is integrated into a business process, such as strategic planning, sales, marketing, or R&D. The respective business process drives the need for the deliverable, and therefore ensures that it will be useful as decision-making support, either directly or indirectly. Also, most strategically valuable intelligence deliverables, regardless of the business processes they serve, focus on the future rather than merely explaining past events.

Integrating intelligence deliverables in business processes sounds simple enough, yet it is an enduring topic even among companies that already have long traditions in conducting high quality intelligence activities. One of the reasons is the business processes themselves. It is not always self-evident that a company has its business processes unambiguously defined, or at least that it has them thought through from the perspective of decision points that will require intelligence support. Even if it has, there may be a disconnect between decision-makers and intelligence professionals in that the latter are not necessarily always aware of what the requested intelligence deliverables relate to, i.e. what decision points in which business processes drive the intelligence needs each time.

Hence, to be able to take its intelligence deliverables to world class levels, a company needs to have:

- Clearly defined business processes

- Decision points needing intelligence support mapped out in context with the business processes

- All of the above communicated to those who regularly produce the intelligence deliverables

- An intelligence team that also proactively invests in understanding the evolving business processes and the requirements that they set on intelligence deliverables

- Active co-creation of intelligence products by the intelligence team and decision-makers

At the end of the day, it is of course *people* who use intelligence deliverables to make decisions, not "business processes". As a rule, the level of interaction in the production and utilization of the intelligence deliverables tends to increase with the maturity of the intelligence deliverables. In practice this is best facilitated in different briefings and workshops, where insights are co-created among decision-makers and intelligence professionals. Regular interaction between the producers and users of the intelligence output speaks of many qualities that truly world class intelligence deliverables have:

- Users of intelligence regularly invest time in discussing the intelligence deliverables, a typical indication of perceived value and usefulness.

- Users and producers of intelligence deliverables have a shared understanding of the (evolving) needs that the deliverables should respond to.

- Producers of intelligence deliverables receive immediate feedback on their work and get to ensure that the investment in the intelligence activity will continue.

DEVELOPING THE INTELLIGENCE OUTPUT AS A PRODUCT PORTFOLIO

In a professionally operated intelligence program, the intelligence team should maintain and develop the intelligence deliverables as a coordinated portfolio of services and eventual intelligence products.

First, attention needs to be paid on the team's service areas. It is not only the intelligence portal and continuous market monitoring that will require development efforts based on the evolving needs of the organization, but also the competencies and capacity of the team to take on ad hoc requests, either those that will need to be conducted in a very quick turnaround time or those that will rather challenge the very analytical competences of the team involved.

What ultimately drives the development needs of the intelligence service areas is the intelligence product portfolio that needs to continuously respond to the requirements of the MI users. In a professionally managed product portfolio, new products are developed on a need basis, and old ones that no longer serve their purpose may also be terminated. Additional content elements, sources, analysis frameworks, or, for example, presentation formats may be created in response to the MI users' requests.

Indeed what should be the goal in intelligence teams is that their intelligence product portfolio responds so well to the MI users' needs that it will engage them in co-creating the intelligence products. This will inevitably lead to favorable development in the value of the intelligence product portfolio for its users, ensuring that the intelligence output in the company will genuinely match business needs.

Case: Managing the Intelligence Product Portfolio at Best Buy

In 2000, Philip Britton, now Senior Manager of Competitive Strategies at Best Buy, a multi-national retailer of technology and entertainment products and services based out of Minneapolis, joined the company's Competitive Pricing team whose job it was literally to go to competitors' stores around the country and harvest price tags. In other words, the intelligence activity in the company was something very basic and tactical. In ten years' time, Britton and his team developed the pricing function into a full-blown global intelligence program that is valued for its high quality deliverables from individual stores all the way up to the CEO's office.

Britton highlights some of the success factors in building an intelligence product portfolio that generate true business impact and help brand the entire MI function. Table 6.1 describes some of the concrete intelligence products in Best Buy's portfolio.

Table 6.1 Some of Best Buy's intelligence products

Product	Product Focus	Client/Audience	Format	Frequency
Board of Directors Review	**Competitive Update** o Mass Channel o Online Channel o Specialty Retailers o International Retailers	o COO (Sponsor) o CEO o BoD	PowerPoint Word	**Quarterly**
Weekly Competitive Edge	**Competitive Landscape** o Quick Updates o Key Intelligence Topics	o Partners o Corp o Field	Wiki PDF	**Weekly**
Pricing Analysis	**Pricing Scorecard** o Top Competitors o Drill down to category level o Interactive Pricing Tool	o Execs o Merchant o Pricing	PDF Excel Tool	**Weekly**
Market Share Analysis	**Market Overview** o Company o Category o Geographic Markets	o Execs o Field	PowerPoint Excel	**Quarterly**
War Game	**Market Overview** o Company o Customers o Employees o Financials	o Field o Execs	PowerPoint	**As Needed**

Establishing a Brand

Hear the needs

Britton and his team were pragmatic about uncovering the intelligence requirements of the Best Buy organization. They discussed with executives and heard openly what they have to say about their intelligence needs. The list of KITs for the coming fiscal year was subsequently made up of the topics that were brought up most frequently by the executives. As the topics came directly from executives, a lot of "pull" was instantly generated for the eventual deliverables of the intelligence team.

Find a patron

Britton also stresses the importance of having "a powerful friend", a patron for the intelligence program who will speak for it preferably at the C-level. In order to identify one, the intelligence team should look at the organization chart and locate people who may also be tracking customers, competitors, and trends: who could be a good ally and help tell the story of the intelligence team? It doesn't hurt to have an eye for psychology in the process: understanding the egos, motivations, and political drivers within the company helps a great deal in identifying potential candidates for the patron's role.

Build a brand name

Building a brand name and logo for the intelligence program may sound cheesy; however, it helps immensely in creating an intelligence product portfolio that won't go unnoticed in the organization. The intelligence team at Best Buy adopted one of the famous "three-letter-acronyms" to label their intelligence function, and even recommend this for a "department of one" in order to enhance credibility and to also represent continuity: persons change over time, so corporate programs should not depend too much on individuals. The same logic also applies to email traffic: rather than sending email to individual persons, the organization should be encouraged to use the intelligence program's mailbox where the team can then pick and allocate the tasks among themselves.

Building Networks

Generate a source portfolio

Building a source portfolio for Best Buy's intelligence deliverables, Britton's team started with the idea that "someone, somewhere in the company already knows what we need to know". They approached both current and past employees, acknowledging that getting people to share their knowledge is all about trading, and sometimes one has to buy people lunch to get them to share what they know. Being properly informed through the internal sources, it is then easier to also approach external experts such as industry specialists or bloggers with something to give them in exchange for their information.

(Continued)

Add value to information

What Britton and his team wanted to avoid from the beginning was just passing on information. Instead, the intelligence team at Best Buy regularly provides recaps, analyses, insights, and opinions about the topics they process into intelligence deliverables. Being consultative and making recommendations is a built in part of the team's daily work.

Delivering

About the eventual intelligence product portfolio, Philip Britton gives a set of recommendations that will help generate and maintain a sustainably branded intelligence product portfolio:

- Understand how each person would like information delivered; executives in particular are typically overloaded with information and have a very short attention span.

- Tailor the message to suit the interests of the audience; the message may change remarkably depending on the audience.

- To reach some executives, make friends with the administrative assistants in the company – they control your access.

- Always summarize the key messages.

- Segment the company's customers and competitors to narrow the focus, as too many distractions will cause problems in digesting the information.

- Control the level of detail in a presentation; however, make sure that the relevant details will be available to support the conclusions.

- Use journalistic standards in producing the deliverables and make sure the look and feel are loyal to the brand image that has been created for the intelligence program (create a style guide!).

SUMMARY

- The deliverables of a world class intelligence program have been organized into four types of service areas: intelligence portal, market monitoring, rapid response research, and strategic analysis and advisory.

- These continuous and ad hoc intelligence services together enable the organization to: 1) pull MI from a central repository, 2) receive Market Intelligence in a "push" fashion, and 3) assign ad hoc research requests to the intelligence team on an "on demand" basis.

- The intelligence service areas will produce five types of intelligence products: market signals, profiles, analysis reports, briefings, and workshops. The eventual intelligence product portfolio that a company adopts is entirely company-specific and will combine elements from all of the above service areas.

- Being world class in intelligence deliverables:

   o A well-managed portfolio of intelligence products exists for recurring decision-making needs.

   o A capability for rapid response research exists through an "industrialized" ad hoc research approach.

   o Strategic analysis projects are handled in a highly customized and consultative manner, delivering not only analysis results but also strategic advisory.

   o A high degree of future orientation is embedded in the intelligence products.

   o Intelligence deliverables contain a high degree of co-creation with end users.

7 Intelligence Tools – Collecting, Storing, and Disseminating Intelligence

INTRODUCTION: INTELLIGENCE TOOLS AS A KEY SUCCESS FACTOR OF WORLD CLASS MARKET INTELLIGENCE

When ambitiously developing MI activities, the need emerges quickly for the intelligence professionals to adopt tools and techniques to help manage the collection, processing, storage, and delivery of the information content. Frequently used tools and techniques include needs analysis questionnaires, information collection templates, and a wide variety of analysis frameworks and approaches, to name just a few. However, by far the most central tool in running a world class intelligence program is an intelligence portal; software that has been designed to support the intelligence activity both at the production end and in accessing and contributing to the deliverables. Hence we will limit the focus in this chapter to intelligence portals only.

An intelligence portal provides a single user interface to screened and organized information content from both external and internal sources. Companies around the world are using a wide range of IT solutions for the general purpose of managing and processing business information; however, the best intelligence portals have been specifically designed and developed to support the requirements of the corporate intelligence process, and the eventual configuration of the software typically follows each company's own intelligence process flow. An intelligence portal usually nests in the organization's intranet and is hosted either in the company's own IT infrastructure or by an external service provider.

An intelligence portal is one of the most tangible elements of an intelligence program, and as such serves as a natural centerpiece of an MI program, even though people, not the software, are doing most of the value-adding intelligence work. Unlike the intelligence process or culture, or other abstract concepts associated with intelligence activities such as needs analyses and workshops, an intelligence portal has a concrete look and feel, and this makes it a great marketing vehicle for the intelligence deliverables and indeed the entire MI program.

While no single intelligence portal will contain all information that decision-makers may want at their fingertips at a given point in time, the efficiency of an intelligence program is greatly enhanced by people simply knowing where to start looking for high quality business information when the need arises, and whom to turn to, when the readily available information will not suffice. Also, efficiencies are achieved by decision-makers gaining continuous exposure to relevant business information through automated and personalized alert services about new and updated information that is being stored and delivered through the intelligence software.

In addition to enhancing the efficiency of storing and delivering business information and providing a tangible platform for marketing the intelligence activity to its internal audiences, an intelligence portal will help maintain the continuity of the intelligence activity at times when either the producers or users of the intelligence deliverables change.

Finally, an intelligence portal facilitates the gradual build-up of an intelligence culture by enabling a two-way flow of information among the user base of the intelligence deliverables: "the wisdom of crowds" applies in the corporate setting in that no centralized intelligence team will be able to deliver all relevant business information to the corporate user base in a one-way manner, but the wisdom of the entire organization should be tapped into for the best results. Again, an intelligence portal will not do this on behalf of the organization, but the best portals will facilitate the process.

Figure 7.1 illustrates the role of an intelligence portal in facilitating the two-way flow of intelligence content: channeling information from a variety of sources to its end users, and serving as a platform for the end users to share their own insights in return.

Although there is a distinct niche market for software specifically aimed at supporting the intelligence process, in reality many companies maintain a combination of different software tools that together respond to the company's intelligence needs. The reasons range from challenges in pure technical integration to confidentiality issues, and most companies seem to have settled with some sort of coexistence among different tools that serve different purposes.

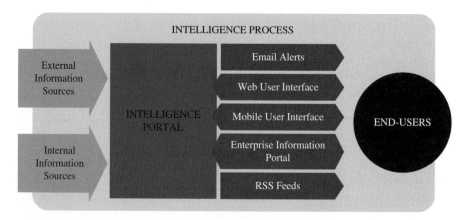

Figure 7.1 The intelligence portal plays an integral part in providing access to the intelligence content and facilitating collaboration among MI users
Source: Global Intelligence Alliance.

GETTING STARTED: PLANNING AND IMPLEMENTING AN INTELLIGENCE PORTAL

There are numerous options for intelligence software, and what will eventually suit a company's needs best will be largely determined by its intelligence process and organization. Most BI tools, frequently also referred to as "number crunching software" are typically considered inappropriate as they focus on quantitative information, whereas, the focus in intelligence system implementation is on qualitative information and processes.

Essentially, a good intelligence portal (Figure 7.2) contributes to the quality with which the intelligence process is run: starting with the information collection phase, an intelligence portal that has been specifically designed to support intelligence work will smother the process flow of any intelligence assignment, whether continuous or ad hoc.

- First, a good intelligence portal pulls in information feeds from a variety of sources, that way easing the process of collecting raw pieces of data. The portal may also

Figure 7.2 Screen shots of an intelligence portal, the Intelligence Plaza®
Source: Global Intelligence Alliance.

contain a list of additional sources (information about access and potential fees included) that may be useful in specific assignments.

- Intelligence portals may also be helpful in tapping into the internal and external sources of primary information, where secondary sources will not be enough to provide the information that's needed.

- For the analysis phase, a good intelligence portal can provide a range of support functionalities, such as project management support and different types of analysis frameworks. Indeed if the analyst team in the company is large (including more than 10–15 people), everyone involved in a project using a centralized interface and the same frameworks may greatly accelerate the completion of the project. Also, as many of the end users of the information will have a great deal of insight about the topics on the radar, features that enable easy collaboration and co-creation of content will add to the level of analysis of the intelligence deliverables.

- Finally, with the mobile devices becoming increasingly sophisticated, smart delivery formats of the produced content will add to the impact of the eventual intelligence deliverables and hence the quality of the intelligence process. If decision-makers can easily read the major conclusions of an analysis project from their mobile device and only later dig deeper into the background of the analysis, the probability simply increases that the vital intelligence content – at least the core of it – has reached everyone that should be aware of it.

Good intelligence portals can also contribute to the quality of the entire intelligence program by providing the administrators with insight into the activity of the internal intelligence community. Those running the intelligence program should have access to statistics about the frequency with which different types of content are received, the popularity of content items, the preferred delivery formats of content, and the usage of different support tools such as analysis frameworks. Based on this information, the intelligence program managers can direct their program development and marketing efforts towards the greatest impact and benefits for the organization.

IT DEPARTMENTS SEEKING MANAGEABILITY AND COST-EFFICIENCY

Over the recent years, browser-based web application platforms have established themselves as the nodal point for internal collaboration and document management in many large organizations. Microsoft's SharePoint has become a de facto standard as the channel for accessing corporate tools and applications.

Frequently, IT departments are pushing this development in the interest of bringing simplicity and cost-efficiency to managing the wide range of IT solutions that serve the different functions of the organization. From the end users' point of view, drivers for the development towards a single platform include ease of access (single sign-on is often required, as typical users do not want to maintain multiple user IDs and passwords), and also the complexity related to using a wide array of software applications. It has become challenging for users to keep track of different interfaces, navigation structures, web addresses, and site owners.

In practice, the increasing dominance of central IT platforms has meant that the applications that support a particular program or function will need to integrate to the main platform, most often SharePoint. At the very least the user's experience should resemble a seamless one even though the tools would not be technically integrated in the background. As a result, corporate functions have also started exploring the possibilities of using SharePoint not only as an access channel but as the very solution to the function's information management needs.

MI tools are no exception among the corporate software tools. Many companies adopting them nowadays require that they either connect to corporate intranets and other relevant applications through RSS feeds, or, increasingly, that they integrate seamlessly with the corporate intranet.

STANDALONE SOFTWARE OR A SHAREPOINT SOLUTION?

At the time of writing this, MI applications built in to SharePoint are still rare in the market, and they co-exist with well-established standalone software tools that emerged during the early years of 2000 in the absence of standard solutions. Here, we refer to commercial products; home-grown IT solutions will continue to exist in many organizations. We will, however, recommend commercial software solutions throughout this book, since there is little evidence of companies successfully managing to run home-grown MI software solutions that would both respond to the specific requirements of MI processes and prevent the internal IT costs from mounting due to the lack of IT skills of typical MI professionals. See the case example Selecting a Standalone Intelligence Software at Heineken Portugal.

Both SharePoint and standalone software solutions have their merits. A standalone MI software "stands alone": when something changes in the corporate intranet platform, one merely needs to worry about re-establishing connectivity, such as access routes and potential feed arrangements. A standalone software is also very quick and easy to implement. Typically a SaaS (Software as a Service) solution, it requires close to nothing from the corporate IT, and also very limited technical input from the MI professionals. Further, the market niche for standalone MI software products is well established, and most of the solutions available are widely used and market-proven. A standalone MI software is a safe and professional choice, with well-established product support.

A SharePoint MI software solution as a commercial product is still only making its way to the market. Essentially it bridges the gap between the need to respond to the MI process requirements and the need to seamlessly integrate with the corporate intranet. With the constantly improving collaboration and navigation functionalities of SharePoint and the competing IT platforms, many companies have over the recent years decided to go with building MI tools using the readily available functionalities that SharePoint offers.

However, the readily available functionalities do not mean that they will always be easy to use or even look appealing, and many companies have come to realize that the expertise required to build MI tool functionalities is beyond the skills of their MI professionals. The IT departments, on the other hand, are typically not familiar with the specific needs of the MI functions: information taxonomies, types of deliverables, email alerting needs, project support, information channeling, and so forth are rarely known to the IT professionals. As a result, internal development projects easily end up consuming a lot of time and effort without necessarily reaching the goals that were set in the first place.

As a response to the mismatch of IT and MI resources in a typical company, Global Intelligence Alliance (GIA) has invested in developing its Intelligence Plaza® product for SharePoint specifically. The product leverages GIA's consultative expertise in MI processes on one hand, and SharePoint's own tools and functionalities on the other. Technically, the product is just another SharePoint site; however, it has the look and feel and functionalities of a full-blown commercial MI application.

The future will see this sort of SharePoint applications for MI becoming common in large companies, first as on premise installed solutions. Over time, they will also become available as SaaS solutions, reducing the need for involvement from the internal IT department to the minimum.

Case: Selecting a Standalone Intelligence Software at Heineken Portugal

Heineken in Portugal started implementing an intelligence program in 2008 in response to the demand for more sophisticated MI by the top management. It soon became apparent that IT tools were a bottleneck in Heineken's effort to reach advanced levels on the MI Roadmap and serve the increasing internal MI user base. The company subsequently started evaluating the intelligence software options available in the market.

Heineken then went through a systematic software selection process:

- Several alternative MI tools were studied through webinars.

- Demo versions were tested, comparing functionalities.

- The Intelligence Plaza® stood out in terms of end user friendliness, scalability, and customer service.

- Heineken Group's strict technical requirements were passed for the Intelligence Plaza®.

In less than one month's time, a customized pilot version of the Intelligence Plaza® was up and running for Heineken's internal tests in the organization. After an additional two months of testing and piloting, the final solution was implemented and rolled out to the users.

FEATURES TO PAY ATTENTION TO WHEN SELECTING INTELLIGENCE SOFTWARE

There are a variety of technical features and functionalities in software tools that can assist the intelligence team to provide great services and the end users to add their own contribution. We have compiled a list of features that have generally proved most valuable and appreciated in global organizations, and that may help the reader assess the options when considering the implementation of intelligence software.

- Content management features:

    o   Storing content in a database and adding metadata

    o   Categorization of content (taxonomy)

    o   Searching and indexing

    o   Automatic translation

    o   Visualization tools and maps

    o   Usage monitoring and statistics

- Data sourcing and input features:

    o   Web crawling/monitoring

    o   RSS feed management

    o   Input through a web interface

    o   Input through a smartphone interface

    o   Ability to do microblogging and use shoutboxes

    o   Integration with external data sources (customer relationships management, enterprise resource planning, application programming interface)

- Security:

    o   Secure authentication and authorization

    o   Encrypted data storage and/or transfer

    o   Granular access rights of users

    o   Single sign-on to save the user from the trouble of logging in separately to the intelligence portal

- Dissemination ("push" from the intelligence team to the MI users):

    o   Automated, personalized email alerts to the users

    o   Newsletter generator and group email functionalities

    o   Integration of external user interfaces (API, XML, RSS, SharePoint)

- Self-service access ("pull" by the MI users):

    o   Dashboards of content that can be customized

    o   Sophisticated search tools

    o   Analysis tools for text-based content (news trends, tag clouds, text-mining, semantic analysis)

    o   Analysis tools for quantitative data (charting, etc.)

    o   Benchmarking (products, companies, markets)

    o   Smartphone user interface/application

- Collaboration:

    o   Commenting on content items

    o   Discussion forums and/or threads

    o   User groups and facilitation of networking

    o   Media and social network monitoring and analytics tools

Another angle to the features and functionalities of intelligence software is the interest group perspective. There are four distinct groups of stakeholders to an intelligence portal in any organization, as has been illustrated in Table 7.1.

- The analysts need to consider how to best make available the content to the end users, manage the content in the system, and collaborate among the analyst team and with the end users.

Table 7.1   Interest groups to an intelligence portal

ANALYST VIEW	HEAD OF MI VIEW
Self-service access	Content management
Content management	Data sourcing and input
Collaboration	Dissemination
USER VIEW	IT VIEW
Collaboration	Security
Dissemination	Data sourcing and input
Self-service access	Dissemination

- The head of MI, in turn, is most interested in internal marketing and branding of MI, usage statistics, managing data sourcing, and making sure that the content will reach the users in an optimal way.

- The users, in addition to being interested in receiving timely and relevant information at their preferred frequency and in a preferred format, will appreciate features that make it easy and engaging to collaborate with the intelligence team and the other users.

- Finally, an important control group is IT; information security and compatibility issues may not be of immediate interest to the users or even to the MI team, yet they need to be properly addressed from the beginning to ensure smooth and secure operation of the intelligence portal and indeed the entire intelligence program.

Companies today are relying increasingly on information that is collected from both external and internal sources, and on increasing collaboration between these two sources. To facilitate this collaboration, intelligence software tools will provide features that support the co-creation of MI: crowd forecasting is one example. Group analysis where several people can contribute to the same pieces of analysis will be more common.

Twitter, Facebook, and other social media platforms are increasingly used as sources of information in the corporate intelligence programs. Channeling content from these sources to the eventual intelligence deliverables is one of the areas where intelligence software can aid the smooth flow of the intelligence process in the future.

On the other hand, with the rapid adoption of social media platforms in the public domain, many companies are also looking to add similar features to their intelligence portals in the interest of increasing collaboration and knowledge sharing among their intelligence community both within business units and between them.

Mobile interfaces have been developed to intelligence portals for years already; however, with the increasingly widespread usage of smartphones and eReaders, they are now genuinely shaping the ways in which business information is shared. For many people, a mobile device is already the primary interface through which information is received, and this sets new requirements for the format in which analytical conclusions should be delivered for them to be digested as well. On the other hand, the mobile interface also offers new possibilities for sharing emerging information in a timely manner, and hopes are high in many companies for the mobile community to start participating in the creation of intelligence content more actively than they have historically.

The multiple formats in which MI is available today, ranging from text and charts to audio files and videos, introduce new challenges to how companies manage MI input and output. While there may seem to be more decentralization in the collection of business information, there also needs to be more centralization in how all this information is filtered, analyzed, and distributed.

Case: Weighing the Pros and Cons between Dedicated Intelligence Software and an Internal IT Development Project

In an effort to make sure that the insights produced by the intelligence team would be easily available to its MI users, a global IT services company decided to adopt an intelligence portal.

At the time, the IT department in the company was running a pilot of MS SharePoint, and since much of the functionality they thought was needed was already available in SharePoint, the company ended up trying to establish an intelligence portal on their own.

Eight months were subsequently spent trying to build their own MI tool on SharePoint. While the idea had worked nicely in theory, the project soon ran into challenges that were not anticipated at first:

- It is surprisingly time-consuming and therefore expensive to try to develop an application in-house that can reliably perform sophisticated tasks.

- The internal IT people were IT experts, yet they had no expertise in intelligence processes, so articulating the intelligence team's requirements to them proved difficult.

- The analysts, in turn, were experts in the intelligence work, but, as was discovered the hard way, they were not SharePoint developers.

- Finally, even if the company had managed to develop a satisfactory MI tool, it would have required continuous efforts from both the analyst team and the internal IT team to maintain and develop it according to the evolving needs: this is not free, either.

Having weighed up the options the company concluded that it would pay to go with a readily available software solution rather than venturing into an internal IT project for which there was no end in sight. Also, getting business analysts to do SharePoint development would be a major waste of high-value analyst time.

Success factors in the eventual implementation process of the intelligence portal included:

- Sufficient budget and senior level sponsorship

- Understanding the internal customers and what they really need. In some cases, they weren't even sure themselves, so the intelligence team often had to interpret on their behalf

- A simple, clear, easy to use interface

- An effective taxonomy

- Daily email alerts are key to making people aware of the centralized intelligence tool

- Getting local champions to further boost internal marketing and to increase people's involvement

- Putting effort into an internal communications plan to support the rollout

CONTINUOUS DEVELOPMENT: TOWARDS WORLD CLASS LEVELS IN INTELLIGENCE TOOLS

ENHANCING COLLABORATION AND CO-CREATION IN THE INTELLIGENCE PROGRAM

Purchasing and implementing intelligence software is easy in the sense that the early phases only take some financial and project management resources. Of course justifying these may be challenging enough if there are legacy issues such as other software tools in use, or the intelligence investment lacks support from senior management. These obstacles are still considered technical in nature, however. What eventually determines the success of any intelligence portal is how its users adopt it.

Characteristics of a world class intelligence portal include that it has gathered an active user base around it that not only pulls out intelligence from it, but also frequently shares their own knowledge about new developments in the business environment. Essentially, a world class intelligence portal facilitates the formation of a knowledge-sharing intelligence community in the organization.

Considering the technical angle, world-class intelligence software has sophisticated functionalities, yet it is not meaningful to nail down exactly what features should be included and what should not, as the requirements vary greatly between organizations. Powerful tools for categorizing data and allowing the individual users to subscribe to whatever categories they find interesting are at the core of any high-quality intelligence software, but the software tools available in the market today no longer differ much from each other on that front. Rather, emphasis should now be placed on functionalities that support active, two-way utilization of the portal regardless of where the user is located. In that sense, featuring multiple user interfaces (such as web, smartphone, and tablet computer) is increasingly critical for engaging the users.

At world class levels, the intelligence portal should also seamlessly link with other IT applications ranging from the corporate intranet to more specific niche tools. Full-blown systems integration is not yet common, but different systems should discuss with each other in a way that does not disturb the user.

> ### Case: SharePoint Integration in a Paints and Coatings Company
>
> A leading paints and coatings company in Northern Europe has implemented innovative ways to deliver intelligence to decision-makers and adapt to their working practices. The management of the company uses a specially designed dashboard, built on Microsoft SharePoint, to get access to various types of information they need in their work. The intelligence team decided to use it as a delivery channel for MI. The two systems were integrated so that competitor and MI show up directly on the management dashboard. This way the management is able to access this information easily using just one access point, while the intelligence team can continue to use its own dedicated intelligence portal to manage the market monitoring process.

What also has been explored but has not materialized yet to the extent that would have a major impact on today's intelligence programs are artificial intelligence applications, text mining tools for analysis support and tools that utilize geographical positioning data. While these advanced applications described above still remain as developments for the future, the currently active development areas include the capability for further collaboration, improved user experiences both in and outside of the office, better reporting tools that allow for multimedia formats, and better integration of MI results into executive dashboards and other internal systems.

Intelligence portal features frequently associated with enabling the above functionalities include:

- Software front pages to become intelligence dashboards that are easy for users to personalize

- Newsletter-style, designed email alerts on desktops

- Capability to personalize RSS feeds

- Ability to add user comments to content items

- Ability to socialize virtually around intelligence topics through own personal profiles and discussion forums

- Advanced reporting tools to support analytical interpretation of business information

- Lightweight web user interfaces to enable full access from smartphones

- Email alerts to support smartphone interfaces

- Improved technical connectivity between intelligence software and corporate intranets

SUMMARY

- An intelligence portal is one of the most tangible elements of an intelligence program. As such, it serves as a natural centerpiece of an MI program, even though people are doing most of the value-adding intelligence work.

- Unlike the intelligence process or culture, or other abstract concepts associated with intelligence activities such as needs analyses and workshops, an intelligence portal has a concrete look and feel, and this makes it a great marketing vehicle for the intelligence deliverables and indeed the entire MI program.

- There is an established market for commercial software applications to support the specific requirements of MI processes. However, the advanced functionalities nowadays included in the corporate intranet platforms such as SharePoint have encouraged some companies to build up home-grown solutions. Experience shows, however, that commercial applications are still in demand: new possibilities offered by SharePoint have not turned MI professionals into application developers, nor have they made the IT professionals better at understanding MI processes. As a result, a market niche for SharePoint MI software applications is emerging.

- Useful features and aspects to consider when implementing an intelligence portal include:

  o   Content management

  o   Data sourcing and input features

  o   Security

  o   Dissemination ("push" from the intelligence team to the MI users)

  o   Self-service access ("pull" by the MI users)

  o   Collaboration

- Being world class in intelligence tools:

  o   All relevant intelligence content is stored in one searchable database.

  o   Personalized email alerts of market developments and new relevant content are being sent to the MI users on a regular basis.

  o   The functionalities support all phases in the intelligence process.

  o   The functionalities facilitate the sharing of field intelligence, networking, and co-creation of intelligence deliverables through an engaging user experience comparable to the existing social media applications.

  o   The functionalities enable integration of intelligence content to various user interfaces (mobile, SharePoint, etc.) and business processes.

8 Intelligence Organization – The People and Resources that Generate the Impact

INTRODUCTION: INTELLIGENCE ORGANIZATION AS A KEY SUCCESS FACTOR OF WORLD CLASS MARKET INTELLIGENCE

"Intelligence organization" refers to the people and information resources that make the intelligence process happen. Appointing someone as the owner of the corporate intelligence activity typically is the starting point of forming an intelligence organization, but the person needs an MI team, information sources, and an internal MI network to support their work. Figure 8.1 illustrates the elements in an intelligence organization. We will briefly introduce them, and explain the evolutionary path that an intelligence organization typically follows after its initiation.

1. At the heart of an intelligence organization is the **MI leadership** – the owner of the activity and the one(s) responsible for steering and managing the daily operations. Organizing the leadership of the intelligence program is the natural first step on the MI development path.

2. The MI leadership will next set up an **MI team**. In many of today's lean organizations, this does not necessarily mean increasing headcount, but the company may engage in cooperation with external partners to organize the ability to centrally serve the MI users in the organization.

3. The MI team will have to set up a **portfolio of external information sources** that will be used in producing the deliverables the MI users need. This source network refers to standard, regularly used sources for which there is typically also a predetermined budget available.

4. The MI users in the organization make up an **internal MI network** that, in addition to being at the receiving end of information delivery, will also contribute to the intelligence process by sharing their own insight.

5. The MI users each will have a network of own contacts outside of the organization that makes up their **personal information source network**, even if a very informal one.

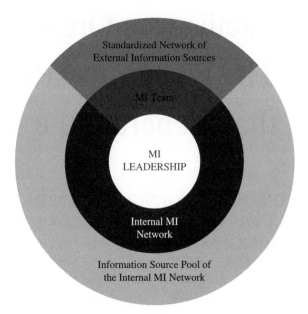

Figure 8.1   An intelligence organization is the combination of internal and external resources (human resources and sources of information) that runs the cyclical intelligence process
Source: Global Intelligence Alliance.

EVOLUTION OF THE INTELLIGENCE ORGANIZATION

In a relatively typical scenario, it takes up to six months for the MI leaders to set up the MI team and the initial information source network. Another six to 12 months is often spent on establishing the initial network of internal MI users, some of which will be very active contributors to the intelligence process, while the majority will remain mostly at the receiving end. Finally, a company usually needs to run its intelligence program for at least one to three years or more before the informal external source network, i.e. the personal networks of the MI users, really starts to contribute to the intelligence process. This is because it takes time to root the newly established intelligence activity in the organization by delivering valuable output, marketing the program, training the users, and essentially engaging them in the activity. Only then will the internal MI network start leveraging their personal external networks for intelligence purposes.

ORGANIZING THE DAILY WORK IN THE INTELLIGENCE PROGRAM

Managing an intelligence program and conducting the daily work typically involves many of the same people, yet their roles may vary. While the MI owner rarely takes part in conducting the regular intelligence work, the head of MI, despite leading the intelligence program, may also be regularly performing hands-on business analysis and writing reports, depending on the resourcing of the intelligence activity. Exactly how the roles and responsibilities will be divided in managing and conducting the intelligence work will typically depend on:

- the size of the company

- its industry

- its geographical location

- the degree of centralization versus decentralization of the intelligence program

- the degree of outsourcing the work

- and, finally, the ultimate budget allocated for the intelligence work

GETTING STARTED: PLANNING FOR AN OPTIMIZED INTELLIGENCE ORGANIZATION

MARKET INTELLIGENCE LEADERSHIP

The Owner/Sponsor

By the time the intelligence organization is established, the scope of the intelligence activity should ideally be defined already. With the purpose, primary target groups, and key topics of the intelligence program determined, the owner and budget holder of the activity should be rather easy to determine. If the primary goal of the intelligence activity is to serve strategic decision-making, the head of strategic planning may be a natural owner for the function. On the other hand, if the key driver of the intelligence activity is more tactical, such as directly supporting sales, the head of sales might be best positioned to own the intelligence program and its budget.

The scoping exercise of the intelligence activity has probably already directed the program towards where the low hanging fruits are: where the greatest impact and benefits can be achieved in relation to the planned investment. This cost–benefit analysis, even if implicit and informal, should be the primary driver for determining the corporate function that will own the intelligence program in order for it to survive the future ups and downs of corporate financial performance. The owner of an intelligence program that has been set up as an "internal luxury service" may find it hard to justify its existence during an economic recession, should the benefits of it be hard to demonstrate.

Along with the corporate function that will own the intelligence program, the seniority of the person who owns the program will also have an influence on its eventual impact. A management team member as the intelligence program owner can take the intelligence topics directly to the top, influencing the corporate strategy, while middle managers will likely need to regularly put time and effort into first getting access to the C-suite and only then being able to influence corporate decision-making.

Managing the Market Intelligence Program

There is no one correct way of organizing the daily management of an intelligence program, but we will introduce roles below that exist in many successful intelligence programs.

- Appoint a **head of MI** to lead the internal MI team:

  o   Ideally, the person responsible for running the daily MI activities should possess qualities that are typically associated with any individual in a leadership role: a networked person who generally enjoys the trust of people around them and has the credibility to lead an educated discussion about strategic topics in a variety of business areas. The person is preferably knowledgeable enough about MI as a topic, yet does not need to have hands on experience about all details involved in carrying out the daily intelligence work. Many successful MI directors have even been appointed to their roles without any prior experience in MI at all.

  o   The right type of person has a persuasive style and uses it to smoothly market the intelligence program both towards top executives and to interest groups around the organization. Regardless of how the intelligence program has been organized, managing it also involves managing a network of external service providers (or prospective ones), which calls for not only social abilities, but also negotiation skills, general knowledge about the information industry, and strategic thinking. Lastly, as the intelligence program will only be successful in the long run if it achieves what the organization needs, the discipline will need to deliver on promises.

- A **steering group** may be appointed to the MI activity that prioritizes the identified MI needs, confirms the usage of resources, and tracks progress of the intelligence program vis-a-vis the set targets. The steering group should involve not only the MI owner and the head of MI, but also some of those that are actively conducting the daily intelligence work (either internal or external people depending on the organization of the work), potentially coupled with representatives of corporate functions that the intelligence program is designed to serve in the first place. The steering group may only be meeting one to a few times per year, depending on what is deemed meaningful in each company.

THE MARKET INTELLIGENCE TEAM

The role of the MI team is to fulfill and manage the expectations of the MI users and to gather feedback from them, conduct internal marketing and training about MI-related topics, activate the internal MI network, manage the content production in-house and by external resources, and own the intelligence portal and other tools. Typically, the core MI team members are either full-time business analysts and MI managers or have something else as their job title but devote a significant part of their regular work to serving the organization's intelligence needs.

Traditionally, intelligence programs have been set up by determining the key intelligence topics, naming an owner for the program and letting them gather a group of people around them to assist in collecting and processing the intelligence that the company requires. The intelligence teams have been groups of in-house business analysts and intelligence professionals that deal with requests that decision-makers from around the organization send them. Headcount has been the primary success factor for the intelligence team. The delivery capability of the intelligence program has been directly dependent on the number of analysts available for working on an assignment.

THE STANDARDIZED NETWORK OF EXTERNAL INFORMATION SOURCES

More recently, outsourcing and offshoring arrangements have emerged as novel ways of setting up intelligence teams, further boosted by the trend of companies concentrating on their core business and reducing fixed costs especially from the headquarter functions. As a result, few companies only hire in-house analysts anymore to carry out intelligence assignments. Rather, a modern intelligence team is often a combination of internal and external resources that contains fixed elements such as in-house professionals, external partners on a long-term contract, as well as continuous subscriptions to various information content services. In addition to these resources, flexible ones that respond to seasonal or irregular peaks in the number and quality of intelligence assignments will also be used.

Hence the relationship between the internal MI team and their external source network is a symbiotic one. Both elements will need each other, while the set up of the combination may evolve over time based on what is the most fruitful and cost-effective way of organizing the whole.

Whatever the division of work will be between the internal MI team and the standardized external network, active management of the information source portfolio and the work of the external partners is an integral part of the internal MI team's role. Secondary information sources vary in content, format, cost, user interface, information retrieval methods, and technical connectivity, and all of these aspects need to be considered when determining which sources the internal MI team will be regularly using.

Furthermore, no parts of the intelligence work should be outsourced without the internal MI team being prepared to manage the outsourced work: communicating the needs, offering guidance, arranging check points and meetings with internal stakeholders, and giving feedback where appropriate. This way, the internal MI team's role is to make sure that the organization will get the most out of the investment in using external partners in the intelligence work.

Ideal Skill Sets of the Market Intelligence Team

Whereas the head of MI ideally is a good leader and a highly networked person with insight into the company's business, for the analyst team the ideal characteristics are somewhat more task-oriented. However, the following example illustrates the typical challenge for "the researcher type" in today's intelligence programs.

John had joined a large oil company as an Analyst fresh out of university, having earned a Master's degree in engineering. John was bright and ambitious and took his work seriously, delivering analyses to management that were always based on thorough research and neatly presented. Hence his manager, the head of MI was quite satisfied with John's performance.

However, John's handicap was that he was somewhat of a "researcher type": he had a lot to say, yet he frequently withdrew to the background and did not take an active role in discussing his analytical conclusions with the management. Paula, the MI head, thought of it as more of a problem with lack of experience and training than a fundamental personal handicap, as John had quite good social skills and he managed well upwards. Hence Paula started to train John, along with some of his analyst colleagues, in adopting more consultative skills. First building more powerful conclusions based on his analyses, adding interpretations from the company's strategic perspective: then essentially selling these conclusions and arguments to the management by presenting them convincingly and being prepared to lead an educated discussion, even a debate, about the results and implications.

Paula knew that the transformation of John and his colleagues from analysts to internal consultants would not happen overnight, yet she also knew that this transformation would be a prerequisite for the intelligence program to raise its status in front of the executive decision-makers. They would love to be challenged by the intelligence team. Only to be able to do that the intelligence team would need the skills to work not only with facts and figures, but also with people, and executive people in particular.

As John's example demonstrates, the primary challenge for many of today's analysts and information professionals is to become internal consultants and trusted advisors to the management (Table 8.1). This is the only way to raise the profile of the intelligence program to a truly appreciated partner to senior management: they will need to experience value in not only receiving analytical reports but also in brainstorming their ideas and leading high quality discussions with the members of the intelligence team.

Table 8.1   The roles and capabilities of MI producers

	Researcher	Analyst	Consultant	Trusted Advisor
Characteristics	Focus on collecting information	Focus on structuring and analyzing information	Focus on strategic analysis and providing recommendations	Focus on providing insights and advice of strategic and business critical value
Impact of deliverables	Operative	Operative/Strategic	Strategic	Strategic/Business critical

Case: Skill Sets for Intelligence at Nycomed

"The skill set of your intelligence team is the factor that ultimately determines your chances of success", says Robin Kirkby, Head of intelligence at Nycomed. "My major principle at recruiting is that I hire for attitude and train for the skills", he says. In order to assess his potential recruits, he has developed a list of attributes to look for and further cultivate for the purposes of intelligence work in the pharmaceuticals sector.

Nycomed Audit for Intelligence Professionals

Adaptability	Elicitation	Listening
Analytical ability	Efficiency	Networking
Approachability	Empathy	Non-judgmental
Business knowledge	Ethics	Observing
Communication	Facilitation	Online research
Commercial acumen	General knowledge	Outside "the box" thinking
Completer/Finisher	Healthily cynical	Presentation skills
Confidence	Influence	Project management
Content management	Insight	Responsiveness
Corporate mentality	Integrity/Trust	See the context of information
Courage	Intellectual curiosity	Soap box enthusiasm
Credibility	Juggle multiple projects	Synthesis
Culturally tolerant	Knowledge of firm	Team worker
Desire to help	Knowledge of industry	Trustworthiness
	Lateral thinking	Unbiased thinking

Kirkby adds that it is also important that the MI team gets broad exposure to various analytical methods and is involved in producing various deliverables. Making sure that the intelligence program contains routine deliverables, strategic deep dives as well as interactive workshops is a way to keep the MI team motivated and open to a broad range of topics.

THE INTERNAL MARKET INTELLIGENCE NETWORK

The internal network of intelligence users and contributors consists of virtually everyone in the organization that has a stake in the intelligence program. The network will not be formed spontaneously, however, but it needs to be facilitated actively, and the head of MI with the support of the MI team will handle the job.

The internal intelligence network should be built utilizing the existing structures of the organization, as the entire program earns its mandate from the current business lines and their intelligence

Figure 8.2   The different roles of the internal MI network members
Source: Global Intelligence Alliance.

needs. An "inner circle" of the intelligence network, as illustrated in Figure 8.2, is typically formed by those involved in performing the regular intelligence work and those that serve as the nodal points in different business units for the intelligence program development. Additional contribution to the intelligence program is obtained from dedicated expert groups.

The internal MI network should ideally be collected into an expertise database, to be maintained in the intelligence portal. This way, it can effectively be communicated to the organization who the experts are in which topics. At the same time, the intelligence organization becomes increasingly live and approachable, as names are put to faces.

In addition, the internal intelligence network can also be expanded into focus groups of experts around specific topics that may cross unit boundaries: some people might start focusing on certain competitors, others on specific customer segments, and still others on the development of strategically relevant technologies.

Recruiting Internal Market Intelligence Network Members

Everyone wants to have good spokespersons for and contributors to their newly established MI program, but how to find and engage them? The following guidelines may help in the process.

I.   Identifying potential network members:

- Look for genuine interest in MI and a willingness to commit to contributing to both content and networking with the rest of the MI users.

- Look for enthusiasm rather than particular skills; being part of the inner circle of an MI network is more about engaging people in working for common goals than being an expert in MI.

     o   Take some time to meet potential members face to face, introducing the intel-ligence program and getting that necessary commitment.

     o   Build the MI network one by one. One active member is better than several passive ones, and an enthusiastic member is the best marketing an intelligence program can get.

2.   Prepare an internal marketing elevator pitch for recruiting enthusiastic contributors to the intelligence program: explain the purpose, target groups and deliverables, and point out the personal benefits for the potential network members.

3.   Once the MI network has been established, have regular meetings with it:

     o   Once a month or once a quarter may be a good frequency, depending on the company.

     o   Face to face meetings are best, yet a combination of occasional live meetings and regular phone meetings works fine. Over the phone/netmeeting/live meeting.

4.   Reward the members for their participation in the intelligence program:

     o   Set targets and measure through the company's normal performance steering and evaluation system.

Case: MI Network Building at Cintas

Cintas, that offers corporate identity uniform programs and related services, runs a sophisti-cated internal MI sales network. Drivers for the initiative included the needs to:

- Quickly identify new business opportunities

- Develop local tactics to attack/defend against the competition

- Develop local competitive binders

- Establish sharing of best practices among regions

- Have greater visibility to the competitive situation at corporate level

The roles and responsibilities:

- Sales directors are responsible for "intelligence formulation", i.e. determining what intelligence is required

- Sales reps are responsible for "data collection"

- Sales managers are responsible for "synthesis and initial analysis"

(Continued)

The process:

Step	Responsible	Activities
1.	Cintas partners/ employees collect information	Sales reps/SSRs/service managers/GMs collect competitor information from the field Competitive info may be invoices, RFPs, brochures, rumours heard, etc. This information is placed in the local intelligence bin, which is a physical box where employees can put their competitive insights
2.	Sales manager identifies field signals	Sales managers review the submissions in the bin on a regular basis Sales managers choose relevant items and post to the Cintas Intelligence Center (CIC) as field signals Something is a "field signal" when it represents a) competitive risk or opportunity, b) best practice for attacking or defending against the competition
3.	Sales/training director selects field signals for discussion	Directors review field signals for their region on a regular basis Directors choose field signals that should be discussed further with their team
4.	Sales/training director emails to sales managers	Prior to the local intelligence meeting, the directors will email the chosen field signals to their sales managers
5.	Sales/training director conducts intelligence meeting	Field signals are discussed in a group and decisions are made on what to do Discussion occurs during any other regularly scheduled meeting **Intelligence meeting agenda** 1) Status updates from previous month's competitive actions 2) Review current month's field signals to identify: a) competitive threats, b) opportunities, c) best practices, d) decide on course of action
6.	Sales/training director records actions	Individual actions/decisions are added to the "Attack & Defend" section in the Intelligence Center

All input can be commented on, discussed, and further analyzed. Says Troy Pfeffer, the head of the intelligence program at Cintas: "The key success factor for this concept was really to go and visit the sales offices we have, talk to people and make them aware of the importance of intelligence in general and the collection and analysis of field signals in particular. Had I not done that, I doubt if we had been able to identify as many field signals by now as we actually have. It is also important for me to be present in many major sales meetings, taking part in the discussion, picking the brains of the sales people regarding competitor issues and alerting them about things they should be aware of."

CENTRALIZED VERSUS DECENTRALIZED INTELLIGENCE ORGANIZATION

Traditionally, establishing corporate intelligence programs has been the responsibility of either the global or regional headquarters of a company. This is because the activity often serves strategic planning, marketing and international business development in particular, and the budgets to support such functions tend to be centralized.

However, as the intelligence program matures and its public recognition increases in the organization, it is typical that the responsibility for producing intelligence deliverables is spread among a larger group of people than it initially was. Hence the activity becomes increasingly decentralized, and local units may start producing their own deliverables that better respond to the local or, for instance, product area specific needs. This type of decentralization is also a means of ensuring that as many people in the organization as possible will be tasked and perhaps incentivized to keep their ears on the ground for weak market signals and emerging trends.

The evolution of an intelligence program may also travel the other way round. Sometimes it is in the local units that the systematic intelligence efforts have been initiated, and the activity is gradually adopted at the regional or global level in an effort to avoid redundant work, coordinate purchases, and leverage the activity for the benefit of a larger user base.

The best way of building up the intelligence organization eventually comes down to the very purpose and target groups, i.e. scope of the intelligence program: a highly centralized organization with up to hundreds of in-house business analysts involved in the activity may make sense if the intelligence program exists to serve mainly corporate level goals. On the other hand, if the company runs very different businesses that may even have separate individual intelligence programs, a decentralized model will likely work best. There are also "best of both worlds" types of examples where an MI team handles the synergistic tasks and runs a common intelligence portal, while each business unit also have their own analysts conducting the very unit-specific intelligence work.

OUTSOURCING VERSUS IN-HOUSE RESOURCING

Organizing the intelligence program entails making decisions not only about centralizing versus decentralizing the activity, but also about whether some of the activities should be outsourced or performed in-house. The list below describes activities that are typically considered by companies as something that can (and even should) be outsourced.

- Collecting information from external sources

  Monitoring news, blogs, websites, and analysis reports will typically be outsourced. Increasingly, companies are also looking to outsource the management of their entire information source portfolio in the interest of optimizing subscription costs.

- Structuring information

  While IT tools already provide some help in structuring the regular flow of information, much of the work still needs to be done manually, and many companies consider that this activity is best outsourced. Examples of outsourced deliverables may be company or industry profiles, regular sales leads reports, or monthly industry briefings.

- IT tools for MI

  Despite the initial interest of many companies to tweak existing corporate IT tools to also serve MI purposes, many have realized that developing and maintaining such in-house tools is so resource-consuming that the company's internal resources are best used elsewhere. Hence IT tools is one of the typical areas where outsourcing takes place.

- MI process set-up

  Especially companies with little previous knowledge about the intelligence processes and tools typically consider using external help in establishing the intelligence program. With the increasing maturity of the profession, however, it is also typical for a company to hire an experienced MI executive from another company to build up the capability, once the mandate has been given by the management.

- Additional viewpoints and methodologies from outside of the own company

  Many companies see value in engaging external consultants in the high level analytical work: outsourcing strategic analysis may bring in additional analytical viewpoints, validation of in-house analysis, and specific methodological skills such as scenario planning or war gaming.

Outsourcing different corporate processes has become commonplace not only in large global organizations, but increasingly in smaller companies as well. So much so that some organizations are already reversing the process and re-insourcing some activities that they have learned are too complicated, costly, or risky to manage with external partners involved.

Managing intelligence programs is not an exception. However, as with all outsourcing arrangements, outsourcing intelligence activities can be done in a high quality manner, or less so. The KSFs of running sustainable, mutually beneficial outsourcing relationships in the area of MI are:

- An appointed in-house manager of the intelligence program that serves as the daily contact point between the companies.

- Well defined intelligence requirements that the deliverables continuously respond to.

- Commitment on both sides to continuously nurturing the outsourcing relationship: long-term outsourcing arrangements have been researched to have the tendency of gradually leading to "sloppiness", the resulting drop in the quality of deliverables, and the eventual termination of the relationship.

CONTINUOUS DEVELOPMENT: TOWARDS WORLD CLASS LEVELS IN INTELLIGENCE ORGANIZATION

For an intelligence organization, growing in maturity ties in with engaging more people in active contribution to the intelligence process – since a world class intelligence program is never a one-man show. This does not mean that more people should be appointed to "overhead positions", but rather that increasingly many people in different parts of the organization will find intelligence work such a vital part of their own roles that contributing to the intelligence process will become "business as usual" for them.

Again, this will hardly happen spontaneously but will require facilitation. In companies approaching world class levels with their MI organization, business unit specific MI coordinators have been named to serve as the local nodes in the internal intelligence network. A case example to validate the argument: for a sales manager working in Japan, it will be a lot easier to approach a local Japanese intelligence coordinator with their (typically local) ideas and requests than to contact an MI head sitting on the other side of the world and looking at the program from a global perspective.

In a world class intelligence program, the internal MI team has earned the position of a trusted advisor to senior management, making use of their analytical and consultative skills and delivering value throughout the intelligence process, i.e. from the needs analysis all the way to delivering the results of their work.

A world class MI organization effectively uses its external intelligence network as a resource:

- to handle regular outsourced tasks

- to ease out peaks in workload

- to complement and validate internal analyses with external views

- to serve as a source of best practices from outside of its own organization

The more of the daily intelligence work being handled by external partners, the tighter the cooperation with the business partners should be. Indeed, a world class MI organization is typically managed by a steering committee that controls and advises the work of both the internal and external intelligence networks.

INTERNAL AND EXTERNAL NETWORKING AS A SUCCESS FACTOR OF A WORLD CLASS INTELLIGENCE ORGANIZATION

A successful intelligence program does not work in isolation from the rest of the organization, but builds its high impact – and lasting buy-in – on a tightly networked strategy. The old truth "it's not what you know, it's who you know" very much applies to establishing a high impact intelligence organization as well:

- **An executive level champion** is needed to promote the program, and this alone may require a great deal of persuasion and networking efforts, should the initiative not come right from the top but rather from the middle management.

- **The deliverables** of the intelligence program should include collaborative elements right from the beginning, such as asking internal experts to add their comments on analysis reports, or arranging short briefings about the findings in them. Experience from many organizations has shown that encouraging people to share their insights through collaborative IT tools may require much more effort, and it may make sense to first go after the low hanging fruits.

- **Demonstrating**, by own initiative, how sharing information benefits everyone will encourage mass engagement.

- **Learning about the market for intelligence services and building external partnerships** selectively will expand the intelligence network for still additional benefits: fresh views from outside coupled with additional resources can further enhance the capabilities of the intelligence program.

- Finally, **networking with companies from different industries** will provide the opportunity to benchmark own operations against others and learn about the experiences of other people facing the same type of challenges.

Case: From Researchers to Trusted Advisors at Merck & Co.

In 2007, the intelligence function at Merck was merely providing answers to questions from management in a library service style. The focus of the intelligence activity was on data retrieval and information collection, while little time was spent on analyzing the content, let alone giving recommendations. By 2011, this had changed completely and the MI team is seen as internal consultants and even trusted advisors to management. A six sigma project was conducted to evaluate the focus of the work, revealing that the intelligence team at Merck now spends the majority of their time on generating insights and producing recommendations, while significantly less time is used at the data collection end.

	Data collection	Information	Analysis	Implications	Recommendations
Work focus	1%	10%	17%	26%	46%

Actions leading to the transformation included:

- Two new analysts/consultants were hired.

- Heads of clinical research for individual projects were recruited internally to become intelligence professionals, hence essentially making MI a career option.

- A service level agreement was established with the internal user groups of MI (strategy, R&D, sales and marketing).

- A Six Sigma project was conducted to improve the process.

- Relationships were enhanced with the company management.

SUMMARY

- The intelligence organization consists of five distinct elements that may take different forms in different companies depending on the level of centralization versus decentralization of the intelligence program on one hand, and in-house resourcing versus outsourcing on the other:

    o **MI leadership**: the owner/sponsor of the activity and the one/ones who are responsible for steering and managing the daily operations

    o **MI team**: a centralized, functional, or local MI team or a combination of several, that serves the MI users in the organization

    o **The external information source portfolio**: a standard, regularly used portfolio of information sources for which there is typically also a predetermined budget

    o **Internal MI network**: MI users that in addition to receiving intelligence deliverables will also share their own insight either randomly or as part of their job role

    o **External information source network**: the informal network of sources that the internal MI network has

- Being world class in intelligence organization:

    o Sponsorship for MI exists in the top management.

    o Head of MI is one of the most networked people in the company.

    o People working in the MI team are well trained and seen as trusted advisors to management.

    o An established internal network of MI users and expert teams enables the collection of field intelligence and analysis that is being done close to decision-making.

    o An external network of information sources has been solidly established for optimized quality of deliverables and cost efficiency.

9 Intelligence Culture – Engaging the Organization in Market Intelligence

> **Case: Promoting Intelligence Software in a Financial Services Company**
>
> When a US-based financial services company decided to adopt a software tool to serve as the concrete nodal point of their intelligence program, they took its internal marketing seriously from the very beginning. The various brochures, T-shirts, mugs, pens, mouse pads, and other promotional items that were distributed made sure that there were no people in the organization who would not have known what MI was and how it could be accessed in the company. While the promotional campaign only lasted a couple of months, it provided a significant boost to the company's intelligence culture: oftentimes, active and bold internal marketing of the intelligence activities is the single most important bottleneck in creating an intelligence culture in the organization. People simply cannot adopt things that they are not aware of.

INTRODUCTION: BUSINESS IMPACT THROUGH AN INTELLIGENCE CULTURE

In the long run, "intelligence culture" is the force that keeps the entire intelligence program together, and by the very definition of "culture", it is born and nurtured inside the organization. Perhaps the most important element in gradually generating an intelligence culture in any organization is senior management's voiced support for the activity. Other important building blocks are demonstrated benefits of the activity, and successful internal training and marketing efforts.

It is almost ironic that "MI culture" as the most complicated, slowly evolving, and ambiguous KSF of MI is also difficult to capture into a graphical illustration that would fully reflect its many facets. Figure 9.1 presents MI branding as the cornerstone of building an intelligence culture. While marketing communication is indeed an important tool for informing the organization about the benefits and characteristics of MI, marketing efforts alone will not yield sustainable results if the business impact of the intelligence activity is not tangible. Hence, "MI branding" should be interpreted broadly, i.e. covering the entire identity of the intelligence program that can take many forms ranging from its name, symbols, and slogans to the quality of content of the intelligence deliverables that eventually create the business impact.

Figure 9.1 Creating an intelligence culture starts with branding the intelligence activity
Source: Global Intelligence Alliance.

One of the most challenging parts of creating a corporate-wide intelligence culture is demonstrating the impact of the intelligence program not to senior management or other limited target groups alone, but to the entire organization. Branding the MI program will essentially serve this purpose: members of the organization should be able to recognize the intelligence program and associate it with a positive influence on the company's business that they themselves can also play a part in.

An important element in the MI branding efforts is top management's support to the intelligence program, without which it will be tough if not impossible to establish a genuine intelligence culture in the organization. Even though this support alone will not create a corporate culture of mutual trust and open knowledge sharing, it can provide many of the necessary elements that facilitate its gradual formation:

- CEO publicly acknowledges the vital role of the intelligence program in facilitating the company's business, sharing concrete examples.

- Senior management is an active group of the MI organization and takes part in co-creating intelligence content with the intelligence team and the rest of the organization.

- MI plays an integral role in all key business processes, typically starting with strategic planning but also in sales, marketing, product management, R&D, and corporate communications.

- Adequate funding and other resources have been made available for conducting the regular intelligence activities.

- Where applicable, involvement in intelligence activities is being used as one component of measuring employees' performance.

- Senior management acknowledges that the organization needs be made aware of the intelligence activity through internal training and marketing efforts, and that this will require its time and resources.

NATIONAL AND ORGANIZATIONAL CULTURES AS THE BASIS FOR CREATING AN INTELLIGENCE CULTURE

In this chapter we are presenting a universal approach to establishing an intelligence culture in the sense that the framework presented in Figure 9.1 can be applied in any organization anywhere in the world. Yet, as our case example at the beginning of this chapter also demonstrates, companies build their intelligence cultures on very different national and organizational traditions, and these backgrounds may have a significant influence on how easy or difficult it will be to establish a culture of open knowledge sharing. The underlying culture may also heavily influence the selection of tools and methods to build an intelligence culture. For instance, the extent to which promotional tools were used in our case company might not even be considered in a company where more subtle marketing styles are generally preferred.

Overall, the culture of openly sharing information tends to be higher where there are relatively low hierarchies. Anglo, Germanic, and Nordic cultures are examples of this, and indeed these geographic areas are also most advanced globally in terms of MI traditions. Along with the national cultures, organizational cultures in large global companies play a big part in setting the scenery for intelligence culture creation. A business unit may be geographically located in say, China, yet being a part of a European company it may have adopted a rather "Western" culture, and enhancing the intelligence culture locally may not be that different from working on it in the other parts of the world.

To bring their corporate intelligence program to world-class levels, the program owner will not be very likely to succeed unless they are aware of the corporate culture type and can adjust their intelligence development efforts accordingly. Even though the elements required for successful development of an intelligence culture do not differ much between companies, applying them will require company-specific organizational insight.

GETTING STARTED: PLANNING FOR AN OPTIMIZED INTELLIGENCE CULTURE

BRANDING THE INTELLIGENCE PROGRAM

We have discussed earlier the importance of building intelligence deliverables into products that can be marketed to their internal audience as a response to intelligence needs. Following the same logic, the entire intelligence program can be built into an established internal support function that validates its existence by continuously responding to the evolving business information needs of the organization.

For the organization to be aware of the support function, however, it has to have an identity, i.e. it needs to become an "internal brand". Many organizations today apply the means of modern marketing to spread awareness about different internal functions: brands are created under HR, spirit raising, or internal communications, all for the purpose of recognition, appreciation, and impact. Eventually, the internal brands may powerfully shape the organizational culture.

Similarly, developing an intelligence culture starts with systematically branding the activity. The effort will take time, but the process described in Figure 9.1 follows the logic presented above:

- Once the brand has been established, people start to recognize the intelligence program, i.e. become aware of its existence.

- Gradually developing an understanding about the value that the intelligence program produces, people start to appreciate it (acceptance).

- Finally, the true impact of an intelligence culture will be reached through assistance, i.e. people joining the intelligence process as not just end users of intelligence deliverables, but as active contributors to generating insights that may shape the organization's future.

Brands are constantly being created and enhanced by well-known individuals lending their status to different products and services. C-level executives voicing their support to internal intelligence programs again follows the same logic: it greatly enhances the credibility and impact of the intelligence program if people know that it's strongly supported from the top. Of course, as with all brand development efforts, the efforts to brand an intelligence program need to be sustainable, and sustainability is measured in actions, not words. Therefore if the intelligence program's brand rides on the CEO's voiced support to the activity, the CEO should be an active user of the deliverables that the program produces, otherwise the "brand promise" is soon proved shallow.

CREATING AWARENESS

The most credible marketing for an intelligence program are its high quality deliverables and their impact on successful business. Yet even the most sophisticated corporate intelligence program may be left with little attention if there is only a handful of people that are aware of the output and its impact. In a typical scenario, there are so many projects and initiatives going on at any given time in an organization that without planned and systematic marketing efforts, few people will ever hear about a corporate intelligence program and how it can benefit the entire company's business.

An intelligence program with little leverage or recognition will be a pity, but the loss can also be measured in financial terms: organizing and running an intelligence program is not free in any circumstances, and a show that runs for an empty house just because no-one remembered to engage the audience will likely not survive any corporate cost-cutting exercise.

Hence an intelligence manager may consider a variety of promotional activities that will help generate awareness of the intelligence program right from the start:

- A logo, colors, and layout for the various intelligence deliverables that will help people recognize them and associate them with certain quality, format, and other desired characteristics.

- Product development and marketing of the intelligence deliverables (including face to face meetings, workshops, and forums that can be built into recognized corporate events that people do not want to miss).

- Training workshops related to using tools (such as intelligence software or specific templates for contributing to the intelligence program).

- Flyers, mugs, pens, mouse pads, t-shirts, hats, or other promotional gear of choice can be considered depending entirely on the culture and the line of business of the company.

REACHING ACCEPTANCE

Building positive awareness of the newly created intelligence program goes a long way in promoting its acceptance. However, over time the promises will have to be met through deliverables that respond to people's needs and help them make well-informed decisions. Here, it pays to share success stories over unit boundaries: the intelligence program at its early stages may only serve a narrow target group in the organization, and relatively few people may therefore have concrete experiences about its delivery capability. However, reaching the low hanging fruits and demonstrating tangible value-add is well worth spreading the word about. If the intelligence activity can facilitate one unit's business, there may be others that might benefit from it as well. Only the others will need to hear about the success stories first and nod to them in approval.

GAINING ASSISTANCE

Convincing people to gradually take an active role in (co-)creating intelligence deliverables stems from the value of the deliverables: people contribute to what they think is meaningful and beneficial, most likely to themselves directly. Hence, a proven track record of the value of the intelligence output likely has people assisting in producing future deliverables as well.

Yet it is not only the end deliverables as such that count when people assess their willingness to contribute to co-creating intelligence. The process of generating the intelligence matters as well: people like to trade information, and to engage the organization in co-creating intelligence output, the intelligence professionals need to be prepared to give something in return for asking for people's contribution already during the process of putting together the eventual deliverables.

Finally, it would be naïve to assume that people are only interested in facts and correct information as such. Rather, people are generally very interested in who else is involved in the process of generating intelligence deliverables, i.e. with whom will they be working if they choose to put some of their time and effort into working on any given intelligence assignment. Hence, it helps to involve thought-leaders and high-ranking executives as spokespersons in an effort to gain assistance from the rest of the organization as well.

Case: Serving the CEO with the Intelligence Program at Dunkin' Brands

Providing MI to the CEO is a fine art, says Michel Bernaiche, Head of the Dunkin Brands' Competitive Intelligence program. While it's challenging enough for the intelligence professionals to earn the trust of senior executives in general, convincing the CEO is often a different story still.

Bernaiche says that the sweet spot for securing CEO buy-in essentially lies in the intersection of a world class intelligence program, the ability to market it persuasively, and the ability to produce actionable results. Making sure that the results of the intelligence team's work are always actionable is the toughest part, says Michel Bernaiche. He lists out ten best practices that will help ensure that the intelligence deliverables are of practical value to the CEO and senior executives.

Ten best practices to ensure actionability of intelligence deliverables

1. Secure agreement on senior management and CEO expectations for the intelligence program.

2. Build personal relationships with the CEO and understand her/his decision-making needs.

3. Position the intelligence function as a decision support function and not just a research department.

4. Get a seat at the decision-making table and get involved in annual strategic planning process.

5. Align the intelligence program with market research to inform both the supply and demand curve.

6. Build a brand around the intelligence program.

7. Be out in front; proactively create business opportunities.

8. Optimize reporting; produce reports and briefings that the CEO actually uses to make decisions.

9. Measure the return on the investments intelligence activities.

10. Benchmark your intelligence program vis-a-vis other companies.

Without having a close a relationship established with the CEO, it is very difficult if not impossible to understand the CEO's needs well enough to provide good intelligence, says Michel Bernaiche and he gives another concrete example about a situation where the company's new CEO came to work on his first day. Bernaiche was one of the first to greet the CEO, and as a result got an excellent opportunity to make a first impression and to brief the CEO on what he could do for him as the head of the intelligence program.

Finally, Michel Bernaiche says, an eye for psychology helps in working with CEOs just like with any people. As individuals, CEOs may be charismatics, thinkers, skeptics, followers, or controllers – or combinations of the above – and each personality type may require a different approach from the intelligence professionals who want to convince the CEO of the value of their work.

CONTINUOUS DEVELOPMENT: TOWARDS WORLD CLASS LEVELS IN INTELLIGENCE CULTURE

Essentially, an intelligence culture means that the organization shares the curiosity towards the external operating environment and the engagement to translating this curiosity into insights and, eventually, successful business.

At world class levels, the intelligence program enjoys a high ranking status in the organization, and its strong brand is being maintained through continuous efforts:

- The intelligence program continuously lives up to its promise, delivering high value to the users throughout the intelligence process and both with regular and ad hoc output.

- Everyone involved in producing the intelligence output follows the uniformly high standards of work.

- The intelligence program is recognized by its own symbols, and the MI brand management also demands that the brand will not be diluted by inconsiderate usage of the symbols.

Even if not every member of the organization will be involved in the intelligence program as part of the internal MI network, virtually everyone in the organization should be aware of the intelligence program when the intelligence culture is on a world class level. An employee does not need to have an MI user status to share an interest in understanding the operating environment and being competitive in it. (Having this interest may in practice quickly earn the person an MI user status, however.)

In a world class intelligence culture, acceptance of the intelligence program is widespread, and practically no-one in the organization questions the importance and value of it. People participate willingly in training about MI topics since they feel that they will receive knowledge and tools that will help them in their own work.

Hence the members of the organization will also contribute: the enthusiasm towards co-creating insights is high, and the assistance takes many forms:

- People share market signals actively through the intelligence portal.

- People are willing to add their comments and insights to intelligence deliverables, whether analysis reports or market signals distributed electronically.

- People participate actively in workshops and briefings, where insight is co-created.

- Those actively involved in producing most of the intelligence deliverables will receive frequent and detailed feedback on their work and its impact.

Case: Branding the Intelligence Deliverables

In a global power solutions company recognition for the MI program and a perception of highly valuable MI deliverables was important from the beginning of the MI development efforts. An intelligence deliverables branding project was launched to reach the goals.

The MI deliverables branding project was outlined as follows:

1. Brand Planning

    o Defining the product: what is MI?

    o Determining the objectives: what do we want to achieve with MI? When? How?

    o Identifying the audience: segmenting the MI users into different groups is a key step in the effort to identify the needs and develop branded intelligence deliverables.

2. Brand Creation

    o Building MI into a brand: the program was named and a logo was created that was used to label all MI products produced by the MI team. Report templates were then made for all MI deliverables such as the MI portal, the MI newsletter, research requests, competitor profiles, and insight.

3. Brand Implementation

    o **Creating awareness**. Ensuring that the user groups understand the purpose and role of intelligence. A communications plan was developed for each of the deliverables in order to ensure that each target group got the appropriate MI marketing message. The awareness was also measured with regards to how many persons were using the different MI deliverables and how many requested MI projects were to be executed and so forth.

o   **Gaining acceptance**. Ensuring that the user groups accept that MI is an important part in order to make the key business processes successful. The quality of the intelligence deliverables is the key at this stage. MI users must feel that the deliverables are timely, have a rich content, and are supporting decision-making in the company.

o   **Garnering advocacy**. Ensuring that people are contributing to the MI work on a practical level. Gaining advocates throughout the organization will lead to quicker development of a mature MI function. Other aspects to serve this purpose are: MI processes integrated into business decision cycles, mature information gathering and distribution processes, MI portal, frequently updated reports, dedicated MI staff throughout regions, and sponsorship by top level executives.

SUMMARY

- An intelligence culture builds on systematic branding of the intelligence activity that will first raise awareness of the intelligence program, then make the organization accept it as an established approach to handling business information, and finally engage the organization in co-creating the intelligence deliverables.

- Creating awareness:

  o   Assigning a logo, colors, and layout for the various intelligence deliverables

  o   Product development and marketing of the intelligence deliverables

  o   Training workshops on using tools

  o   Promotional efforts

- Reaching acceptance:

  o   Delivering on promises; quality of deliverables is key

  o   Sharing success stories

- Gaining assistance:

  o   Engaging people in regularly sharing their insights related to the external operating environment

- Being world class in intelligence culture:

  o   Top management voices support to MI and serves as an example of using the deliverables.

  o   The intelligence program and its deliverables have been branded well and they enjoy a high level of internal recognition.

  o   Curiosity towards the operating environment and a culture of open information sharing are reflected in the way people work in the company.

  o   Field intelligence is being actively shared and utilized.

  o   A culture of "counterintelligence" has also been established, with people around the organization safeguarding the company's market insights.

PART 3

Market Intelligence for Key User Groups

**10   Market Intelligence for Current Awareness Across the
Organization** 143
Pulling in the "Must Know" While Keeping Out
    the "Nice to Know" 143
Linking Market Monitoring to the Company Strategy 146
Early Warning and Opportunity System 154
Summary 156

11   Market Intelligence for Strategic Planning 157
Challenges in Strategic Planning 157
Strategic Decision Topics Demanding Market Intelligence
    Support 160
Market Intelligence Deliverables to Support Strategic Planning 165
Summary 172

**12   Market Intelligence for Marketing, Sales,
and Account Management** 175
Understanding the Customers and Competition 175
Market Intelligence Deliverables to Support
    the Customer Processes 180
Support Tools for the Customer Processes: Intelligence Portal
    and Market Monitoring 186
Summary 186

13 Market Intelligence for Innovation and Product Life Cycle Management 189

Innovation and Product Life Cycle Management............................ 189

Market Intelligence Needs in Innovation and Product Life Cycle
  Management.. 192

Market Intelligence Deliverables to Support Innovation
  and Product Life Cycle Management 196

Summary 201

14 Market Intelligence for Supply Chain Management 203

Introduction 203

Supply Chain Management Functions 204

Market Intelligence Needs in Various SCM Functions 207

Market Intelligence Deliverables to Support Supply Chain
  Management.. 210

Summary 213

10 Market Intelligence for Current Awareness Across the Organization

PULLING IN THE "MUST KNOW" WHILE KEEPING OUT THE "NICE TO KNOW"

Case: Targeted Market Monitoring Helps Avoid Information Overload in an Energy Company

"We didn't want to bother our people with 'nice to know' information, but wanted to support their work with targeted intelligence content that each of them would find relevant and useful", says the Business Intelligence (BI) manager in a Nordic energy company, having established a market monitoring service for a group of 200 executives and experts inside the organization. "As our people have been getting increasingly overwhelmed by the amounts of available information, we now only take in information that is relevant for the company, and our people can further narrow the scope to only cover topics of interest to them individually", she continues. "As the market signals have also been geared at supporting sales work specifically, our sales people are essentially getting leads directly to their desktop, which puts an additional twist to the service and increases our motivation to stay tuned to the current developments in the marketplace."

When executives and professionals are asked about their methods of maintaining awareness about the daily developments in their industry, it is not uncommon to hear comments along the lines of "I'm reading business newspapers and subscribing to four different news services to keep abreast of what's happening", or "Our competitive environment changes so rapidly that I don't even know all our competitors and customers, hence I try to keep an eye on the ones I do", or "When I need business information I usually go to Google first".

The comments speak of three things:

1. Executives and professionals need information pre-selected for them on a daily basis, hence they follow news services.

2. However, their information needs vary so much and evolve so quickly that few generic news services serve anyone's needs very well.

3. Once a situation comes up where information is needed for a specific purpose, there's no database of pre-selected information available, and people start searching the internet.

It is sometimes hard to establish the direct connection between the business that the company generates and Market Intelligence (MI) that simply keeps people aware of the daily developments in the operating environment. Yet it is obvious that companies need to spot the relevant opportunities and threats in a timely manner while simultaneously accumulating a searchable database of past intelligence content that matches the company's interests.

In a typical organization, people for whom it is an essential part of their job roles to maintain awareness about the current market developments include:

*   Top management

*   Middle management

*   Various expert positions

As a response to this need, organizations should establish "Push" and "Pull" types of continuous MI services, as first introduced in Chapter 6 about intelligence deliverables.

CONTINUOUS INTELLIGENCE SERVICES: "THE PUSH AND PULL SERVICES"

1. **Intelligence portal:** central storage and delivery software for MI content that stores the information in an organized manner and makes it accessible to its audience at different locations.

The intelligence portal ideally features both "push" and "pull" functionalities: at the very least users can pull information from the portal based on their needs in a self-service fashion, and they can also tailor the portal interface to match their individual interests. The more sophisticated intelligence portals also push information to the users, and this functionality, too, can be tailored by the users themselves in a self-service fashion.

2. **Market monitoring:** continuous, standardized deliverables that the intelligence team produces for the organization to stay on top of the relevant developments in the company's business environment.

Examples of continuous market monitoring deliverables are daily or weekly market signals monitoring and different types of recurring reviews and analyses that respond to continuous intelligence needs. "Continuous" in this context refers to especially the intelligence need, as the exact content of the deliverables changes each time.

ANALYTICAL MARKET MONITORING: FACILITATING CURRENT AWARENESS OF THE IMPORTANT TOPICS

Market monitoring often serves as the bedrock of the intelligence product portfolio, as it facilitates continuous awareness of the past, present, and future developments in the business environment, and it frequently also feeds into the rest of the intelligence products. A high quality market monitoring service has a number of benefits:

- While keeping the organization on top of the latest market developments on a daily basis, market monitoring also forms a database that may be used as a validated source of information when working on more analytical intelligence products such as regular reviews and ad hoc reports. This way, the cost of the analysis reports can be reduced and quality improved as opposed to a scenario where they would be produced from the ground up each time.

- Often, establishing a market signals service for a business unit or even a larger group of internal customers is a "low hanging fruit"; one can quickly achieve something visible and continue the further intelligence development efforts from there.

- With the growing role of social media among both the sources of MI and the applications through which people share information with each other, the inherent level of analysis of even simple market signals is increasing: they may already contain meanings and interpretations that may very quickly shape the operating environment of the company. This is especially true with market signals originated from the internal community as opposed to a centralized market monitoring service.

- Continuous market monitoring and actively shared internal signals serve as an effective marketing vehicle for the entire intelligence program, as the signals will reach a large user base frequently, reminding them about its existence and the very topics that are relevant for the company's future.

Despite the benefits of systematic market monitoring, it is sometimes perceived in organizations as merely tracking online publications in isolation from the other activities in the company. In order to avoid this perception from the very beginning, it is important to establish a solid connection between the company's strategy and the market monitoring process. Ideally, market monitoring should be harnessed to serve both the formulation and implementation of strategy, and in the following we will discuss ways to accomplish this.

LINKING MARKET MONITORING
TO THE COMPANY STRATEGY

A clear distinction needs to be made about whether the information delivered by market monitoring is supposed to help the company in *implementing* a strategy or whether it is supposed to help it in *formulating* a strategy. In this chapter, we present market monitoring as the very bedrock for the entire MI process, but further divide it into two (Figure 10.1):

- Market Monitoring System (MAMOS)

- Early Warning and Opportunity System (EWOS)

MAMOS specifically helps companies in implementing a strategy (most currently existing market monitoring processes in companies globally are of this type), while EWOS is designed to support the formulation of strategy in particular.

What is required from the market monitoring process for the formulation and implementation of strategy is quite different. Experience shows that, because it is easier to implement than EWOS, it is best to start with MAMOS, the market monitoring process for supporting the implementation of strategy. Here, the topics under the coverage of the market monitoring are derived from the existing strategy; hence the strategy sets the boundaries of the market monitoring.

MAMOS serves a wide range of internal users, as everyone in the company is involved in the implementation of a strategy. The sales function is trying to generate revenue, so the MAMOS can provide them with leads. The marketing function is trying to generate market share, so the MAMOS can inform them about competitor behavior. The procurement function is trying to secure resources at low costs, so the MAMOS can assist them by monitoring suppliers and market prices. All of these activities are parts of strategy implementation.

Once the strategy-driven MAMOS is in place and it is operating as planned, it can be extended to EWOS, i.e. to also support strategy formulation that involves strategic planning and self-assessment, and eventually leads to decisions regarding the company's strategic intent and goals. Here, the context is necessarily wider than the current strategy dictates, and the EWOS therefore covers

Figure 10.1   Continuous market monitoring divides into two: the Market Monitoring System (MAMOS) that supports the implementation of strategy, and Early Warning and Opportunity System (EWOS) that supports the formulation of strategy

also topics that are outside of the current business scope and may indeed never be part of it. The whole point in operating an EWOS is to look beyond the most immediate and obvious topics in the business environment and to detect weak signals that may indicate changes in the business environment that may also necessitate changes in the company strategy. EWOS is often linked with scenario work, and the market monitoring system is set up to provide evidence about the possible realization of some of the alternative future scenarios that the company has developed.

FUTURE ORIENTATION AND THE TIMING OF ACTIONS

It is often recognized that in order to provide valuable support for strategic planning and strategy formulation, any system monitoring the business environment should be able to foresee, at least to some degree of accuracy, future developments. Being able to grasp opportunities early on when, say, a new consumer trend emerges, regulation changes, or new technologies are introduced, is valuable in itself. But being able to capture these opportunities before the competitors do gives a company the additional first-mover benefits of market share, high margins, or improved brand image. Figure 10.2 illustrates this idea.

Without a future-oriented market monitoring system events in the marketplace are detected only after they occur. As a result, the company is able to take action only after the implications of the event have already realized and after the competitors have taken action (Figure 10.3). The result is a less than optimal allocation of resources, low margins, and low market shares.

With a forward-looking system in place, the company is able to anticipate the event which enables it to take action and allocate resources before the event occurs and before the competition acts. This way the company may be able to pre-empt competitive action as well as capture higher market shares and higher margins.

There is, however, one caveat. In case the market monitoring system, however future-oriented it may be, is not reaching its intended audience or the decision-makers in the company are not committed to act based on the delivered information, then action is not taken even though critical events can be foreseen. This is illustrated in Figure 10.4.

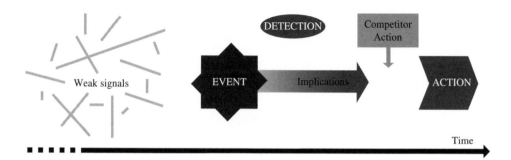

Figure 10.2   No future-oriented market monitoring in place

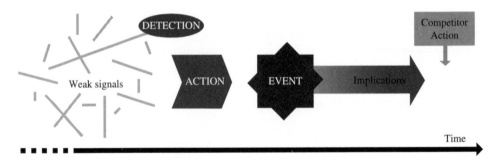

Figure 10.3   Market monitoring enables action before competitors move

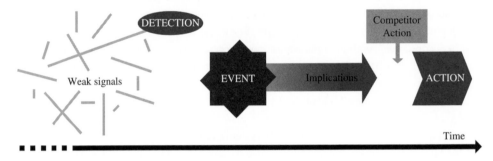

Figure 10.4   Events are detected on time through market monitoring, yet the response is delayed due to poor utilization of the collected signals

It is therefore vital that the decision-making structures in the company are receptive and responsive to the signals that the market monitoring system provides. This requires two things:

● Top management commitment

● Integration with functional processes

The latter point means that the market monitoring system should be sensitive to the various functions in an organization, as each of them has different intelligence needs and their own types of decisions to make. If the MI system is not integrated into the specific decision-making structures of each corporate function, detection of marketplace events does not lead to actions and opportunities are missed.

THE BIG PICTURE OF THE MARKET MONITORING PROCESS

Any kind of market monitoring process follows a certain basic logic, which is illustrated in Figure 10.5. The three fundamental stages of the process are the sourcing of information, the processing of information into intelligence deliverables, and the delivery of the intelligence deliverables to decision-makers. Within each of these stages there are multiple variations, but the basic structure of the process is fairly universal.

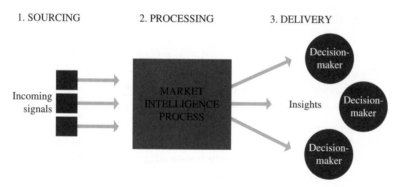

Figure 10.5 MI process adds value to the incoming market signals

We will call the basic unit of information a market signal. The market monitoring process is thus a system for capturing market signals from a variety of sources, processing these signals into an actionable format, and then delivering the processed signals to decision-makers.

When setting up a market monitoring process, good results can be achieved by planning these three stages each in turn. There are, of course, common denominators as well, and before the process can properly run, the big picture must also be coordinated. Before elaborating the big picture further, Table 10.1 provides a closer look at the Key Success Factors (KSFs) for each of the three stages of the process.

Table 10.1 KSFs for the three stages of the market monitoring process

Key success factors when setting up a three-stage market monitoring process

Sourcing	Processing	Delivery
Data sources can be push or pull. Prepare for both and don't assume that everything can be pushed or pulled.	Signal processing is a very demanding job which requires a combination of skills and tools.	The delivery process needs to adapt to the working processes of the MI user.
The relevance of a signal may not be apparent immediately. It is safer to allow more inflow of signals and to filter them out in the processing stage rather than to limit the inflow too strictly.	Incoming signals need to be evaluated, filtered, archived and transformed into intelligence deliverables by editing, analyzing, reformatting, and tagging them.	The preferences of each MI user should be considered individually.
The inflow of signals can be automated to a high degree, but sourcing also involves active search and evaluation of new sources, which requires human work.	Every market signal must have a point or a purpose.	MI users' own involvement in the process should be encouraged. Different signals have different meanings to people, and context is also created at the receiving end.
	The processing stage should put the signal into a context that is familiar and meaningful to the MI users.	The format, channel, and time of delivery should be such that it fits the workflow of the MI users so they can easily absorb the information and act on it.
		The variety of delivery formats is considerable: emails, documents, RSS feeds, text messages, SharePoint, etc.

TECHNOLOGY AND HUMAN WORK

For each of the three stages in the market monitoring process there is a variety of ways to implement them. The optimal set up varies greatly depending on the size of the company, the industry, and many other factors. As a general notion, however, each stage can employ a combination of technology and human resources. In order to make the process as cost-efficient and productive as possible, many tasks in each stage of the process can be automated and enhanced using various technological solutions. On-line publications, websites, and databases can be scanned automatically using keyword searches and text-mining technology. Market signals can be tagged, stored, and grouped automatically using a predefined logic and delivered using automated emailing systems and RSS feeds.

At the same time, however, there are certain tasks that can never be fully automated. The evaluation and search for new information sources requires human work, as do most tasks in the processing stage. It is precisely the human contribution that decision-makers perceive as particularly insightful and valuable. That is why the process should seek to employ both technology and human resources in an optimal combination – the first to improve the efficiency and productivity of the process and the latter to create insight.

Another point related to the relation between technology and people has to do with the delivery of information. There is a big difference in how actionable or useful the intelligence is perceived to be depending on the way in which it is delivered. The market monitoring process is there to help the decision-makers in their day-to-day jobs, not the other way around. Therefore, when planning the delivery stage of the market monitoring process, one should make note of the communication methods preferred by the decision-makers, and adapt the market monitoring process to these working practices.

Market monitoring should not exist in isolation of other business processes in a company. The market monitoring process is a knowledge process whose purpose is to improve the quality and productivity of other processes. Therefore any output of the market monitoring process will serve as an input in another process. When setting up a market monitoring process, one should therefore have a clear understanding about what other processes are involved. It should be kept in mind, however, that with regards to market monitoring, the strategic planning process has a special status, as was explained and illustrated in the beginning of this chapter.

CONTENT AND CONTEXT

Some of the biggest challenges in market monitoring have to do with the delivered content itself. When there are large volumes of irrelevant information, the content delivered by the market monitoring process is considered noise rather than information. To avoid this perception, the process should instead deliver concise and relevant information in a timely manner and in a format that makes the information easy to absorb.

For the information to be valuable and actionable, it has to have meaning to the decision-maker. Meaning, in turn, can be established by reference to a context. Indeed, it is the lack of context that so often renders content meaningless. Context is derived directly from the current strategy of the company and refers to the framework of concepts, topics, themes, and priorities that are chosen to be the focus of attention throughout the company. Naturally, people working in different functions may focus only on a subset of the context while the top management of the company is concerned with the entirety.

The importance of context is easy to defend in theory, but how can context be established in practice in a market monitoring system? The answer lies in taxonomies, as first introduced in Chapter 4 about the intelligence scope. A taxonomy is a set of categories or classes that are organized hierarchically. It is derived from strategy, and it is used for classifying the content in the market monitoring system.

Each content item in the market monitoring system is tagged, in other words marked as belonging to one or more of the categories. Tagging has already become a standard practice in many kinds of information systems, but the purpose and value of the practice in market monitoring is sometimes poorly understood. The key benefit from tagging is to establish a business context to any piece of information, thus pointing out to the decision-maker how it fits in with the big picture of business strategy. To add value, however, the taxonomy has to be built carefully.

The following sums up the general structure of a good taxonomy, derived from Figure 10.6 that illustrates the competitive landscape of an organization and was discussed in more detail in

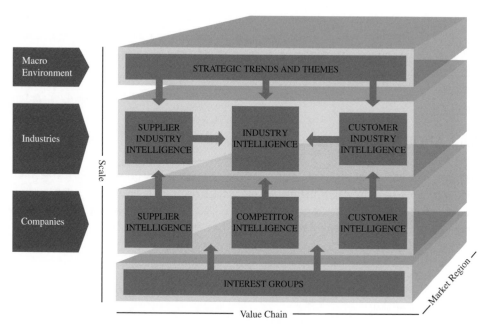

Figure 10.6   Along with strategy, the competitive landscape defines the taxonomy of the company

Chapter 4 about the scope of the intelligence program. The illustration serves as the basis for the taxonomy, i.e. the list of things in the external business environment that are relevant for the organization:

- Competitors, customers, suppliers, partners and regulators

- Geographies, customer segments and product lines

- Strategic themes

The following list provides some additional advice on how to build a good taxonomy.

- Strategy determines what kind of information is relevant for the market monitoring process. Taxonomy should be a representation of the context implied by the company's strategy.

- Consider the needs of different business functions, but use a common taxonomy. The taxonomy should reflect the relevant external business environment of the company, rather than its own organizational structure.

- Don't exaggerate the number of categories. Evaluate the usefulness of each individual category carefully based on whether it can provide insight to the decision-maker. There is no point in having categories that are rarely or never used, or categories that are outdated or have no meaning in the mind of the decision-maker. Become suspicious if there are more than one hundred categories in the taxonomy.

- Understand the difference of implementing strategies and formulating strategies. Most market monitoring systems are designed for implementing strategies. Taxonomies for supporting strategic planning require special considerations, which are discussed in conjunction with the EWOS.

COLLABORATION AND SOCIAL MEDIA

The rapid growth of online social interaction has also opened up new possibilities in market monitoring. While the basic model of the market monitoring process, as presented earlier, follows a linear structure, information exchange can also take place in a more complex fashion. We can identify at least three ways in which the process can be extended (Figure 10.7):

- New kinds of information sources (social media websites)

- Market signals (field signals) coming directly from end-users, acting as a kind of feedback loop

- Collaboration in the form of discussion about market signals, providing additional insight to market signals

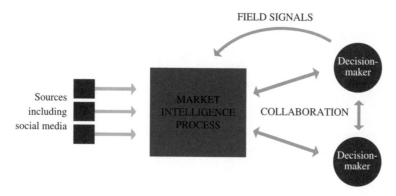

Figure 10.7   Collaboration and social media as part of the market intelligence process

We will illustrate these possibilities and discuss each in turn.

The most straightforward way to benefit from social media is to tap into public social media as one additional source of information. Services such as LinkedIn, Facebook, Twitter, and many more provide information about competitor actions, customer trends, and other potentially important topics. One has to keep in mind, however, that the information that can be extracted from these services is founded on open discussion between people and as such is generally subject to particular scrutiny in regards to its trustworthiness, thus requiring special attention in the processing stage of the monitoring process.

Case: Monitoring Blogs and Discussion Forums at Outotec

Outotec is a leading provider of process solutions, technologies, and services for the mining and metallurgical industries. Already covering a wide range of information sources, the company wanted to expand their market monitoring process even further to also extract market signals from public social media. After testing some blogs and discussion forums related to their industry, the company found that these sources indeed can provide interesting information. Therefore they decided to continue monitoring these sources and to provide decision-makers with regular reports about the top trends, themes, and opinions that appear in these media.

Using similar features and tools found on social media services, collaboration can be facilitated also within the market monitoring process. Some delivery formats such as web interfaces or mobile services can be outfitted with tools for user interaction such as commenting features, on-line discussions or rating mechanisms. These services can encourage decision-makers to participate in the MI process and lead to providing additional information. The delivery of market signals to the decision-makers can thus induce the inflow of additional signals, or field signals, leading to a kind of feedback loop and therefore strengthening the entire process.

> ## Case: Field Signals in a Global IT Services Company
>
> For many years, the company's European operations have developed their market monitoring process with the aim of delivering MI to decision-makers as effectively as possible. The intelligence team understands the value of market signals coming from their own employees, so the team has set up tools for increasing end user participation and collaboration. While the end users receive MI from the market monitoring system, they are also able to feed back their own field signals, thus providing additional insight to decision-makers.

In addition to enabling the inflow of field signals, the collaboration tools, such as comments or discussions about market signals, also act as an additional validation mechanism for the original market signals. Although a market signal is evaluated already at the sourcing stage, and further scrutinized in the processing stage, its value can be enhanced even further when it is rated or discussed at the delivery stage. Rating mechanisms are widely used in any kind of on-line services, but for a market monitoring application, ratings that enhance the regular tagging mechanism would be of particular use. For example, letting decision-makers tag individual content items as, say, competitive threats or business opportunities will add additional context.

EARLY WARNING AND OPPORTUNITY SYSTEM

Lastly, we will elaborate on market monitoring systems designed specifically to help the *formulation* of strategies, called Early Warning and Opportunity Systems (EWOS). These systems are best set up after a market monitoring system for strategy implementation is already in place, because the basic structure is the same. What is different, however, is the coverage of information sources and the criteria for the relevance of incoming market signals. Also, for an EWOS, uncertainty is more acceptable and even desirable. Collaboration and social media are likely to play a much greater role in an EWOS compared to a regular market monitoring process.

An EWOS is a process for scanning an environment that is broader than what the current strategy dictates. This means that it is often difficult to specify precisely which information sources should be monitored. Instead, more broad definitions can be used. For example, instead of monitoring one particular website, the process monitors any websites of a certain kind. An EWOS is often described as a somewhat fuzzy process.

When sourcing for information, an EWOS is specifically looking for weak market signals rather than market signals with a high degree of certainty. These weaker signals are often described as outliers, disruptive, unusual events, irregularities, or any hints of significant changes. It is acknowledged that many of the incoming signals are unconfirmed information, lack validation, and might turn out to be false alarms. This is acceptable, because otherwise potentially valuable weak signals would also be missed.

The relevant context guiding the EWOS process is also broader than with regular market monitoring systems. Just as with sourcing, relevance of individual market signals cannot easily be determined. It is useful to start with the context and taxonomy derived from the company's current strategy, but in the EWOS process it should be interpreted more liberally and it should be expanded with additional strategic themes that represent potential new avenues and unexplored territories.

It is also noteworthy that the competitive landscape considered relevant in an EWOS includes the whole macroeconomic environment, which is often considered less important in a regular market monitoring system. Macroeconomic developments are looked at closely when formulating new strategies, so monitoring and analyzing them should be considered an essential part of an EWOS.

The processing and delivery of market signals coming out of an EWOS process is allowed to be more provocative. Since the process will eventually lead to a reformulation of strategy, it is acceptable to challenge existing preconceptions, to raise questions rather than answer them, and to provide alternative points of view to familiar topics. From a resourcing perspective, it is important to realize that this significantly raises the bar for the resources used in the processing and delivery stages of the EWOS. The tasks require much more human work compared to a regular market monitoring process and should be assigned to the most experienced analysts available, who also should be able to communicate fluently with the top management.

The time horizon considered in an EWOS is also much longer than in regular market monitoring systems. While strategy implementation usually operates with a time horizon of one to three years, strategy formulation is concerned with time horizons beyond three years.

An EWOS is also the perfect tool for supplementing other processes or tasks related to strategic planning. For example, scenario analysis is a method that is commonly used in conjunction with strategy formulation. An EWOS is just the right process for tracking scenarios and their drivers and to perform the follow-up work that is needed to make scenario analysis truly valuable.

To sum up these ideas, Table 10.2 compares the two kinds of market monitoring processes.

Table 10.2   Two kinds of market monitoring processes

Market Monitoring System	Early Warning and Opportunity System
Market monitoring for strategy implementation	Market monitoring for strategy formulation
"Traditional" market monitoring	"Futuristic" market monitoring
Information that helps to achieve strategic goals	Information that helps to set strategic goals
Delivers information that is relevant	Delivers information that might be relevant
Seeks opportunities within given strategy	Seeks opportunities outside current strategy
Strict business context	Loosely defined business context
Short- to medium-term time horizon	Medium- to long-term time horizon
Well-defined set of information sources	Open-ended set of information sources
Identify competitor moves and business leads	Identify weak signals, outliers and disruptions
Seeks to reduce uncertainty	Seeks to embrace uncertainty
Process is well-defined	Process is fuzzy
Process under fairly strict centralized control	Process involves lots of peer to peer interaction
Social media provide additional insight	Social media plays a major role in the process
Collaboration is used to validate signals	Collaboration is used to create signals

Case: Competitive Action Item Lists at Cintas

Cintas designs, manufactures, and implements corporate identity uniform programs and provide entrance mats, restroom cleaning and supplies, promotional products, first aid and safety products, fire protection services, and document management services. Working in such a versatile industry, Cintas' strategic planning team is constantly monitoring the business environment and looking for new and emerging strategic opportunities. The scope of this inquiry is very broad as opportunities might arise in previously unexplored business areas and industries. To make this task more effective, Cintas has adopted a practice of keeping a competitive action items list of new potential strategic opportunities identified during the market monitoring process, along with implications, opportunities, and further investigation suggestions. This intelligence product is submitted to the strategy team, which uses it in their strategic planning process to further analyze it and develop new potential strategic avenues.

SUMMARY

- A market monitoring system is a continuous activity whose purpose is to facilitate organization-wide current awareness by collecting information about the competitive landscape, processing and analyzing that information, and eventually feeding it into decision-making processes. While the concept of actionable MI is well accepted and understood, companies often find it challenging to implement a market monitoring process that would deliver actionable and insightful intelligence. In this chapter we have presented ideas on how to tackle that challenge.

- When setting up a market monitoring system, one should first of all understand the difference between the implementation and the formulation of strategies, as these set quite different requirements for the market monitoring process. In this chapter, a MAMOS is presented as the means to support the implementation of strategy, while an EWOS supports the formulation of strategy. Organizations should typically start with establishing MAMOS and only consider setting up EWOS later on if deemed relevant.

- Strategy determines what kinds of market signals are relevant and why they are relevant. Strategy implies a business context which is comprised of the competitive landscape and strategic themes. The business context is represented by a taxonomy in the market monitoring process. The taxonomy should be constructed carefully to accurately reflect the strategic priorities of the company.

- In any kind of market monitoring process the market signals that are delivered to the decision-maker must be processed before delivery. Decision-makers cannot act on raw data alone, but need the information to be put into context and presented meaningfully. While many tasks in a market monitoring process can be automated, that particular task requires a skillful analyst.

Market Intelligence for Strategic Planning

Fred was looking forward to next week's strategic planning workshop. As the head of business development at a large financial services company, he had been preparing for the workshop for two months already. He now felt he had an excellent package of facts and figures to present to his colleagues. His plan suggested that the company should go ahead and introduce its equity trading services to a new customer segment.

Fred had been supported in his task by Sue, the MI director, who had worked with a partner company to collect and analyze the data that Fred needed to back up his plans. Not that all evidence in the market would have supported Fred's plans, though: Sue and the analyst team had been able to bring up market insights that would provoke lively discussion among the executive team next week, Fred was sure. His plan might even be put on hold for the moment, but, whatever the eventual decision, it would be based on solid information and a high quality discussion, Fred thought.

CHALLENGES IN STRATEGIC PLANNING

Fred, in our example, is well prepared for the upcoming strategic planning round, having perhaps learned from past mistakes: all too often business unit heads and strategic planners leave the preparations for the planning workshop to the last minute, then try to make up for the lack of groundwork by desperately searching for relevant data through Google.

Admittedly, the strategic decision-makers' task is not easy: the complex business environment combined with a massive overload of unprocessed information are making it increasingly challenging for strategic decision-makers to cut through the clutter and form clear views about the future.

- There's so much available data in different sources that finding the relevant pieces requires expertise that few executives have.

- The topics to be understood emerge at an increasingly fast pace.

- As a result, the "information paralysis" slows down strategic decision-making and increases the risk of poor decisions that are based on inaccurate or downright faulty information.

Fred was in the fortunate position to have a corporate MI program supporting him. In fact, he should not be alone: running an MI program that provides actionable insights to the strategy and planning processes is virtually mandatory in today's turbulent business environments.

In this chapter, we will demonstrate how MI can be integrated with corporate strategic planning processes in an organized fashion. Three sub-processes under strategic planning are presented that should interact: the Future Watch process, the Planning Process and the Early Warning and Opportunity System (EWOS), all of which can be supported with a specific set of MI products. These products represent a combination of a historic, present, and future oriented outlook to an organizations' business environment.

Most large organizations have what can be called a formal strategic planning process. However, the quality with which it is implemented varies, as has been discovered in many studies conducted around strategic management and MI. This book is not about the quality of corporate business processes as such, yet we want to underline that the impact of MI efforts cannot be developed and evaluated in isolation from the corporate processes that they serve. In this case, without a solidly implemented strategy process, it will be difficult for the organization to make the most of the supporting MI deliverables either. Hence we recommend that attention should be paid not only to the intelligence deliverables alone but also to how they will be utilized in decision-making.

There are many ways in which companies conduct strategic planning, ranging from annual strategy clocks to more irregularly performed processes. However, the basic elements of a strategy process are largely the same for every company, as is illustrated in Figure 11.1. It highlights four steps towards a strategy in action, and MI plays a specifically big part in "environmental scanning" in the beginning of the strategy process. Towards the end of the process, continuous market monitoring and ad hoc analyses about rapidly emerging topics of interest will respond to the strategic decision-making needs.

ENVIRONMENTAL SCANNING   STRATEGY FORMULATION   STRATEGY IMPLEMENTATION   EVALUATION AND CONTROL

Figure 11.1   Traditional description of the strategic planning process

Case: Integration of MI into the Annual Planning Clock with a Focus on Risk Management at Luvata

Interviewed for this case was Fredrik Vejgarden, Senior Vice President of Operational Excellence. Luvata is a world-leader in metal fabrication, component manufacturing, and related engineering and design services.

At Luvata, intelligence activities for the strategy and planning process have been integrated into the company's turnaround and change management program with the purpose of ensuring effective corporate planning on both strategic and operational level.

Luvata operates in many market segments that each includes a variety of sub-segments. The challenge therefore to MI is to focus the information gathering and analysis on a sufficient level of detail, while at the same time maintaining an overview on the whole business. Subsequently, Luvata is concentrating the most part of its intelligence efforts on identifying specific driving forces in each end-market in order to build foresight into complex market scenarios under different circumstances.

Luvata has a structured MI process in place that follows the company's "annual planning clock", the phases of which have been described in the following, along with the related MI requirements and output.

1. Management Conference

   The specific focus in the management conference is on growth areas. Luvata's management discusses the strategic business situation and identifies growth opportunities, a process that will result in a list of issues that need to be researched for a more in-depth understanding.

2. Market Insight Creation

   Through the market insight creation process, answers to the above listed MI requirements are provided along with an overview of the likely market developments during the next 12–18 months. A large part of Luvata's intelligence output is produced at this stage.

3. Divisional Strategy Making

   Luvata's divisions and business units will develop their own strategic plans based on the input received through the market insight creation phase.

(Continued)

4.   Risk Map Evaluations

Luvata uses a structured risk management approach through which various categories of risk are analyzed. Three specific risk areas have been identified: business
risks, operational risks, and strategic risks. Examples of strategic risk areas are substitute solutions, competitor actions, or commodity versus special product strategies.
All risks are analyzed with regards to their likelihood on the one hand and their
potential impact on the industry and the company on the other.

5.   Strategic Review

At this point, the company strategy that was confirmed in January will be challenged
and either reconfirmed or altered based on the business situation half way through
the calendar year.

6.   Strategic Workshop Summit

The Strategic Workshop Summit is a one to two day yearly conference that involves
all senior managers in the company. The updated company strategy is presented and
its implications for all divisions are discussed.

Many companies today consider the strategic planning process too important and demanding to
be conducted once a year only. Rather, strategic planning may be conducted throughout the year
at varying intensity, which naturally is resource-consuming. The positive thing from MI's perspective
is that the required efforts will be spread out evenly over the course of the year, and the related
workload is easier to manage than with only one annual strategy round.

Although the strategic planning process in many organizations is already being supported by systematic MI activities, a frequent finding in MI surveys and interviews with executives is that this
support could generate still more impact. This chapter presents a conceptual framework that will
help assign a very specific role and purpose for every intelligence product in the strategic planning
process and the related decision topics.

STRATEGIC DECISION TOPICS DEMANDING
MARKET INTELLIGENCE SUPPORT

Illustrated in Figure 11.2 are strategic themes under different elements in the organization's operating environment: strategic decisions should be made about the market territories where the
company will operate, the segments that the product and service portfolio should cover, key players
whose actions will have relevance for the company, key figures (e.g. macroeconomic indicators and
price developments) that will impact the company, potential merger and acquisition plans, and so
forth. The idea of MI in support for the strategy process is to feed in directly to the specific strategic theme/decision topic to generate an impact on decision-making.

STRATEGIC THEMES

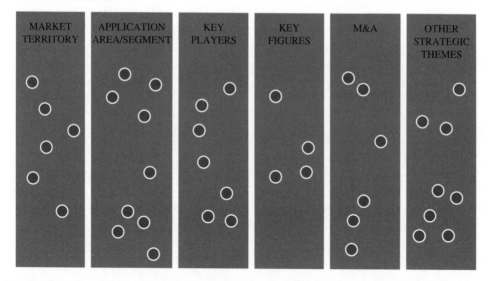

Figure 11.2   Strategic themes relate to a number of areas requiring decision-makers' attention

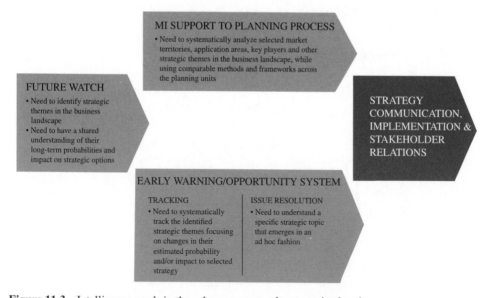

Figure 11.3   Intelligence needs in the sub-processes under strategic planning

The different strategic themes described already may relate to different parts of the strategy process: the Future Watch, Strategic Planning, and EWOS that are illustrated in Figure 11.3. These three processes have varying objectives and focus, and they demand different analytical approaches from the intelligence deliverables. The output of these processes serves as an input to communicating the strategy; the implementation and dialogue with stakeholders.

The processes also differ from each other with regards to continuity and timing. The Future Watch process that spans a long analysis horizon, ranging from three to 20 years ahead, is normally conducted as an input to the Planning Process, while the planning work where the analysis horizon typically covers the next one to five years often takes place throughout the year. The EWOS including continuous tracking and issue resolution with the associated ad hoc analysis projects build on the other two processes and provide the continuous tracking and analysis of how the strategic themes develop over time.

Each sub-process to the strategy process demands different types of MI support, as has been illustrated in Figure 11.3.

Case: Towards Excellence in Running an Intelligence Program at Orange UK

Interviewed for this case was Andrew Beurschgens, Business Intelligence (BI) manager at Orange UK. Beurschgens now works as head of business market insights at Everything Everywhere Ltd., the UK joint venture managing the two brands Orange and T-Mobile.

Intelligence and the Strategy Process at Orange UK

"Everyone in the organization should sing from the same song sheet" says Andrew Beurschgens, summarizing the role and purpose of BI in the company's strategic planning process.

Beurschgens speaks from the point of view of making sure that the strategy process is being served with such BI that everyone involved is on the same page regarding the anticipated market developments. At the same time, he acknowledges the challenge: "It may be difficult sometimes for the intelligence program to take into account different intra-organizational and political issues that may pull the analyses and conclusions into different directions. Our BI program really exists to ensure that it ultimately drives sound decision-making through insight for the internal business groups it serves, and secondly for those individuals who have mandates to make decisions within those business groups."

The initial focus in Orange UK's intelligence activity was on relatively operational and tactical issues. The idea was to develop a solid intelligence framework and a platform of knowledge that would eventually support strategic decision-making. Organizationally, the intelligence team was placed in the market insight unit under the strategy and business performance operation. The market insight unit in turn hosts market research, strategic insights, and the competitive analysis sub-units.

Main target groups for the BI program at Orange UK are top management and the strategic planning team, management teams in the consumer and broadband business segments, and people involved in sales, distribution, and finance.

Beurschgens reflects on the challenging parts in the set up process of the intelligence program: "Organizational culture and internal politics are an area where I think most companies face challenges when establishing an intelligence capability, especially when it is geared at serving the strategy process. People typically have a lot of own ideas and perceptions of the company's strategy, and intelligence professionals may find it tough to feed in neutrally positioned insight for every different unit's needs."

He continues: "Strategy is also under constant revision, and it is not always so simple to serve the insight needs of the old strategy while waiting for it to be replaced by an updated one. And on top of serving the strategy process, our unit is also responsible for addressing intelligence requests from all of our business areas. This makes the intelligence scope very broad, which makes it important to think and work on many levels at the same time."

Business Intelligence Framework for Orange UK's Strategy Process

It takes time to establish and solidify a corporate intelligence program. Beurschgens highlights the stepwise nature of this development process: "Initially, we had little structure in our intelligence activities. Most assignments were conducted on an ad hoc basis, using very basic information sources."

"It was a bit like stick-fetching", Beurschgens describes. "A manager says he needs something and someone tries to deliver that, without knowing much about the purpose of the request, let alone the larger context. Over time, we have developed a more structured approach by digging deeper into the end users' true intelligence needs, and by utilizing an increasing variety of information sources and analysis methods", he continues.

It is important to understand the relationship between intelligence end users and intelligence providers, respectively. The challenge for the intelligence manager has been to understand the perspective from both sides – the strategically focused consumer and that of the practitioner. Then deliver the "what's next" rather than the "so what" to that strategic issue.

Management typically looks at the intelligence program from the results and value perspective, asking the "what's next" questions, rather than "so what does this mean for our business?" Intelligence practitioners on the other hand are naturally more focused on the insight creation process and techniques.

The middle ground is an important area to define and develop in order to allow for efficient exchange of information between these groups. It is vital to first agree on the expected outcome of the intelligence process and then to design a process with roles and responsibilities to ensure smooth insight delivery.

"Our intelligence program produces anything from single customized ppt slides to comprehensive research studies, scenario reports and early warning signals reports",

(Continued)

Andrew Beurschgens describes. For the strategic planning process, Beurschgens and his team have developed a specific framework with building blocks that focus on specific topics which are listed out in the following.

1.   Intelligence briefing packs. With input from Orange UK's own win–loss sales analysis and information collection, coupled with internal field signals, an overview is provided of the existing market situation on both macro and micro levels.

2.   Scenario analysis workshops. Based on the briefing packs, a workshop will be run where the participants identify and analyze issues that will likely impact Orange UK's present and future business. For each issue, the scope of impact will be determined, along with the probability of the event. Finally, a set of scenarios will be developed that might or might not actualize in the future. For each of the scenarios, opportunities and threats will be identified from the perspective of Orange UK's business.

3.   Competitor reactions analysis. Orange UK also tries to understand how their competitors' anticipated actions would fit to each of these scenarios. War gaming has also been used in order to build a more profound understanding of the competitive moves in the market.

4.   Orange action options. Based on the above activities, Orange UK will determine strategies for obtaining and maintaining favorable positions in its different market segments. The strategic overview provides a basis on which different unit managers will need to build their unit-specific strategies.

Once again, it is vital for the intelligence professionals to maintain awareness of how the output of the intelligence processes will be used by the organization's decision-makers. When several people are involved in producing intelligence input to the strategy processes of different business units, the risk exists that the "right hand does not know what the left hand is doing", i.e. especially tacit information is lost in handing over an analysis product from one person to another for further processing before its final delivery.

Lessons Learned: Intelligence Professional, be Bold and Daring!

Being asked about the key success factors in Orange UK's intelligence program for the strategy process, Beurschgens says: "You need to understand where the highest impact can be made, i.e. to develop methods and processes for winning the battles that you want to win." He continues: "In our company, decision issues often stem from the bottom up but they are decided by top management. It is therefore of obvious importance to have an impact on middle management and BU directors, since they will bring the important issues to top management's attention."

Another distinct success factor in Beurschgen's experience is the delivery of intelligence. "It is essential to have multiple ways to deliver intelligence; from face to face meetings and public presentations to memos, documents, and emails. Personal meetings are very important since managers will typically not only give you feedback, but will also share their views on the issues discussed. Here you have to be bold."

Finally, Beurschgens comments on what the team might have done differently in the past, looking back now: "We would probably have been more bullish and direct about the inferences on the analysis and its insight that we have provided. We have sometimes conformed to the traditional way of thinking, having done things based on intra-political agendas. Now, we feel that we need to develop a bit more independency, stand up for what we believe given the work we have done. This is proving to be beneficial to both the team and the wider business as demonstrated by the fact that the strategy door is still open to us."

MARKET INTELLIGENCE DELIVERABLES TO SUPPORT STRATEGIC PLANNING

With the intelligence needs in the strategy process described, we can now leverage the intelligence program for the support of planning and implementation of strategy. Figure 11.4 illustrates intelligence deliverables that will support the different phases in the strategy process. Admittedly, for a relatively simple business and/or limited budget, the approach that we are presenting may be even too comprehensive. However, significant strategic decisions should never be made without supporting them with MI, as researched facts will greatly improve the probability of success, while reducing the risk of making expensive mistakes.

Hence the core MI elements to support the strategy process need to be there: the company needs to have an educated view about the long-term future, a good grasp of the immediate competitive

Figure 11.4 MI Products for the Strategic Planning Process

environment and customer demands, and a way of keeping track of how the above things will evolve over the current planning horizon. With these things in mind, we will now move on to explaining how the different sub-processes to the strategy process can be supported with analytical intelligence deliverables.

MARKET INTELLIGENCE SUPPORT FOR THE FUTURE WATCH PROCESS

The Future Watch process is inherently forward-looking, and also considers factors outside of the company's most immediate business environment, such as the macroeconomic and political conditions. Hence at this stage the strategic planners should adopt the role of a visionary; building alternative scenarios of how the future may unfold and what will be the preconditions for doing successful business under the different scenarios. In the following we will outline some useful methods for assessing the future business outlook.

PESTEL Analysis

Purpose   To identify trends and critical topics in the external business environment. The focus is on political, economic, social, technological, ecological, and legal topics.

Work process   A PESTEL analysis includes in-depth secondary and primary research and aims at foreseeing significant changes in the macro-level business environment over a time horizon of typically two to five years. PESTEL analysis is often conducted as preparation for scenario and trend analyses in the process of identifying trends and uncertainties.

Forecasting

Purpose   To anticipate market developments.

Work process   Statistical analysis is applied when there are sufficiently high quality data available to make precise estimates. Judgmental analysis is used for qualitative portions of the assignment. Gathering the available analyst forecasts and consensus estimates may also be a part of the forecasting assignment. Forecasting works best in stable industries, and relying solely on forecasting is historically not very successful. Hence additional analysis approaches are recommended to effectively triangulate the results of the forecasting effort.

Case: MI for the Technology Strategy in an Oil Company

The intelligence team in our case company has developed a concept for mapping out alternative future technologies and key player strategies with regards to them. The resulting technology map consists of five building blocks:

I.   Issue Framing

Having an active dialogue with top management in order to determine the key issues that the analytical efforts should focus on.

2. Information Collection from Internal Sources

   Typically people inside the company already have a lot of knowledge about any specific intelligence topic, and this knowledge should just be utilized in a systematic and documented fashion.

3. Information Collection from External Sources

   Once the internal research has been completed, the results are complemented, verified, and triangulated using information from external sources: publications, online research, IP research, and external expert interviews.

4. Analysis

   The analysis phase combines profiling, positioning, patent analysis, partner analysis, benchmarking, and five forces analysis into a comprehensive overview of the emerging technology trends, uncertainties, challenges, and market players. Based on the analysis, competencies will be identified that the company itself will need in order to stay on top of the industry developments.

5. Workshops

   Eventually, strategic workshops will be run that involve people who can confirm and challenge the analyses. Based on the workshops, the challenges and opportunities identified in the analysis phase will be reviewed and updated.

Strategic Options

The end result of the entire technology mapping process is a set of strategic options that the company management needs to evaluate and make decisions on.

Scenario Analysis and Workshops

Purpose To identify possible future outcomes for an industry, a business unit, a product, or other topic of strategic importance.

Work process Scenario analysis works best with a future horizon of three to 30 years. Some of the most critical present and future uncertainties will be identified in the business environment. The result from PESTEL analysis may be good input here. An uncertainty impact matrix is developed, along with scenario axes for the most important uncertainties. Scenario crosses are formed by combining two uncertainties. The four scenarios that have thus been developed will be named.

The scenarios are refined by enriching the content. The scenarios could be written as a story, a newspaper article, or similar. The results are verified by sending them out to stakeholders or running another workshop. The present and future strategic options will be matched with the different scenarios in order to find the best strategy.

To follow up on a scenario exercise, key indicators can be identified for each scenario and tracked with an EWOS. Scenarios can also be used as a basic framework for value chain analysis, war games, and/or competitor analysis.

War Game

Purpose   To understand potential actions of competitors and other important stakeholders in the business environment.

Work process   A war game is a powerful tool for boosting involvement and insight co-creation among the participants. War games work best on a one to three years future horizon, and competitor profiles, trends, and scenarios serve as useful input to the process. In a war game, the idea is to "become" the competitors and use their mindset and perspectives. First, the purpose for the war game will be defined. Teams will then be created with extensive knowledge about the different competitors. Background information is provided for the teams about the war game exercise and the specific competitor that has been assigned to each team. Interesting future scenarios/events will be constructed that the teams shall respond to. The teams will present their responses to various scenarios, including a business/product/marketing plan for the own organization. The workshop outcomes will be shared among the participants. The results will be used as an input to the strategy process.

Is it necessary to conduct all of the above described Future Watch related analyses and workshops? It will depend on how much uncertainty there is that needs to be addressed in the Future Watch process. If the company operates in a relatively stable industry, the approach may be rather straightforward. However, even in stable industries, changes will eventually occur. Using the analytical approaches described, companies will stand a better chance of capitalizing on change as opposed to merely adopting a reactive market follower's role.

In Figure 11.5, the analysis methods typically used in the Future Watch process have been combined with the earlier presented strategic themes related to the strategy process. The most frequently used combinations of analysis methods and strategic themes have been highlighted.

	MARKET TERRITORY	APPLICATION AREA/SEGMENT	KEY PLAYERS	KEY FIGURES	M&A	OTHER STRATEGIC THEMES
PESTEL Analysis	●					●
Forecasting	●	●		●		●
Trend Analysis	●	●				●
Scenario Analysis	●	●				●
War Gaming			●	●	●	

Figure 11.5   MI Products for the Future Watch Process

MARKET INTELLIGENCE SUPPORT FOR THE PLANNING PROCESS

To support the planning process, common MI products include market attractiveness analysis, market size and share analysis, M&A analysis, industry analysis, and key player profiles.

Figure 11.6 provides an overview of how MI products can support the planning process. While the eventual number of intelligence products and their very names is less relevant, it is recommended to use different analysis methods in order to approach the strategic themes from several perspectives.

Macroeconomic Analysis

Purpose To provide an overview of the macroeconomic environment that sets the background for the more specific strategic plans.

Work process Typically the macroeconomic analysis includes PESTEL type of approaches ranging from assessing the political and regulatory environment to assessing the general economic conditions and indicators over the next quarters to years. Many companies also include raw material price indices in macroeconomic reports.

Market Attractiveness Analysis

Purpose To identify attractive market segments either in the existing or new market areas.

Work process The markets or segments to be included in the analysis will first be prioritized, and research will be carried out on region, country, or segment-specific topics to evaluate

STRATEGIC THEMES

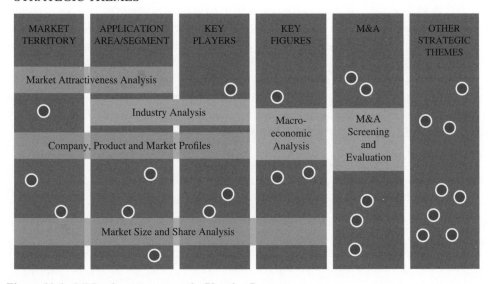

Figure 11.6 MI Products to support the Planning Process

the business opportunities in the selected market areas. The content of the report may include, for example, the macro perspective (PESTEL analysis) market size assessments, and analysis about distribution channels, the presence of competitors, local production, and pricing. Once the external analysis has been completed, the resources required to obtain the desired market position will be assessed internally, and a decision will be made as to which market or segments will be focused on.

Case: Assessment of the Russian Industrial Diesel Engines Market

One of the world's leading producers of industrial and marine engines wanted to understand the potential of the industrial diesel engines market in Russia in order to decide on whether to invest more in business development in the country. Secondary research was conducted on the topic, followed by 25 in-depth interviews with potential customers. The research results were built into an in-depth analysis report, where the following parameters were addressed: market size, position of key competitors, key demand drivers, main market trends, and key decision-making factors. Finally, the customer's potential to increase its market share was estimated and recommendations were made on how to increase sales, including required product portfolio, most promising target segments, and promotion initiatives. As a result, the company got to improve its strategy in Russia by concentrating on the most promising segments and client types. Subsequently, the company's engine and spare parts sales in Russia increased significantly.

M&A Screening and Evaluation

Purpose   To provide decision-making support to M&A considerations.

Work process   Analysis to support M&A decision-making can be undertaken at any stage of the M&A process and the focus and methods of the analysis will differ in each phase: evaluating the viability of the M&A strategy overall, identifying potential target companies, screening and analyzing the most potential targets, analyzing them during M&A discussions, and conducting a commercial due diligence analysis.

Case: Entering a New Geographical Market Area through an M&A Analysis Project

An environmental management and property and plant maintenance company wanted to identify suitable acquisition candidates and get a review of recent M&A activity on a new market, in order to enter that market. A combination of interviews with branch organizations, trade unions, select customers, and select facility management companies was conducted, complemented by extensive secondary research on news archives, industry reports, and company databases. A large number of companies was analyzed and profiled. Thirteen companies were selected as potential acquisition candidates based on parameters selected by the company's management team. One of these was eventually acquired by the company's competitor and three were acquired by the company itself.

How companies handle the M&A process varies remarkably depending on their strategic orientation. Some companies are constantly scanning the business environment for possible M&A targets, whereas others consider the topic as an ad hoc issue. Yet even companies that are not running an active M&A strategy are greatly affected by the potential M&A activity of other companies around them. Hence the M&A aspect should always be taken into account when conducting strategic planning.

Profiles

Purpose To provide structured information, typically about a competitor, customer, product, or country. Profiles may be used as standalone intelligence products, or they may also be needed as input to a benchmarking process.

Work process Profiles follow a uniform structure that will be determined in the needs analysis: what will be the relevant aspects to cover in a strategically meaningful profile snapshot? The collected information is typically something that can be obtained from secondary sources, and the added value really comes from the structure that also allows benchmarking the market player to others in the market when conducting strategic planning. The profiles may be produced into Word or PowerPoint format, or they may also make up a database.

MARKET INTELLIGENCE SUPPORT FOR THE EARLY WARNING AND OPPORTUNITY SYSTEM

Companies that have conducted the strategy process with the support of organized MI for years already should typically also have the capability to systematically track the indicators suggesting that a scenario, risk, or forecast may be about to realize. An EWOS fits this purpose, as was already discussed in Chapter 10 about MI for current awareness. In conjunction with the discussion of strategy work, we also count in issue resolution as part of the EWOS, as MI sometimes needs to address rapidly emerging ad hoc topics that have strategic relevance to the company. Figure 11.7 highlights the MI deliverables under EWOS tracking and issue resolution that may relate to the various strategic themes prevailing in the operating environment.

Strategic themes monitoring is essentially advanced current awareness tracking, where the level of analysis may differ a lot between companies. Some have built up sophisticated indicator systems involving signposts: when an indicator reaches a signpost, an analyst should alert their colleagues, and the topic should be addressed in an appropriate manner.

At times, workshops will be arranged around a topic of strategic significance. The greatest value of workshops lies in content co-creation, i.e. knowledgeable people sharing their views about the topic. To maximize the benefit of a workshop around a strategic theme, analysis should be produced beforehand for the participants to prepare themselves with. In the eventual workshop, the role of the intelligence professionals will be to objectively facilitate the discussion and point to the facts supporting the analyses where necessary.

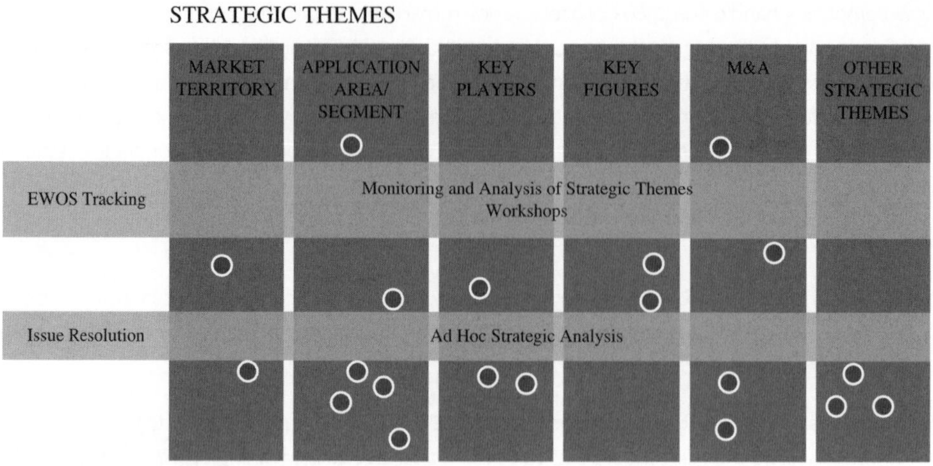

STRATEGIC THEMES

	MARKET TERRITORY	APPLICATION AREA/ SEGMENT	KEY PLAYERS	KEY FIGURES	M&A	OTHER STRATEGIC THEMES

EWOS Tracking — Monitoring and Analysis of Strategic Themes Workshops

Issue Resolution — Ad Hoc Strategic Analysis

Figure 11.7   MI Products to support the EWOS

Issue Resolution: Ad Hoc Analyses to Address Emerging Strategic Issues

Whereas the EWOS process is an on-going process with pre-established focus areas, the issue resolution process is an ad hoc approach to handling rapidly emerging, unforeseen topics.

While the issue resolution capability is an important element of a full-blown intelligence program, relying on this capability only will easily have the organization falling into the "ad hoc trap" with the associated reactive mode. Ideally, the intelligence team has already spotted the potentially emerging issue through the research in conjunction with the Future Watch, Planning, and EWOS processes, and the ad hoc analysis will swiftly complement the strategic planning process. In a high quality intelligence program, the intelligence team has bandwidth to deal with both continuous, pre-planned intelligence deliverables, and emerging ad hoc requests.

SUMMARY

- Organizations should always back up important strategic decisions with properly researched and analyzed facts.

- Organizations have a number of decision points related to the strategy process that can be supported with targeted MI:

  o Future Watch: need to identify strategic themes in the business landscape and develop a shared understanding about their probability and impact on the company's business. Typical intelligence products: PESTEL analysis, forecasting, trend analysis, war gaming, scenario analysis.

○   Planning process: need to systematically analyze selected strategic themes in order to develop an actionable strategy. Typical intelligence products: market attractiveness analysis, market size and share analysis, industry analysis, key player profiles.

○   EWOS

   ◆   EWO tracking: need to systematically track the identified strategic themes with an eye on changes and signs of the realization of certain strategies. MI products: strategic theme alerts, strategic theme workshops.

   ◆   Issue resolution: need to have the ad hoc capability to address emerging, unforeseen strategic topics. Typical intelligence output: analytical deliverables, the format of which will be dictated by each topic at hand.

12 Market Intelligence for Marketing, Sales, and Account Management

UNDERSTANDING THE CUSTOMERS AND COMPETITION

Laura had a new job. She had just started as a senior consultant in a company specialized in the recruitment of executives and white-collar professionals, and, with her ambitious sales targets, she was eager to start contacting the prospective customers. She had a purchased list of prospects to work with, but she soon realized she would need more than that to be able to maximize her productivity.

- She would need more information about the companies she was trying to turn from prospects to customers: how were they doing financially, what were their future plans, and what were their drivers for recruiting new people?

- She would need competitive pricing information: now she felt like she was flying blind, trying to do guesswork around how her proposals were doing against the competition.

- She would also need better market insight to help gear her efforts at the most lucrative market segments.

In other words, Laura would need Market Intelligence (MI) to add insight – and improved results – to her sales efforts.

Laura is not an exception among many of today's sales professionals: she is capable and knowledgeable about sales work; however, she has already had several jobs at the age of 35, and to be able to quickly become productive in yet another company she needs MI support to make up for her lack of long experience with this particular company and industry.

Figure 12.1   The customer processes

MARKET INTELLIGENCE NEEDS IN THE CUSTOMER PROCESSES

Customers are the most important interest group for any organization. To add value for customers, the organization must understand their wants and needs, to the extent that sales consultants and account managers can sometimes advise the customers in situations where their wants may differ from what they eventually need.

Prior to even getting in contact with the eventual customers, i.e. in order to reach the customer's end of the sales funnel, an organization of course needs a great deal of information about its customers and the competing offerings: marketing communications and sales planning should be supported with accurate information about market size and segmentation, competitive strategies and offerings, and prevailing trends.

In this chapter, we will discuss MI related specifically to the customer processes. Under the umbrella term of "customer processes", we will present four different sub-processes that all need MI support: marketing and sales planning and management, the marketing process, the sales process, and the account management process (Figure 12.1).

There are many stakeholders involved in the customer processes whose focus and objectives differ depending on which part of the customer management process they are at. Accordingly, their MI needs range from highly strategic brand and media planning to supporting, on a very concrete level, sales productivity through targeted business information.

Typical Intelligence Needs of Marketing Directors and Marketing Managers

- Understanding the market segments and developing the marketing strategies accordingly

- Targeting marketing messages to different market segments

- Choosing the right marketing mix

- Timing marketing activities optimally

Typical Intelligence Needs of Sales Directors and Sales Managers

- Understanding customer needs and competitive offerings

- Being able to swiftly adjust product and service offerings

- Identifying opportunities to increase sales, margins, and market share

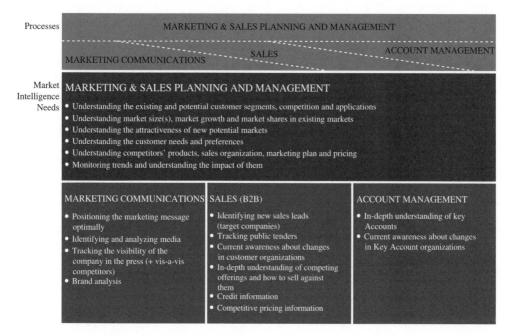

Figure 12.2   MI needs in the customer processes

Typical Intelligence Needs of Sales Representatives and Account Managers

- Understanding customer needs

- Having sales leads

- Understanding competitive offerings and pricing

In Figure 12.2, we are presenting a framework to highlight the MI needs of the above groups in their roles. The focus of the framework is mainly on business-to-business (B2B) markets; however, many aspects of it can also be applied in the business-to-consumers (B2C) context.

MI Needs in Marketing and Sales Planning and Management

In order to conduct effective marketing and sales planning that directs all activities at the customer front, companies need systematic MI support. Understanding the existing and potential customer segments, competition, and applications is vital for developing sustainable sales and marketing strategies, as is building a solid view over how the market dynamics in the competitive environment will affect the company.

Researching previously unknown market territories is one of the most obvious MI needs in organizations today, given the accelerating globalization. Generating insights into the customer needs in different cultural environments is a natural prerequisite for entering new markets, and the competitive environment will also need to be analyzed in a structured manner.

MI Needs in the Marketing Process

Positioning the marketing message optimally requires MI support in order for the organization to make sure the right message will reach the target groups in the marketplace. Analyzing the available media options will also be necessary, and systematically tracking the company's own media visibility along with that of the competition will aid the company in gearing the marketing message at the right target groups.

Analyzing the company's brand value and perceptions in different market areas is becoming increasingly important as the marketplace evolves into the direction of virtual value creation. While the MI needs under the marketing process are relatively continuous in nature, analyzing the company's brand is more tightly linked with strategic marketing planning, and the need for it therefore tends to emerge periodically in conjunction with the strategic planning process.

Related to brand perceptions, social media has emerged as another viable channel to reach the interest groups even for B2B companies that traditionally have been very far from the consumer. Hence it does matter how the general public perceives the company, and most companies nowadays need to cover social media sources in staying on top of marketing-related topics.

Market Intelligence Needs in Sales

Sales process is probably one of the most concrete areas where MI can directly support the generation of new business if the needs have been properly identified. Identifying target companies, tracking public tenders, or increasing current awareness about both the customers' decision-making processes and how to sell against competition are areas where effective MI can help win new business.

Throughout the sales process, MI should provide arguments to demonstrate the benefits of the company's own product or service compared to that of the competitors. Post-sale analysis will sometimes also be needed from MI: by learning from past sales successes and failures, sales tactics and the product can be improved in order for it to yield better future earnings.

Market Intelligence Needs in the Account Management Process

MI is also needed in the account management process in order for the company to enhance their understanding of the existing customers and develop and implement account plans. It is important to identify internal stakeholders such as units, projects, and persons in the customer organization that will likely have an influence on the future sales. Competitor products and solutions must also be monitored on a continuous basis.

Case: MI for Key Account Management at Rettig ICC

Interviewed for this case was Julian Stocks, at that time the key account manager for Europe at Rettig ICC. Rettig ICC manufactures and markets Europe's leading brands for radiators, underfloor heating, valves, and controls.

Key account managers analyze customer accounts that are of strategic importance, determine the needs and challenges of these particular customers, and implement procedures to ensure that they receive premium customer service and to increase customer satisfaction. Success is often measured by the ability to maintain existing and/or identify new sales opportunities. The ability to build long-term relations is key; even in the face of changes to customer personnel, market dynamics, or business cycles.

Over the course of the economic crisis of 2008/09, key account management at Rettig ICC has become even more crucial as customer markets underwent the drastic impact of the global economic crisis in 2009 and significant slowdown in construction and renovation activity. As the senior point of contact for Rettig's key accounts that are located in different parts of Europe, it was essential for Stocks to keep abreast of individual customer markets as well as the changes to the European business environment in general.

How is MI used in Account Management?

According to Stocks, MI can be very beneficial in managing key accounts when used to:

- Monitor developments in customer markets, particularly complex ones, e.g. different business cycles, many stakeholders, government involvement in legislation and subsidies.

- Provide a good overview of regional or country-based sales trends, particularly when customers are spread out geographically.

- Predict changes in the customer markets which will impact Rettig sales so they can be addressed in advance.

- Gather industry and raw material insights which will help in customer negotiations.

- Keep track of personnel movements across the industry.

- Fine tune the intelligence process with customer intelligence gathered.

A handful of Rettig's customers are publicly listed companies that release a lot of information. The benefit of using a market monitoring system is that information which is not readily available in the public domain, such as industry reports, can also be included so that more comprehensive views on customer markets can be formed.

At Rettig, information gathered is reviewed on a daily basis and is used in different formats across various presentations. It can be shared throughout the company and with customers, either electronically or by phone.

Some examples of how Rettig has been able to proactively respond to changes in its business environment with the market information gathered include:

- Being the first key supplier to request an update meeting with the CEO at a customer organization after one of their directors left.

(Continued)

- Recognized payment issues at customer subsidiaries beforehand and re-negotiated credit terms as a result.

- Compared information provided from the market versus information gathered independently to derive balanced and informed views. (Larger customers follow raw material price movements very closely, so it is important to be able to manage and drive the resultant negotiations for the benefit of both parties).

- Created "killer" arguments that produce win–win situations for both parties in the market.

- Won new contracts on the back of reported house-building schemes.

MARKET INTELLIGENCE DELIVERABLES TO SUPPORT THE CUSTOMER PROCESSES

Having set out the needs in the customer processes, we will now direct the intelligence program to systematically support marketing, sales, and account management. Figure 12.3 illustrates how

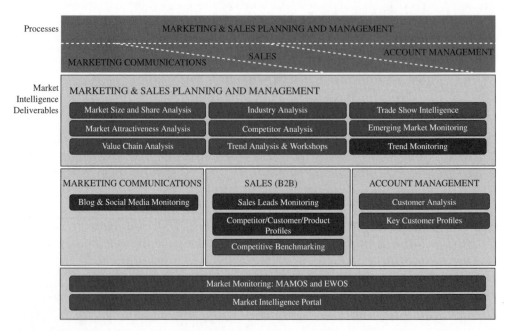

Figure 12.3 MI deliverables to support the customer processes. Recurring intelligence products have been differentiated from the analysis products of one time/ad hoc nature using color codes

organizations can leverage a variety of intelligence products to develop a solid understanding of the present and future needs of the customers.

Here, we are presenting a comprehensive approach to MI for customer processes that, if fully implemented, will require a relatively sizable investment of time and money. We are encouraging the readers to weigh the expected benefits of each intelligence product – that at the customer front may be more easily measured than in many other areas of the organization – against the investment and make decisions based on that as to what kind of customer intelligence the organization will need most. At the very least the company must stay tuned to their customers' evolving needs in the long run, hence both strategic and operative customer planning will need MI support. Whether additional sales could be generated through, for instance, targeted sales leads monitoring, should be considered based on the available resources and ambitions.

We will now discuss the MI deliverables in more detail that will support the customer processes.

MARKET INTELLIGENCE SUPPORT FOR THE MARKETING AND SALES PLANNING AND MANAGEMENT

The first steps of the marketing and sales process involve planning, customer identification, and segmentation. At this stage, the opportunities and risks related to customers and customer segments should be analyzed from a broad perspective, and typical intelligence products responding to the need include analyses about industries, value chains, competitors, customer markets, and geographical regions. We will provide a few examples, including a description of the work process related to producing the intelligence output.

Market Size and Share Analysis

Purpose   To analyze the market size and market shares for various market segments. The analysis often also includes future growth opportunities.

Understanding market sizes and shares is important for companies not only in formulating strategy, but for them to be able to provide relevant information for their investors and other stakeholders. Market share and the related sales targets are also something that can be used in measuring the performance of both sales people and the executive team.

Work process   Start with analyzing the earlier market size and market share figures. Estimate future market size growth based on supply and demand-related scenarios, trends, and forecasts. Estimate the future market shares based on competitors' objectives, strategies, strengths, and weaknesses. Rely on both secondary sources and expert insights gathered through interviews.

Case: Definition of Optimal Market Segmentation for a Medical Equipment Company

A manufacturer of medical equipment wanted to size the demand for testing products in Greater China. Multiple-level demand sizing and segmentation approach was taken, including validation of overall market size, segmentation of customer types, and definition of channel shares for each customer type. Both secondary and primary research methods were used in order to collect the information that was subsequently analyzed. As a result, it was confirmed that the demand opportunity for testing products was promising. Channels and customer groups were identified that would drive the greatest sales volumes within the shortest timeframe. The size of greatest opportunity customer and channel segments was quantified, thus supporting the efforts to increase market share.

Industry Analysis

Purpose To provide a high-level overview of the industry landscape. Normally covers the value chain, industry dynamics, competitive developments, and demand and supply trends.

Work process Define the appropriate scope of analysis (e.g. whether to focus primarily on the competitor landscape, or to include the entire value chain or value net in the analysis) and select applicable analysis frameworks to use. Collect information and conduct the analyses. Pay special attention to concise reporting of findings while including all supporting data in the materials clearly documented as well.

Case: Mobile Gaming Industry Analysis

In preparing a go-to-market strategy for a new concept, a mobile phone manufacturer wanted to understand the global mobile gaming industry dynamics, competitive situation, and opportunities and threats for their planned offering. To address the need, several methods were combined: secondary research using various databases was supplemented with primary research and scenario workshops. As a result, a comprehensive analysis of the industry was produced, with recommendations for go-to-market strategy. The company gained improved insights on mobile gaming industry and the possible competitive scenarios in the marketplace.

All of the above described analysis reports can be leveraged for productive strategic workshops that involve some of the key decision-makers in the customer front. Even the customers themselves could be involved in parts of the workshop, that way bringing in hands on views about their demands and priorities.

Market Intelligence Support for Marketing, Sales, and Account Management (B2B)

Having analyzed the customer segments from a broad perspective, we now need to ensure that the MI is detailed enough in order to win new business on an operational level. The individual customers and competitors will need to be understood in order for the organization to stay competitive in its chosen market segments. MI will need to cover angles such as:

- Customer demands and the customer industry's trends and developments.

- Customer's financial development.

- Competitive offerings.

- Competitive positioning.

Again, we will provide a few examples of intelligence products supporting the daily hands-on work at the customer front.

Customer Profiles

Purpose   To provide structured information about a customer. Profiles may be used as standalone intelligence products, or they may also be needed as input to a benchmarking process.

Work process   Profiles follow a uniform structure that will be determined in the needs analysis: what will be the relevant aspects to cover in a strategically meaningful profile snapshot? The collected information is typically something that can be obtained from secondary sources, and the added value really comes from the structure that also allows benchmarking the market player to others in the market. The profiles may be produced in Word or PowerPoint format, or they may also make up a database.

Case: Comprehensive SWOT and Competitor Analysis in a Retailer Company

As part of its strategic planning process, a large Southern hemisphere retailer wanted a SWOT and a competitor analysis conducted on its key competitors in its core business categories, namely home, beauty, clothing, and food. Suppliers and industry analysts were interviewed, and insight from over 1,600 consumers was gathered in order to gain a sharper image of the market and key competitors. Competitor profiling and benchmarking techniques were used to convert this insight into intelligence identifying competitor core strengths and weaknesses and possible strategies. Eventually, a comprehensive SWOT and

(Continued)

competitor analysis model was delivered to management and presented to the Board. The MI was subsequently used across the retailer's operating countries. As a result, the company understood its competitors' key strengths and weaknesses, as well as their opportunities and threats in the market, and was able to utilize this insight in strategic planning, with a strong focus on company competitive advantage.

Benchmarking

Purpose   To understand similarities and differences between different organizations and competing products, and so on.

Work process   At the customer front, targets for benchmarking may include, for instance, competitors' sales process, products, or services. Based on criteria that are defined by the purpose of the benchmarking exercise, the company's own approaches can be compared with competing offerings.

Case: Benchmarking Flu Vaccine Manufacturers in China and Korea

A pharmaceutical company wanted to benchmark its flu vaccine product and sales and marketing strategy with the market leaders in the Chinese and Korean market areas. The MI team conducted interviews with vaccine sales executives, clinical physicians, hospital pharmacists, and hospital administrators, along with reviewing competitor product brochures. As a result, the fastest growing segments and distribution channels were identified and competitors' offerings were benchmarked against the company's own. The company gained a better understanding of competitors' flu vaccine products and sales and marketing strategies in China and Korea.

Sales Leads Monitoring (B2B Industries)

Purpose   To identify potential customers that meet the requirements identified in the planning and market segmentation phases.

Work process   Lists of prospective companies will be produced based on market presence, market size, product needs, previous purchase patterns, or other suitable criteria. Research will be conducted as the first step through global or country-specific company databases. The short-listed companies may then be targeted in different forms of marketing and sales campaigns.

Case: New Ship Building Projects Monitoring for Ship Engine Manufacturer

A ship engine company wanted to continuously monitor new ship-building projects globally in order to cross-check whether its sales staff is aware of all available opportunities and to know of such opportunities early enough to enable participating in bidding contests. They had the MI analysts collect information on new ship-building projects on a weekly basis from a number of secondary sources, such as tender databases. The findings were collected into a weekly Excel report that contained key information per each new ship-building project, such as country, parties involved, bidding deadlines, and so on. As a result, the company's sales organization had an up-to-date list of all ship projects available, which enabled participating in bidding contests and keeping the sales force's activity level high.

Case: Identifying Potential Customers and Collecting Contact Information to Support Marketing and Sales

A supplier of magnet generator and converter packages for new energy applications was planning a marketing campaign that was targeted to wind turbine manufacturers. The sales and marketing management had realized the company did not have enough contact details in-house for the campaign and needed to gather more contacts globally. The task for MI was to generate a list of all wind turbine manufacturers globally, with relevant contact details. In addition to the marketing campaign, the idea was to also utilize the contact database in their direct sales efforts by sales personnel contacting the most promising prospects directly.

Existing secondary information was first utilized in order to identify wind turbine manufacturers globally, with their sales figures and company contact details. In order to gather contact information for purchasing and technical directors in each identified company, primary research was used. Overall, 30% of the work ended up being secondary research and 70% of the information was obtained through primary research. In total 269 companies were contacted. As a result, a list of identified wind turbine manufacturers with their sales figures (total corporate sales) and company contact details was produced. In addition, contact information was delivered for purchasing and technical directors in each identified company. Marketing and sales was hence well equipped to run the planned marketing campaign and also contact potential customers directly.

SUPPORT TOOLS FOR THE CUSTOMER PROCESSES: INTELLIGENCE PORTAL AND MARKET MONITORING

We have summarized and showcased a number of analysis deliverables that can be utilized in providing MI for the customer processes. Since many of these studies need to be repeated over time, and significant volumes of market information data needs to be analyzed, continuous market monitoring and IT tools are required to support the process as follows:

1. **Continuous monitoring of market signals ("push" type of intelligence deliverables).** The two current awareness systems, i.e. the market monitoring system that supports the implementation of strategy and the EWOS that supports the formulation of strategy were introduced in Chapter 10. Without repeating the details already discussed, we emphasize that the market monitoring systems should be built up so that they readily support customer processes as one of the most important user groups of MI in the organization.

    People working at the customer front should be continuously supported with relevant information about key customers, competitors, and market trends.

2. **IT tools to help manage the intelligence content related to customer processes ("pull" type of intelligence deliverables):**

    a. A dedicated MI portal typically contains lots of qualitative information about customers and customer industries.

    b. Building technical bridges between the company's CRM system and the intelligence portal is often considered, as both contain information that is relevant for people working at the customer front. Whether a connection is technically feasible needs to be considered case by case, and it may also be easiest to continue running separate systems, avoiding overlaps in the content. The main thing is to make the relevant customer information easily accessible to the users.

SUMMARY

- The customer processes: sales and marketing planning and management, marketing communications, sales, and account management are a distinct internal user group to the deliverables that the MI program produces.

- While measuring the impact of MI in concrete financial terms is generally challenging, supporting marketing and especially sales through MI is one of the areas where new business generation may be directly attributable to the MI efforts.

- In modern organizations, the productivity of employees working at the customer front is much more dependent on support functions such as MI than it has been traditionally, and they should therefore be supplied with high quality market insights by the MI team. At the same time, people at the customer front are also the first ones to hear weak signals about emerging opportunities and threats, and they should in turn be engaged in producing some of the critical insights.

- The customer processes can be supported through a wide range of analysis output, examples of which have been provided in this chapter. In addition to the analytical reports, it is important to also keep track of the customer-related themes and trends on a continuous basis so as to support the organizations capability of swiftly spotting new business opportunities and utilizing them.

13 Market Intelligence for Innovation and Product Life Cycle Management

Case: Competitive Technical Intelligence (CTI) for a Car Tire Manufacturer

The car tire company had decided to invest in setting up a competitive technical intelligence (CTI) capability that was determined to monitor changes and spot potentially interesting technological advances that could critically influence the company's competitive position. At the same time, the CTI initiative was to facilitate sharing of internal knowledge about technical topics that were of competitive value to the company.

At first, the CTI function was established "as an experiment" under the company's R&D unit, but it soon evolved into a program of its own, having proved its worth as part of the company's innovation management activity. The primary focus of the CTI activities was patent monitoring, since it was the main source of detailed technical information about the innovation activity of the company's competitors. Later on, the objectives of the CTI activities supporting innovation and product development were broadened to include:

- Keeping an eye on competitors' activities

- Monitoring the tire technology domain and the related technologies

- Monitoring the macroeconomic trends and constructing regulatory scenarios

INNOVATION AND PRODUCT LIFE CYCLE MANAGEMENT

Similarly to other business processes, R&D and the related innovation and product life cycle management need solid support from timely and relevant Market Intelligence (MI). Turning ideas into marketable products involves multiple decision points, and decision-making will need to be backed up by accurate information. The potential benefits and costs related to making right versus wrong decisions in innovation and product management are so substantial that investing in accurate MI during the process is not only justified but often mandatory.

A number of MI products will be introduced in this chapter that will help support and further improve corporate innovation processes by means of MI.

There are numerous benefits in using MI to support innovation and the product life cycle process, as has been illustrated in Table 13.1. The benefits differ depending on the person or group that requires MI, and the users have been divided into two groups accordingly:

- The innovation management team including innovation directors, R&D directors, and technology directors

- The product management team including product directors, product portfolio directors, product managers, marketing managers, and project managers

Table 13.2 introduces the concepts and terms that will be used in this chapter.

Inventions, the output of inventive activity, are relatively hard to define and measure. The output of innovative work might be an invention – an addition to the set of blueprints – or more generally it may be advancement in knowledge creation or the acquisition of further information. Novelty is essential; an invention must include something new that adds to the current knowledge about the topic.

To become an innovation, an invention or idea must be commercialized. The innovation can therefore be defined as a successfully commercialized invention. As such, an innovation is a commercially successful improvement to a system, process, method, product, or service, which has been widely accepted.

Table 13.1   Benefits of MI in the innovation and product management process

Innovation Management – Technology and R&D Directors	Product Management – Offering and Product Directors and Product Managers
• Improved understanding about trends in the market	• Improved understanding of customer needs and their likely development in the future
• Early alerts about disruptive technologies/ innovations within or outside own industry	• Improved understanding of competitive offerings and related future developments
• Identification of partner networks in the operating environment	• Higher quality product portfolio planning and strategic development
• Unbiased information about the viability of short-listed innovations and existing technologies and products	• Enhanced positioning, specifications, and pricing of the products at the time of product launch and afterwards
Summary: more efficient allocation of R&D and innovation management resources and improved marketability of the company's innovations	Summary: more efficient allocation of product management resources and improved marketability of the company's products

Table 13.2 Explanation of concepts and terminology in innovation and product life cycle management

Concept	Description
Invention	An invention is an object, process, or technique that contains an element of novelty
Innovation	Commercialization of a new object, product, or process or technique, e.g. an invention
	Types of innovation: product, business, process, service, marketing, supply chain, or financial
Innovation Management	Management of the innovation process in order to ensure that a strategy and business culture exists that promotes innovation
Product Life Cycle	Product life cycle is the chronological path that a product's development, sales, and profits will follow over time. The stages of a product life cycle are conception, product development, market launch, growth, maturity, and decline
Product Management	Product management handles the product strategy and planning and/or marketing the product at all stages of its life cycle

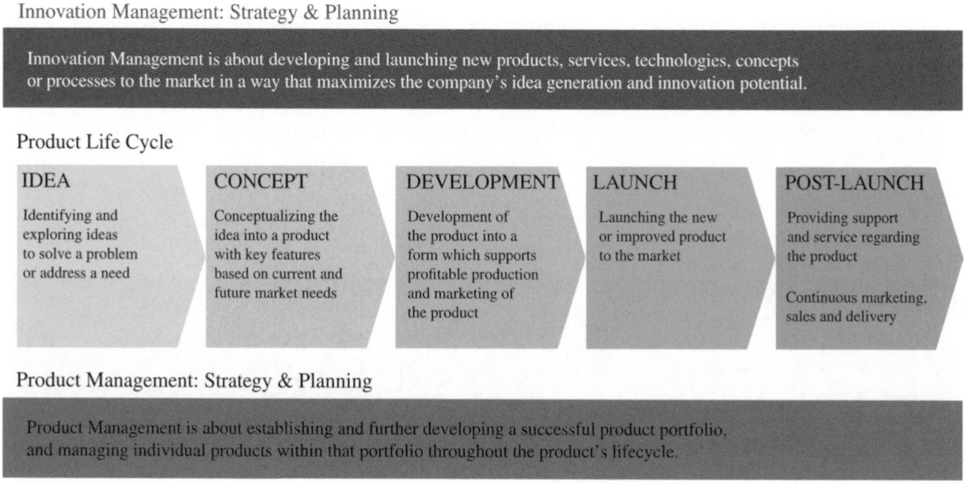

Innovation Management: Strategy & Planning

Innovation Management is about developing and launching new products, services, technologies, concepts or processes to the market in a way that maximizes the company's idea generation and innovation potential.

Product Life Cycle

IDEA	CONCEPT	DEVELOPMENT	LAUNCH	POST-LAUNCH
Identifying and exploring ideas to solve a problem or address a need	Conceptualizing the idea into a product with key features based on current and future market needs	Development of the product into a form which supports profitable production and marketing of the product	Launching the new or improved product to the market	Providing support and service regarding the product

Continuous marketing, sales and delivery |

Product Management: Strategy & Planning

Product Management is about establishing and further developing a successful product portfolio, and managing individual products within that portfolio throughout the product's lifecycle.

Figure 13.1 Concept overview: innovation and product life cycle management

Innovations can be either incremental or radical. Incremental innovations involve the adaptation, refinement, or enhancement of existing systems, processes, and methods. Radical innovations generate new knowledge that is not necessarily related to existing solutions.

In this chapter, the product life cycle process will be used as the core framework within which the utilization of MI for innovation and product development will be explored. There are several phases and decision points in the process, and various types of MI output will therefore be needed to serve the specific decision support needs. In the framework illustrated in Figure 13.1 that will be used throughout this chapter, innovation management is presented as the strategic "umbrella view", whereas product management will focus on more tactical and operative issues related to the existing and future product portfolios.

MARKET INTELLIGENCE NEEDS IN INNOVATION AND PRODUCT LIFE CYCLE MANAGEMENT

Intelligence professionals need to understand the innovation and product life cycle process in order to be able to serve it with appropriate MI deliverables. People in the innovation and product management roles in turn need to understand how MI can help improve this process and make the organization more innovative. To explore MI needs in innovation and product life cycle management (Figure 13.2), we are using a structured stop/go decision approach in which a number of decision points are defined as tollgates: at the end of each phase, a decision must be taken as to whether to move on to the next phase. Figure 13.3 presents a relatively generic view of the typical decision points within the product life cycle management process.

IDEA PHASE

Idea generation and idea screening is the first step in the innovation and product life cycle process. Ideas can come from customers (user innovations), focus groups, employees, salespeople, trade shows, or through innovation discovery methods and tools such as research for user habits and patterns, patent databases and trend research, and so forth. Formal idea generation methods can also be used such as brainstorming, problem-based analysis, and scenario analysis.

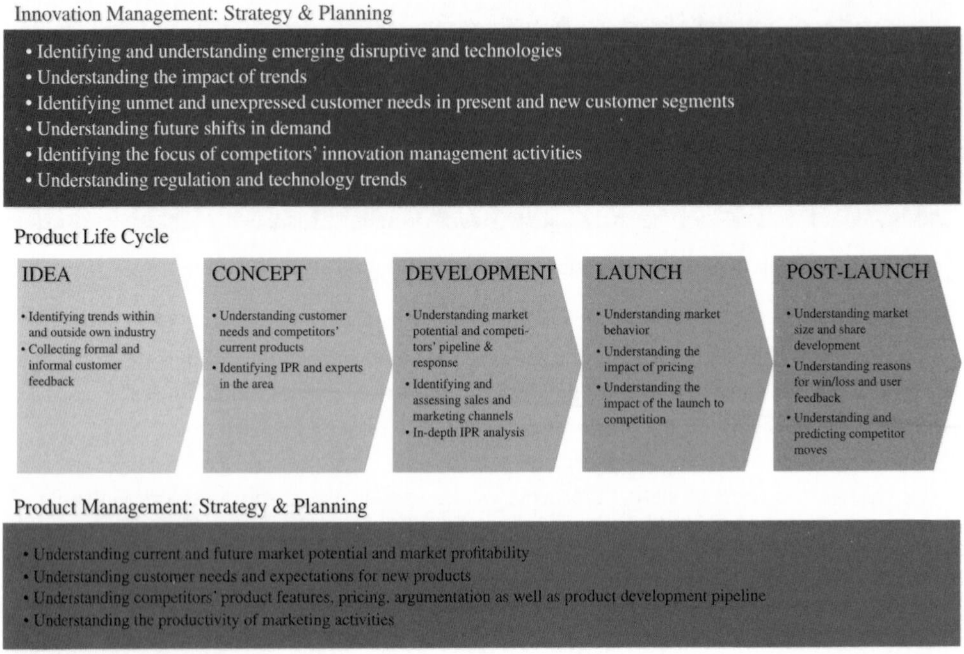

Innovation Management: Strategy & Planning

- Identifying and understanding emerging disruptive and technologies
- Understanding the impact of trends
- Identifying unmet and unexpressed customer needs in present and new customer segments
- Understanding future shifts in demand
- Identifying the focus of competitors' innovation management activities
- Understanding regulation and technology trends

Product Life Cycle

IDEA	CONCEPT	DEVELOPMENT	LAUNCH	POST-LAUNCH
• Identifying trends within and outside own industry • Collecting formal and informal customer feedback	• Understanding customer needs and competitors' current products • Identifying IPR and experts in the area	• Understanding market potential and competitors' pipeline & response • Identifying and assessing sales and marketing channels • In-depth IPR analysis	• Understanding market behavior • Understanding the impact of pricing • Understanding the impact of the launch to competition	• Understanding market size and share development • Understanding reasons for win/loss and user feedback • Understanding and predicting competitor moves

Product Management: Strategy & Planning

- Understanding current and future market potential and market profitability
- Understanding customer needs and expectations for new products
- Understanding competitors' product features, pricing, argumentation as well as product development pipeline
- Understanding the productivity of marketing activities

Figure 13.2   MI needs in the different phases of the innovation and product life cycle management process

Product Life Cycle

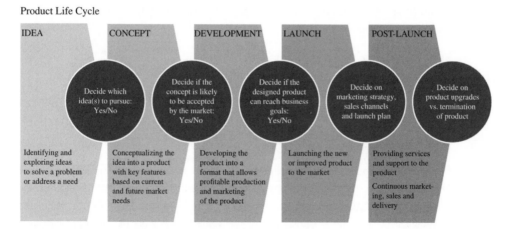

Figure 13.3   Decision points in product life cycle management

The development of ideas is a creative process where people should be exposed to a variety of different information from different sources. Information must flow freely so that the exchange of ideas and experiences is efficient. An organization can thus promote internal innovation by enhancing the transfer of ideas, knowledge, and thoughts both within and outside the organization.

The resulting inventions must be carefully selected for commercialization given that resources are usually limited and not all inventions can be commercialized. Throughout the phases of the innovation management process, selection takes place: not all ideas will be turned into inventions, and only selected inventions will be commercialized. Despite the scarcity of resources, however, consideration must be given to how rigorous the selection process for ideas will be in the early stages. The company's strategy and goals should be reflected on, and space should be given to ideas that could potentially radically improve the chances of achieving those goals.

Examples of intelligence needs in the idea phase:

- Understanding trends within the industry
  - Competitors' product portfolio and product development activities
  - Technological developments
- Understanding trends outside the industry
  - Emerging technologies that might have an impact in the future
  - Macro-level trends related to political, environmental, or legal environment
- Understanding the customers
  - Usage of existing products
  - Unmet market needs

Decision point: decide if the idea has commercial potential. Ideas that meet this requirement are allowed to enter the concept phase.

CONCEPT PHASE

The goal of the concept phase is to develop the idea into a product, service, or solution with key features that will meet an assumed present or future market need.

An idea that has been selected in the concept phase will be conceptualized further, i.e. a more detailed description of the eventual product will be developed that will highlight its features and demonstrate how it will successfully meet the demand in the marketplace. The product should also have an advantage over competing solutions. An initial understanding about the entire competitive environment for the product should therefore be developed at this stage. Also, a market size analysis should be carried out to estimate whether the eventual market will be large enough to justify the investment in product development, commercialization, and marketing.

Patents and other intellectual property rights will need to be analyzed at this stage to ensure that no rights will be infringed. Potential partners for developing and/or distributing the solution also need to be identified during this phase since the involvement of the partners will have a significant bearing on the development and sales costs.

Examples of intelligence needs in the concept phase:

- Understanding customer needs
- Understanding current competition
- Understanding intellectual property rights related to the innovation
- Understanding who the experts are within this specific area

Decision point: decide if the concept is likely to be accepted in the marketplace. The concepts that meet this requirement are allowed to enter the development phase.

DEVELOPMENT PHASE

In the development phase, a concrete appearance for the product will be developed which is in line with what is required from profitable production and marketing of the eventual product. Key aspects to address include:

- Production costs
- Features the product must incorporate

- Developing and testing the product beta version

- Understanding how the product will be received in the marketplace

- Securing partnerships with the product suppliers, producers, and distributors

Examples of intelligence needs in the development phase:

- In-depth understanding of the market potential

- Awareness of the competitors' product pipeline

- Detailed knowledge about all intellectual property rights (IPR)-related issues

- Anticipating competitors' responses to the new product in the marketplace

- Identifying and assessing sales channels

Decision point: decide whether or not the concept can achieve the business goals that will be set to it. The products that meet this requirement are allowed to enter the launch phase.

LAUNCH PHASE

During the launch phase, preparations will be made for the launch, and the innovation will subsequently be launched to the market. Prior to the actual launch, a detailed marketing plan will be made including the traditional marketing mix (pricing, promotion, product, and place).

Examples of intelligence needs in the launch phase:

- Understanding the impact of different pricing options

- Anticipating the competitive response to the final launch plan

- Anticipating the market response to the final launch plan

Decision point: decide on the sales and marketing strategy. After the product or service has been launched, the post-launch phase begins.

POST-LAUNCH PHASE

The post-launch phase covers all the remaining phases in the life cycle of a product after it has been developed into a product and brought to the market: growth, maturity, and decline. For each phase, product managers need to decide on potential changes in the marketing and sales strategy for the product. Market size and market share analysis should determine when and how these changes will be made.

Incremental product innovation may also be considered along the way to make the product more attractive to the customers.

Examples of intelligence needs in the post-launch phase:

- Understanding market size and market share developments

- Understanding why the company is winning/losing sales bids

- Anticipating competitor moves based on the competitors' product portfolios

- IPR analysis in order to protect the organization's own products

Decision point: decide on product upgrades and changes in product strategy.

Overall, it is important to acknowledge that not all ideas, concepts, or readily developed products will be launched, let alone become commercially successful. However, by using the tollgate approach with the related decision points, going through the development process should be safer.

MARKET INTELLIGENCE DELIVERABLES TO SUPPORT INNOVATION AND PRODUCT LIFE CYCLE MANAGEMENT

Having described what kinds of MI requirements innovation and product life cycle management processes typically have, we can now design a comprehensive intelligence product portfolio to support the activity. Figure 13.4 illustrates how companies can use concrete, targeted MI products to cater to the information needs in the product life cycle management process. Some of the individual products will be briefly introduced and showcased in the following.

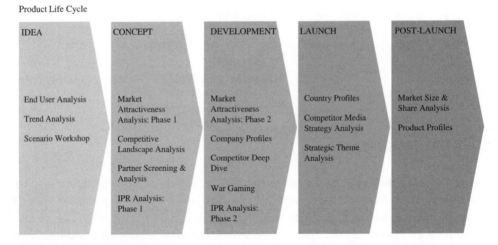

Figure 13.4   MI products for decision support in innovation and product life cycle management

ANALYTICAL SUPPORT FOR THE STAGES OF THE PRODUCT LIFE CYCLE

Trend Analysis

Purpose   To identify present and future trends and their impact on the company's business. Macro trends might be as important as micro trends. Trend analysis can be either focused (conducted on a specific topic) or generic, where the purpose is to look into what trends there are that have an impact on the company's business environment. Conducting trend analysis regularly is a useful way of avoiding the formation of business blindspots.

Work process   The subject of the analysis (general, company level, product level, BU level, and so on) will be defined. Trends will be identified that will likely affect the subject in a positive way along with ones that will likely have a negative impact. The strengths and likelihood of these trends will be assessed. Analytical conclusions will be formed based on the assessment above, and the results should be used as input for evaluating which ideas to pursue and which ones to drop or put on hold.

Case: Trend Monitoring at Rettig ICC

Rettig ICC, a Nordic producer of radiator and heating equipment, wanted to have a systematic analysis of raw material pricing fluctuations coupled with general economic outlook indicators to produce a meaningful trend analysis allowing their sales and marketing operations to quickly react to changing market conditions. The existing secondary information and price indices were utilized to create various timelines for raw material price variations. The research was done using secondary sources only, and it was repeated on a monthly basis. A monthly update was then provided for the company's management of all relevant raw material price variations (globally) and targeted monitoring of demand indicators as well as the monitoring of various commodity prices, OECD Economic Outlook reviews and competitor and supplier stock prices.

Partner Screening and Analysis

Purpose   Partner analysis identifies potential business partners with specific technologies, resources, skills, or capabilities that would enable the successful development and launch of the innovation.

Work process   Information is collected from secondary sources such as databases, industry associations, newspapers, and so on. The prospective partner companies will be screened based on aspects such as technology, resources, methodologies, and finances. The analysis results in a short list of companies or profiles of companies that might be suitable partners.

> **Case: Partner Screening for a Manufacturing Company**
>
> A building and emergency lighting manufacturer needed to identify potential reseller partners in the German language market area. Secondary research was used in compiling a long list of potential partners based on predefined criteria. More detailed information was collected through secondary sources on the most interesting partner prospects. Both the long list of companies and the shortlisted ones, with additional analysis included, were delivered in Excel files.

IPR Analysis

Purpose   To analyze the IPR related activities and strategies of competitors or other relevant interest groups.

Work process   Information sources like patent databases and industry reports are utilized to provide input to the analysis. The analysis uses quantitative methods to study levels and focus areas regarding the innovation area. Patent analysis and patent citation analysis are examples of methods used.

An IPR analysis should make it clear as to whether there are any intellectual property rights which might block or hinder the innovation when it is launched. The analysis may also establish whether the proper IPR protection can be obtained for the innovation in the form of patents and trademarks, and so on.

Competitor Analysis

Purpose   To provide insight into specific aspects of a competitor's strategy, operations, products, or similar. Potential topics could be, for example, understanding a specific competing technology or product strategy.

Work process   Information will be collected from both secondary sources and through interviews with experts about the specific topics of interest. Various analytical approaches may be used in processing the information depending entirely on the nature of the assignment. The scope normally covers historical, current, and potential future moves of the competitor.

MARKET MONITORING SUPPORT FOR INNOVATION AND PRODUCT LIFE CYCLE MANAGEMENT

MI support to the innovation and product life cycle management process cannot be built around predetermined decision points only. To properly facilitate innovation activity in the company, a process needs to exist for continuously identifying signals in the external business environment that may trigger ideas and thus bring new material to work on in the early stages of the product life cycle process.

Continuous market monitoring, i.e. the earlier introduced MAMOS and EWOS systems, can be leveraged to benefit innovation and product management processes as well. The key is to go through the specific intelligence needs of the R&D and product management in order to gear the monitoring activity towards supporting these activities. The set up may also require adding new information sources to the market monitoring: patent databases and scientific papers may be the best sources for gaining an understanding about what the competition is doing on this front, and, overall, what kinds of innovative solutions are being pursued that may challenge the currently offered products and services in the marketplace.

Case: Intelligence Driving the Open Innovation Process at DSM

DSM is a life sciences and performance materials company employing 23,000 people in total. The company's net sales in 2007 amounted to EUR 8,757 billion.

Interviewed for this case article was Mr. Ubald Kragten, manager, business and MI in the DSM Innovation Center. Ubald Kragten held a number of different positions at DSM, such as technology manager and technology portfolio manager before taking responsibility of the company's intelligence operations. Kragten's educational background is in chemistry.

Innovation Intelligence Needed for Reaching the Company Vision

At DSM, it has been explicitly stated that "innovation is key for reaching DSM's Vision 2010". Market driven growth and innovation along with increased presence in emerging economies have further been listed as the company's strategic objectives. By 2010, DSM should have generated EUR 1 billion in additional revenues through active innovation efforts. With a vision and objectives like this, it is hardly surprising that intelligence activities play a vital role in facilitating innovation and product development at DSM.

Intelligence Organization at DSM

At DSM, intelligence has been organized in different units as a staff function, i.e. several people are involved in the process on a full- or part-time basis. Corporate marketing is targeted to own DSM's intelligence process.

Intelligence for the Innovation and Product Life Cycle Process

Intelligence activities specifically related to innovation have been organized under the DSM Innovation Center that consists of three units:

1. Innovation services: working on issues related to patents, trademarks, and other intellectual property issues

(Continued)

2.   Emerging business areas: setting up and managing projects and companies within DSM's "innovation funnel"; includes a business incubator

3.   Intelligence services: focused on the emerging business areas

Intelligence output at DSM has been divided into three categories based on the level of analysis that different organizational activities require:

1.   Strategic – business strategic dialogue: the intelligence team at DSM is responsible for developing and updating a strategic data set for top management with which management can discuss and make decisions based on intelligence from the external business environment.

2.   Tactical – project/business plans: the intelligence team is heavily involved in helping business managers develop business plans throughout the innovation and product launch process.

3.   Operational: DSM have identified four key innovation pockets which form the foundation for innovation towards the vision:

    o   Biotechnology

    o   Process technology

    o   Nanotechnology

    o   Information technology

These technology areas and trends relate to trends in the society such as aging and the growth of the world's population, environmental, health and safety awareness, individualization of the society, and global networking. The present intelligence activities aim at developing a better understanding of these trends and topics in order to identify new business opportunities.

Examples of opportunities that have developed into emerging business areas are biomedical materials, specialty packaging, personalized nutrition, and white biotechnology. It is important that the intelligence process focuses both on the initial idea development, patenting, and market launch and on the full commercialization process. Intelligence therefore plays a vital role in both the value creation process and the value capturing process.

Feedback on a Job Well Done

At DSM, there is an annual evaluation process in place to measure the success of the intelligence efforts. Each individual within the intelligence function as well as the operation as a whole are evaluated for timeliness, thoroughness, sufficient levels of analysis, and efficiency of communication. "This is a very important process for us", Kragten says, "it helps us understand where we need to improve our intelligence work."

Kragten lists out critical success factors that are being used at DSM to measure the value of intelligence in and around the innovation and product management processes:

1.   Customer orientation

It is vital to have an in-depth understanding of the needs of the decision-makers that should be supported through intelligence work.

2.   Outside-in thinking

The intelligence team needs to bring in external perspectives to the company.

3.   Being independent

By remaining an independent staff function, the intelligence team at DSM is able to stay clear of any intra-political issues that might cloud their judgment. The analysts must be able to stand up for their analysis without fear of risking their own position.

4.   MI + technology intelligence = justified decisions

It is vital not to be driven by the technology perspective alone, but to add the market perspective in order to properly estimate the business potential of each initiative.

5.   Managing external partners

The reporting of consultants and other information providers should be made to follow the same format and structures as DSM's intelligence team in order to facilitate seamless integration of both internal and external input in the intelligence process.

SUMMARY

- The financial worth of decisions related to innovation and product life cycle management is typically huge: consistently succeeding or failing in bringing marketable products to customers has determined the fate of countless companies, and even single go/no go decisions in product development have dictated the success of many companies for years to come. To base the critical decisions on a solid understanding about the factors determining the success of new innovations and products, companies should invest in high quality MI.

- We have presented and discussed an innovation and product management process where distinct decision points will determine whether an idea will be taken to the next stage of development. MI deliverables can support the decisions at each stage.

  - Idea phase: conducting trend and scenario analyses

  - Concept phase: analyzing market attractiveness, competitive landscape, potential partners, and IPR topics

○   Development phase: analyzing competition and IPR topics, conducting war games

○   Launch phase: country profiles, analyzing media strategies

○   Post-launch phase: assessing market size and share, benchmarking products

- Continuous market monitoring (the MAMOS and EWOS systems) will also support innovation and product life cycle processes, but a separate needs analysis will have to be conducted for that purpose, and additional data sources will likely need to be included in the source portfolio, most notably patent databases and scientific papers.

14 Market Intelligence for Supply Chain Management

INTRODUCTION

Case: Purchasing Dry Ice in Pharma Services

A buyer working for a pharmaceutical company was asked to issue an RFP (request for proposal) for dry ice – which is used in shipping bio-samples to labs to keep the shipments cold.

The buyer then attempted to determine who to invite to bid in the RFP:

- Google searches came up with companies that supply dry ice machines for making cloud effects at high school dances and Halloween parties.

- After asking the incumbent supplier who its competitors are, the buyer had three suppliers to issue the RFP to.

- In the end, the buyer discovered that there were numerous companies offering this service on the international scale, but this information arrived too late.

What the buyer would have needed in the first place was targeted Market Intelligence (MI) about the dry ice sector's competitive landscape and the names of players. As a lesson learned, the company decided that, going forward, an extra amount of time and money would be set aside for comprehensive industry research in all sourcing projects where the spend would be more than $100,000 per year.

Supply chain management (SCM) experts claim that properly focused efforts to manage a firm's supply chain create cost savings, which are better than any money spent on creating profits – think of this as 100% ROI (return on investment). It is thus in every firm's interest to constantly keep costs in check.

Firms need to focus on relationships with suppliers and the movement and storage of goods to maximize profitable outcomes while minimizing risks and costs. Various areas of supply chain management rely on different types of information inputs. This chapter discusses the role of MI in SCM strategy. MI offers insights into what is happening, presently and in the future, in an industry, sector, market, niche, cluster, company, and so forth. Knowing what suppliers, competitors, and customers are expecting helps a firm plan its next strategic move.

The better information that is made available to SCM professionals, the more efficiently and effectively an SCM function can be accomplished. However, SCM professionals do not always receive the research and analysis training required to perform professional MI, making a cooperative model with MI specialists an optimal solution.

SUPPLY CHAIN MANAGEMENT FUNCTIONS

The multiple facets of SCM and the strategic focus of each function are not all commonly known or the same worldwide. Geographic distinctions vary the definition of SCM, and thus the strategic focus of firms in different parts of the world. For example, when one mentions SCM in North America, people usually think of purchasing, while Europeans usually assume one is talking about logistics management. The logistics focus in the Middle East is on infrastructure building, while the focus in Asia is on developing an infrastructure in a politicized geography. In fact, SCM is made up of purchasing, procurement, logistics (which is then broken down into deployment, inventory management, and operations management), and strategic sourcing. All of which are at different stages of evolution in different regions of the world, and all of which have different intelligence requirements.

The particular role of intelligence in each facet of SCM varies, but the underlying theme is that the better information there is available, the more efficiently the SCM function can be accomplished. MI deliverables enable strategic planning by combining on-going monitoring, research, and analysis with deep needs assessment, a future focus, and problem solving.

As has been illustrated in Figure 14.1, the main arenas of SCM are purchasing, procurement, logistics, and strategic sourcing. It should be noted that SCM has indirect functions within knowledge management, marketing, and finance as well.

Purchasing is the function of buying goods or services:

- The purchasing process in the large corporate environment with a centralized purchasing department will usually follow the process of identifying a need, creating a requisition which records the budget owner with the expenditure, followed by the buyer transforming the requisition into a purchase order (PO). The buyer will either have relied on an approved vendor listing (AVL) to know the appropriate vendor and price for the PO, or will have conducted a request for quotation (RFQ) from the most qualified suppliers in the buyer's network. The buyer may be responsible for

SUPPLY CHAIN MANAGEMENT FUNCTIONS

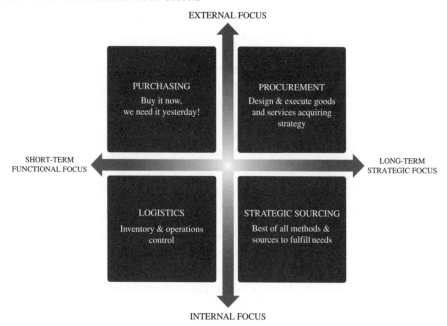

Figure 14.1   The SCM functions as on scales of functional versus strategic, short term versus long term, as well as internal versus external focuses

coordinating delivery and customs clearance. The buyer will usually also be responsible for ensuring the supplier's invoice matches the PO, and arranging with accounts payable for payment.

- AVL – approved vendor listing – is a company's internal database of suppliers that can be purchased from, including catalogue or negotiated pricing, lead times, volume discounts, delivery terms, and so on.

Procurement is the act of designing and executing the strategy for the on-going purchasing of goods and services:

- Procurement design process. A company pursuing procurement organization first maps its purchasing function and then looks for bottlenecks and unmet needs. Benchmarking exercises enable the firm to know best practices and alternatives. This is followed by reorganizing the purchasing function into either teams that service the company's lines of business, or centralized resources that cater to all internal customers' needs. Goals and metrics are organized around encouraging specific behaviors and outcomes. For example:

  o   Maximized savings targets

  o   Maximized percentage of spend using suppliers from approved vendor listings

- o   Maximized volume of requisition to PO transactions completed in less than one day

- o   Maximized volume of PO and invoice mismatches resolved in less than seven days

- Ongoing duties of the procurement department include creation and maintenance of the AVL, and maintaining the contract management process: negotiate contracts with suppliers for best pricing and other terms, every two to five years.

Logistics is the management of inventory after purchase, or after being considered part of the overall operation:

- The process for inventory management can be complicated and depends heavily on the industry and sector the company is involved in.

- Production processes which rely on the input of goods often count those goods as different kinds of inventory: purchased, needed but not yet fulfilled, created just in time, work in progress, and so on. Managing all of the inputs in order to optimize efficiency and production is called inbound logistics management.

- Outbound logistics management focuses on getting an operation's finished products to where they need to be: either as finished goods for end users, or as inputs to another operation's process. Logistics managers are often involved in strategic decision-making regarding the approach to inventory deployment, distribution center locations and operations, and other such tasks.

Strategic sourcing is problem solving and needs fulfillment using the best combination of methods and sources available:

- The strategic sourcing process involves internal needs assessment, evaluation of supply markets, management of the bid process (RFP, RFQ, RFI) with efforts to achieve best costs, quality, and schedule while minimizing risk.

- RFQ – request for quotation. Suppliers are asked to bid on a standard set of goods or services. The quote with the best price, amongst other characteristics, wins the business for a set period of time. The next best quote may win the position of being a secondary/backup source of the goods or services.

- RFP – request for proposal. Suppliers are asked to propose the best overall solution to a firm's problem or scenario. The firm describes its needs; however, specific schedules and quantities are not listed. Often the buying firm dictates the format of the suppliers' proposals. Suppliers propose solutions, sometimes turn-key solutions, to the buying firm. Proposals are compared and weighted based on combinations of factors, usually including cost, quality, schedule, and relationship and/or credibility of the supplier. One, or a combination of suppliers, may win the business based on their proposals or some variance of them.

- RFI – request for information. Suppliers are asked to provide information about their product/service offering as it relates to the buying firm's requirements. The suppliers are being sought as experts in the industry to educate the buying firm about its options. The results of an RFI often lead to some of the participants being invited to bid in a subsequent RFP.

MARKET INTELLIGENCE NEEDS IN VARIOUS SCM FUNCTIONS

PURCHASING

Purchasers' core competencies are negotiating, contract language writing and editing, and coordination. Often a buyer will know an industry or sector well enough to know who all the players are. Alternatively, they may be networked with people who can share this information with them. But there are also circumstances wherein a buyer does not know who the suppliers are for certain goods and services, and a buyer often begins their search using the internet. Not all businesses advertise on the internet. In fact, even if they do, they may not be found using the same key word searches that the buyer chooses. In-depth research and economic analysis are not always core strengths for buyers.

What the buyer often needs is someone to conduct a targeted search and inform them in a clear and concise way of the sector's competitive landscape. The firm needs to know that all information retrieval methods had been exhausted, and that the list of suppliers is comprehensive. Not having access to complete information at the right time means that the firm may be paying too much, or buying from a non-reputable source. And this mistake may have large consequences when three to five year purchase contracts are negotiated, or when the product or service is very expensive. Or worse – when the product or service is more directly ingrained in the firm's core business offering, meaning that if a company buys widgets, turns them into wonkas, and then sells those wonkas for profit, it ought to know everything it can about the widget supplier and the best price for widgets on the market today. This is particularly painful since the purchasing department is responsible for saving the company money every time it buys something.

PROCUREMENT

Procurement involves the longer term planning of how a firm sets up their purchasing function. It aims to answer the following types of strategic questions:

- Should there be a centralized department that serves all lines of business?

- Should the firm engage employees in the simple task of turning requisitions into purchase orders?

- Should there be those whose function it is to solve immediate purchase requirements on a daily basis?

- Should the department use an AVL?

- Who should be responsible for researching suppliers and their industries?

Understanding how the competitors have set up their procurement departments can give the firm ideas about how to set up their own procedures in order to best meet their needs. Best-in-class information is usually sought after by those companies involved in operations that are heavily measured using operation control methods like Six Sigma and Operational Excellence; often asking questions like, "what is the most efficient and economical way to get those parts into inventory on time?" As well, when considering signing a purchase contract with a supplier for any length of time, a firm usually wants to know who else the supplier is doing business with, and the rough ranking of the supplier's client list, in order to know how clients are prioritized in case of stock shortage.

Without benchmarking programs managers may not even know what is possible in terms of styles and metrics around procurement functions. As one firm may be pushing to get their requisition-to-PO process under five days, they may be surprised to learn that the best in class is averaging 2 hours for the same metric. In such a case, it is valuable to "know what you don't know" since it enables the firm to focus on learning how to get from point A to point B, rather than wondering what to work on to become more efficient. So now that the firm knows it is possible to achieve a two-hour requisition-to-PO standard, they can try to achieve it.

LOGISTICS

Inventory and logistics managers have the complicated task of balancing forecasted requirements with the cost of buying and carrying inventory which is not always sold right away. To further complicate matters, some corporations invest in their supply chains heavily, working closely with suppliers to create a just-in-time delivery system. This means that inventory managers need to know that production schedules can be met by the limitations of the production schedules of suppliers, and how wasted efforts, wasted materials, and wasted time can be eliminated. Put this on an international scale and you can see that factors in between production and warehousing begin to have large effects on the tight management of inventory. These factors include external macroeconomic events, politics, regulations, and technological innovations and limitations.

The information needs of logistics managers can be local, in terms of whom the third party logistics providers are, and what their competitive landscape looks like; or the needs can be global, in terms of what the customs requirements are in other countries, and what it takes to move inventory in countries with differing rules. It takes out-of-the-box strategic thinking to be efficient and effective in varying countries and cultures, and often the logistics manager is not a geopolitical expert. Inventory managers have a real need for political and cultural country profiling to compliment their economic and strategic analyses.

Many inventory management systems, or inventory modules within enterprise resource planning systems, are capable of calculating the complex equation involved in forecasting demand. This is a combination of facts and assumptions including costs, shelf life, storage and shipping requirements, lead time, and so on. However, predicting how demand may be affected by irregular cycles and exogenous factors cannot come from a closed computer system. Rather, it takes a strategic thinker with access to information – a serious pain-point for local inventory and logistics managers, since they are often the last ones to find out about the factors affecting demand for their inventory.

STRATEGIC SOURCING

While sourcing is the act of looking for the best supplier for goods and services, strategic sourcing is more about looking internally for the best big picture solution and considering the total cost of buying and owning goods. Often an internal customer will ask its supply chain department to find it a supplier of certain goods or services. When investigated at a deeper level with a wider scope, it may turn out that there are multiple departments seeking the same goods for other functions, and a bulk purchase for the whole company could result in cost savings. Alternatively, the investigation may result in determining that the department does not really require the goods after all, what it actually requires is process re-engineering.

This function is often employed in concert with Lean Sigma, or an equivalent philosophy, where experts attempt to determine what is really driving the need for this purchase by looking at the entire process and the whole supply chain. Is there something that can be done by the SCM department that can enable the operations to work more efficiently? Alternatively, while the firm may be experiencing changes in its strategic direction, sourcing may be required to adapt, and the sourcing specialist is required to explore sourcing options that may not have been discovered before.

While strategic sourcing professionals are able to perform a deep internal needs assessment, and determine the resources and capabilities available within the organization, they do not always have the resources to perform the same level of investigation outside the firm. Strategic sourcing requires benchmarking breakdowns, best-in-class studies, competitive landscape reporting, and strategic analyses. A report that advises the sourcing specialist of who does what, where, how well, and for whom, could be the difference between mediocre sourcing and real strategic sourcing. Strategic sourcing, to be effective, requires a change in the view of the supply chain, from the traditional to the alternatives, as described in Figures 14.2 and 14.3.

Figure 14.2   The traditional view of the supply chain is the understanding of where the goods have been coming from; the alternative view of the supply chain provides an understanding of all possible alternatives for supply from a network of manufacturers, distributors, sellers, and licensors.

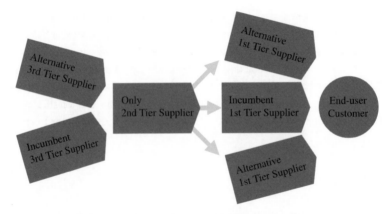

Figure 14.3   The alternative view of the supply chain becomes even more important to the strategic sourcing manager when a supplier, or alternative supplier, is also the competition. It is essential for the strategy manager to know when M&A activity may affect supply priorities, for example, when a competitor acquires a supplier, and prioritizes the supply of components to its own process first.

MARKET INTELLIGENCE DELIVERABLES TO SUPPORT SUPPLY CHAIN MANAGEMENT

PURCHASING

Strategic analysis reports can provide buyers with comprehensive supplier lists by industry sector, and with the confidence that all relevant information retrieval methods have been exhausted. At the same time, a deep dive report on a specific supplier can reassure a buyer that a supplier is legitimate, reliable, and trustworthy; this can be the approval stage for including a supplier in a company's AVL. In situations where a supplier's brand or behavior may directly affect its clients' reputation, it may also be important for a buyer to continuously monitor the companies in its supply chain. Continuous market monitoring can also be the early warning system a company uses to ensure that the competition is not encroaching on a critical source of supply.

PROCUREMENT

Value-chain analyses investigating the firm amongst its competition can enable a procurement manager to benchmark processes and work toward a best-in-class scenario. Continuous monitoring of competitors can also aid in the benchmarking efforts of a procurement department pursuing a continuous monitoring program.

MI is not always competitive intelligence (CI) and pricing exercises. This field includes benchmarking circles, best-in-class information, education, and workshops. All of these services cater to the organization that is interested in learning and open to changing. Getting exposure to how others run their businesses is made possible with MI programs; what a company does with this experience can create great successes.

Anonymous industry surveys enable a firm to understand how other firms in the same industry are managing their sources, and choosing their priorities via operational metrics. Benchmarking circles involve firms from similar or different industries coming together to share best practices and to encourage and enable transformations to becoming more efficient. Workshops are customized classes focused on teaching team members how to perform their functions differently by incorporating intelligence in their thinking and their routines.

LOGISTICS

Market profiles and country risk analyses can be an important resource for logistics managers seeking locations for distribution centers. Rather than simply weighing the factors of input and set up costs, labor, and proximity to suppliers and customers, an MI report can include explanations of local cultures and politics as well. This can inform the logistics manager of where and how to deal with corruption, and how much red tape to expect to get tangled up in when engaging with local governments. Scenario analyses can aid in terms of understanding which combination of factors will yield the best results – this can be particularly useful when making decisions around how much of a limited supply of inventory to keep at which depot within a network of warehouses. Macroeconomic analyses result in forecasts of commodity prices, short supplies, and runs on demand – all of which a logistics manager might otherwise rely on a crystal ball to predict.

On-going monitoring of local, national, and international regulations governing transportation and logistics can enable logistics managers to make new strategic decisions on the fly; redirecting shipments via air or ocean, relying on different hubs, and even moving processing steps to different countries as news of proposed regulation changes becomes known.

STRATEGIC SOURCING

The more strategic the supply chain decision, the more MI can help. While a buyer may be considering only the cost and the ability of the supplier to provide the required goods or services, a strategic sourcing manager may require an analysis report to determine who else the supplier is providing the same goods or services to, and with what other firms the supplier is associated.

As well, a customized company profile can inform the strategic sourcing manager of the relationship between a competitor and a supplier; whether the competition is getting preferential treatment, or whether the firms are owned by the same parent company. Understanding a supplier's approach toward its client base, its strategic direction and its business model can enable the sourcing manager to determine how well it is aligned with its supply chain, and to determine if a potential supplier is geared toward offering the kind of service and supply the company seeks over time.

Another type of strategic analysis reporting is market size and forecasting. Sourcing managers benefit from market information because it enables them to know whether to be simply customers of a sector, or to become players in the industry. For example, an accurate analysis will enable a firm to decide between buying enough raw materials to use for its own purposes and trading the goods. Purchasing and storing goods for resale or later use will also affect the logistics manager's decisions.

But relying solely on one-time reporting and profiling may not be the most cost-effective solution in the long run. Continuous market monitoring can offer the supply chain manager insights from the effects of macroeconomic changes, and changes in political and corporate power. A firm may choose to continuously monitor its competition and its suppliers, and thereby be the first to know when M&A activity occurs, when new contracts are won, or when new innovations are put into use. Marketing activity is a key indicator for a company's supply chain requirements, since what a company offers for sale is made up of components and services bought from suppliers. Sourcing managers may also choose to monitor price levels and commodity trends which enable them to know when to buy materials in bulk and store them, and when to buy items just-in-time for processing.

Case: Logistics in Aerospace

The manager of spare parts inventory and forecasting for a global aerospace company describes the scenario of moving plane parts around the world to various depots. The goal is to have the part available in the local depot whenever a customer asks for it, but carrying as many parts as customers might ask for is too expensive. The inventory manager says that forecasting is part art and part science. "You can have all the right analysts working with all the right technological tools with the right goals in mind, and still be negatively affected by some event from outside your control." Knowing in advance that the government of a certain country is going to use their bureaucracy to trap your inventory would be extremely valuable. As well, knowing what effects the changing price of raw materials or fuel will have on the inventory logistics line of business would make the logistics manager's job a lot easier.

The aerospace spare parts manager describes how the company he works for opened a distribution center in south Asia, thinking that this would enable the company to have spare parts close to customers in the Middle East and Eurasia, and the cost of running the DC would be low based on the Asian price levels. However, once the parts arrived the local government blocked the company from selling or removing the inventory.

It would cost the company an enormous amount of money to unravel the bureaucratic red tape and enable it to remove the parts from the country, and yet it was paying monthly for them to sit in a warehouse with no opportunity to go to customers. Ideally, before opening the DC, the aerospace company could have used an MI report describing the advantages and disadvantages of operating its DC in any number of locations. Factors would include the number of customers that could be served from each location, the cost of running the DC (land, labor, etc.), as well as the cooperation of the local governments.

As the inventory manager describes it: a key MI factor in this case would be the informal infrastructure – where governments might block business for arbitrary, political, or other reasons, or where high ranking officials expect bribes. This kind of information is not readily available, but is absolutely necessary in order for this type of business to function properly.

As it turns out, this particular aerospace manufacturer learned its lesson from this mistake. While it has paid dearly for the South Asian DC, every strategic location decision from this point onward gave clear and deep consideration to politics and local culture, and further-more, acknowledged each team members' core competencies, recognizing that this valuable research is not usually the first priority of a time-constrained logistics team.

SUMMARY

Properly focused efforts to manage a company's supply chain may create cost savings that will exceed any money spent on creating profits. Companies also need to focus on relationships with suppliers and the movement and storage of goods to maximize profitable outcomes while minimiz-ing risks and costs.

Many areas of SCM rely on MI inputs that can indirectly contribute to achieving greater profitability. Each area of supply chain management requires different MI support:

- Purchasing
    - Comprehensive supplier lists by industry sector
    - Deep dive reports on specific suppliers
    - Continuous monitoring of the companies in the supply chain
    - Ad hoc research
- Procurement
    - Value chain analyses investigating the firm amongst the competition
    - Continuous monitoring of competitors
    - Survey analyses, benchmarking circles, intelligence workshops

- Logistics

    o   Market profiles and country risk analyses for seeking locations for distribution centers

    o   Scenario analyses to support inventory decisions

    o   Macroeconomic analyses to forecast commodity prices, short supplies, and runs on demand

    o   On-going monitoring of local, national, and international regulations

- Strategic sourcing

    o   Analysis report about the value chain

    o   Company profiles about the players in the value chain

    o   Market sizing and forecasting

    o   Continuous market monitoring

PART 4

Developing World Class Market Intelligence Programs

15   Implementing Market Intelligence Programs 217
The Challenge of a Newly Appointed Head
  of Market Intelligence 217
"It's Time to Modernize Our Market Intelligence Approach" 217
The Market Intelligence Roadmap 218
Initial Success Indicators 222
So Now, How to Get There? 223
One and a Half Years Later 225
Towards World Class Levels 226
Summary 226

**16   How to Develop an Existing Market Intelligence Program
for Greater Impact** 227
Benchmarking Market Intelligence for Global Best Practices 227
Assessing the Status of Market Intelligence 232
Learn, Plan – and Execute 238
Summary 239

17   Demonstrating the Impact of Market Intelligence 241
First Things First: Market Intelligence is Only Impactful
  When it is Used 242
Return on Market Intelligence Investment – The Case
  for and Against Financial Calculations 243
The Long-Term, Qualitative Benefits of Market Intelligence 247
Summary 250

18   Trends in Market Intelligence 253
       Intelligence Scope 253
       Intelligence Process 255
       Intelligence Deliverables 257
       Intelligence Tools 260
       Intelligence Organization 262
       Intelligence Culture 264
       Summary 265

15 Implementing Market Intelligence Programs

THE CHALLENGE OF A NEWLY APPOINTED HEAD OF MARKET INTELLIGENCE

Mark was smiling inwards. He was quite happy with the presentation he had prepared for a conference where he had been invited to speak about setting up a Market Intelligence (MI) program. In his mind, he had gone through once again the multiple initiatives that had kept him occupied for the last one and a half years, reflecting on his past experiences and selecting some of the key things to discuss in his presentation. One thing clearly stood out: never before had he had such an extensive network of people around him, all of whom were stakeholders to the intelligence program that he was leading. Mark felt somewhat pressured – he felt personal responsibility for delivering on the promises that his program continuously made to the organization – while at the same time he thought nothing could be more rewarding than this: being able to support the managers and experts around him by providing top notch intelligence to their needs. As a people person, he really enjoyed his job. This was what he would start his presentation with.

Mark was working in a relatively large logistics company whose services covered express delivery, freight, warehousing, and distribution. Originally, the initiative to establish a systematic intelligence program in the company had come from one of the Board members who had previous experience of a solid intelligence program in operation. It was not like Mark's company hadn't had any previous MI activity at all, though. On the contrary, information about market players and trends had been collected by various local units for their own purposes.

Only there was no central coordination in collecting and processing information, and no-one really knew just how many resources were being put into the activity and what the concrete benefits were at the end of the day. In addition, the top management felt they were not being served with good enough MI for their strategic needs that had become very apparent in the increasingly complex competitive landscape.

"IT'S TIME TO MODERNIZE OUR MARKET INTELLIGENCE APPROACH"

To further add to the challenge, the organization was burdened with some old traditions that the management now felt should be replaced by a new level of professionalism in collecting and using business information: there were very experienced long time employees in the company who were knowledgeable about the business and were more than happy to serve as the trusted sources of information for the rest of the organization. Valuable as they were, the management viewed this as a potential risk for several reasons:

- Getting accurate business information should not be dependent on individual persons. This would make the company very vulnerable to changes in personnel.

- While person to person communication is vital in exchanging business information, without any central information management, only a very limited group of people would benefit from the insights of the random individuals who were willing to share theirs.

- The changes in the business environment happened so fast these days that the process of collective insight creation just needed to be faster than it had been traditionally.

- Finally, the company was looking to soon bring on board hundreds of new employees, following the decision to expand its business to new market areas in the emerging economies. These employees would need to be brought up to speed rapidly, and the management simply felt the modern way of contributing to this goal was to have a professional MI program in place. Naturally the modernization of the MI approach would simultaneously serve the entire organization regularly needing business information, not just the new employees.

Hence Mark had been appointed as the Head of MI, reporting to the vice president of strategic planning who was part of the management team. Mark's background was in sales and, more recently, corporate development, so he was not new to the company and he already had insight into where some of the pain points were regarding market information – or the lack of it. Yet Mark was in no way familiar with MI as a discipline, and while he was waiting to have the chance to talk to the MI savvy Board member about his experiences, Mark had simply started running Google searches on market and competitive intelligence.

THE MARKET INTELLIGENCE ROADMAP

Mark was clicking through his conference presentation, repeating the storyline once again in his mind. Back then, one and a half years ago, running his Google searches Mark had come across the Global Intelligence Alliance (GIA)'s World Class MI Development Roadmap (Table 15.1) that he had put as the next slide of his presentation. Rather overwhelming as the Roadmap looked at first – and Mark knew his audience wouldn't be able to read the small font from the screen – he had immediately found it useful for three reasons:

- The Roadmap concretized the things that he would need to address from the beginning.

- Setting the ambition level for the entire MI initiative was easy with the Roadmap.

- The Roadmap mercifully presented the necessary development efforts in steps, making it easy for Mark to set intermediate targets rather than suggesting the world class levels should be achieved at once.

Table 15.1 The World Class MI Roadmap

Description	Informal MI "Firefighters"	Basic MI "Beginners"	Intermediate MI "Coordinators"	Advanced MI "Directors"	World Class MI "Futurists"
Intelligence Scope	No Specific focus has been determined. Ad hoc needs drive the scope.	Limited scope, seeking quick wins. Focus typically on competitors or customers only.	Wide scope with the attempt to cover the current operating environment comprehensively.	Analytical deep dives about specific topics complement the comprehensive monitoring of the operating environment.	Broad, deep and future-oriented scope that also covers topics outside of the immediately relevant operating environment.
Intelligence Process	Reactive ad hoc process puts out fires as they emerge. Uncoordinated purchases of information.	Needs analysis made. Establishing info collection from secondary external sources. Little or no analysis involved in the process.	Secondary info sourcing complemented by well established primary info collection and analysis.	Advanced market monitoring and analysis processes established. Targeted communication of output to specific business processes and decision points.	Intelligence process deeply rooted in both global and local levels of the organization. MI fully integrated with key business processes; two-way communication.
Intelligence Deliverables	Ad hoc deliverables quickly put together from scratch.	Regular newsletters and profiles complement ad hoc deliverables.	Systematic market monitoring and analysis reports emerge as new, structured MI output.	Two-way communication is increased in both production and utilization of MI output. Highly analytical deliverables.	High degree of future orientation and collaborative insight creation in producing and delivering the MI output.
Intelligence Tools	Email and shared folders as the primary means for sharing and archiving information.	Corporate intranet is emerging as a central storage for intelligence output.	Web-based MI portal established that provides access to structured MI output. Users receive email alerts about new info in the system.	Sophisticated channeling of both internally and externally produced MI content to the MI portal. Multiple access interfaces to the portal in use.	Seamless integration of the MI portal to other relevant IT tools. Lively collaboration of users through the MI portal.
Intelligence Organization	No resources specifically dedicated to MI. Individuals conducting MI activities on a non-structured basis.	One person appointed as responsible for MI. Increasing coordination of MI work in the company. Loose relationships with external info providers.	A fully dedicated person manages MI and coordinates activities. Centralized, internally or externally resourced info collection and analysis capabilities exist.	Advanced analytical and consultative skills in the intelligence team. MI network with dedicated resources in business units for collecting local market info. Non-core MI activities outsourced.	MI team has reached the status of trusted advisors to management. Internal MI network collaborating actively. Internal MI organization smoothly integrated with the outsourced resources.
Intelligence Culture	No shared understanding exists of the role and benefits of systematic MI operations.	Some awareness exists of MI, but the organizational culture overall is still neural towards MI.	MI awareness in a moderate level. Sharing of info is encouraged through internal training and marketing of MI.	MI awareness is high and people participate actively in producing MI content. Top management voices its continuous support to MI efforts.	A strong MI mindset is reflected in the way people are curious towards the operating environment and co-create insights about it.

The World Class MI Roadmap contained six Key Success Factors (KSFs) for an MI program (Figure 15.1) that would have a professional ambition level, and Mark had quickly introduced the KSFs on his next slide, reflecting on the status in his company back then with each of the KSFs.

- **1. Intelligence scope.** The purpose of the program should be derived from the management's initial drivers for assigning Mark in his role in the first place. Working on the required breadth and depth of the intelligence program would be one of Mark's first tasks.

- **2. Intelligence process**. How to organize the production of whatever deliverables the MI program was to produce? Mark knew he would have to run a proper assessment of what MI exactly would be needed in the company and, importantly, what the company already had in different parts of the organization.

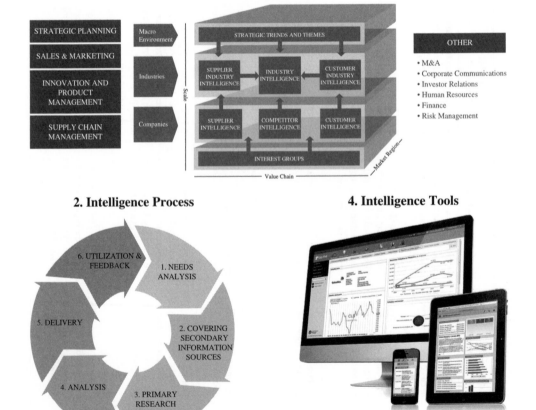

Figure 15.1   The six KSFs in the World Class MI Roadmap

3. Intelligence Deliverables

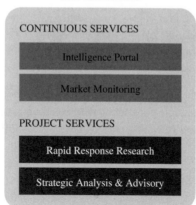

5. Intelligence Organization

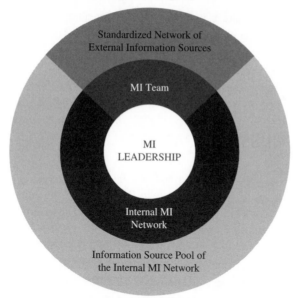

6. Intelligence Culture

Figure 15.1 (*Continued*)

- **3. Intelligence deliverables**. First things first – from day one, Mark knew his MI program would have to deliver value, even in the middle of only resourcing the activity and developing the related processes.

- **4. Intelligence tools**. In the beginning, there was no existing dedicated MI software, and Mark intended to look into how people were storing and delivering whatever MI content was being stored and delivered.

- **5. Intelligence organization**. Now this was a complicated one. Mark knew he would need to evaluate the resourcing situation, considering who could be assigned with intelligence tasks even as a part time role, let alone full time. As a separate area, Mark would need to familiarize himself with what services were available out in the market for outsourcing any of the MI activities. As well, Mark would need to start building a network of stakeholders internally, at the same time avoiding stepping on the toes of the "self made intelligence professionals" who might feel intimidated by his efforts. They would be immensely valuable as allies, but Mark would need to treat them delicately to generate goodwill.

- **6. Intelligence culture**. In the beginning, Mark didn't think the company had much of an intelligence culture to speak of: MI efforts existed but they were too random and local to have achieved anything like a uniform culture towards MI. "If an intelligence culture rests on branding the MI activity, there's not much to brand", he thought. He would need to change that.

INITIAL SUCCESS INDICATORS

Now, the World Class MI Roadmap had given Mark the topics to work with and even the frameworks to use; however, his next challenge was to determine exactly where he would start. He thought of the initial indicators of success that he would like to achieve quite quickly in order to demonstrate value and results to the management team:

- Success stories: Mark would be able to point out decisions that had been successful for the company because the background work was well done, i.e. the decision-makers had the insights that were needed to make an educated decision.

- Requests for intelligence inputs would be flowing in.

- The intelligence program would start to be recognized in the company.

- People would view the MI program positively, so much so that they would willingly contribute by sharing their own information.

Having thus determined how he would like his MI program to be characterized after a while, Mark adopted another development framework, the stages of which he was determined to go through in the next one and a half years. Initially, he thought he would like to be at the

"Intermediate" level 3 on the World Class MI Roadmap once the initial development efforts had been completed; yet the exact results would have to be evaluated afterwards. If, Mark thought, he could honestly say that his earlier mentioned success indicators were actually there after one and a half years of MI development, his company's status couldn't be very bad on the MI Roadmap either.

SO NOW, HOW TO GET THERE?

Mark flipped to the next slide (Figure 15.2) that was presenting his initial MI development framework for the setup phase.

Even though Mark had been appointed by the management team to take on the task of establishing an MI program, and their drivers for doing this were quite clear from the very beginning, Mark thought he would still need to further deepen the needs analysis for the intelligence program. He concluded that he had several options for conducting a needs analysis, ranging from using questionnaires and templates to running interviews and workshops. "Questionnaires are too impersonal and I want to start building a personal network", Mark thought, while at the same time acknowledging that he probably would not get the entire busy management team to attend an MI workshop any time soon.

Hence Mark ended up scheduling a few one-on-one interviews with high ranking executives. Based on the information gained he would make thorough preparations for a suggested MI plan. The management team would subsequently review, discuss, and approve the plan.

Mark's discussion topics with his interviewees included:

- What should be the primary purpose for the MI program? Any secondary purposes?

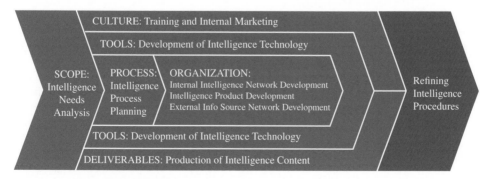

Figure 15.2   Setting up a MI program

- Who should be initially served with the MI deliverables (in addition to top management of course)? Which corporate functions and business processes? In other words, where were the fires that should be put out first?

- What information would the MI users need? On which market players? Which industries? Which geographies? Which trends and themes?

- How frequently and in which format would the information be needed by the users? Also, what level of analysis would be expected from the MI content; would the focus have to be in giving consultative advice based on market analysis, or rather just keeping the users on top of the current market developments?

Based on his interviews, Mark prepared his initial MI plan. The purpose of the MI program would be to serve primarily top management with highly analytical intelligence deliverables that would support strategic decision-making. As a secondary goal, the MI efforts should also support generating more sales, especially in the areas of express services and freight. Mapping out the detailed topics on which each of these user groups would need information would be on Mark's task list; however, the primary topic areas would be understanding customers and customers' customers, the competitive offerings, as well as the trends and drivers that were shaping the logistics industry.

As an immediate ad hoc topic, the planned expansion into selected emerging markets would need to be supported with analyses about the local industry landscape. As the information content needs ranged from both analytical deliverables to market and sales leads monitoring, and the users of MI would be in various locations around the world, the need was also quite immediate for the company to have a software tool for storing and distributing the MI deliverables.

Mark had now completed a needs analysis and the subsequent action plan for his MI program, and he would next explain to his audience how he had gone about building up the deliverables and structures needed to accomplish his goals. He flipped on to the next slide that showed an assessment of his resources in the beginning.

1. The available team

    1. One full-time analyst

    2. Four part-time analysts in business units (roles need to be clarified and confirmed)

    3. Vice president, strategic planning as the MI program owner (very limited time available)

    4. Various potential beneficiaries of the MI deliverables (need to be recruited as contributors and spokespersons as well)

2. Budget

    1. Limited in the beginning, any sizable investments subject to decision by the management team based on detailed plans

3.   Data sources

    1.   Two separate news feeds

    2.   A subscription to industry analysis reports

    3.   No dedicated software tools

ONE AND A HALF YEARS LATER

Combining his MI plan with the available resources, Mark had subsequently put the required efforts on a timeline and moved forward to execute the plan:

- Responding to the immediate need of preparing industry landscape analyses about three separate geographical regions. Delivering to management in a showcase style. Using external resources as help where needed: the quality of the first analytical deliverables would set the expectation level for a long time to come, hence the ambition level would need to be high.

- Setting up and launching MI software that would first contain daily market monitoring for the purposes of current awareness about strategic and operative hot topics, and to support sales work.

- Organizing the resources: deciding on whether the market monitoring should be performed in-house or whether it should be outsourced for resource optimization. The necessary information sources portfolio would also have an impact on this decision.

- Organizing the processing of information from data sourcing to analysis to delivery and utilization. This would be done in close linkage to software implementation, resourcing decisions, and intelligence product portfolio design.

- Once the pilot version of the software was up and running, starting to recruit MI network members with something tangible to show them right from the beginning.

- Once the pilot phase with the software and the related intelligence deliverables was over, starting to conduct road shows to promote the intelligence program to still wider user groups, at the same time establishing personal contacts and building engagement in the MI topic.

- Keeping all the time in mind the traditional "self made intelligence people", trying to recruit them as special spokespersons for the intelligence program.

As a result of the initial development efforts, Mark's company was now in a situation where they had initially addressed all relevant aspects of MI. The purpose and coverage of the program were quite clear, the intelligence process ran relatively smoothly, the deliverables of the program were of high quality, there was a dedicated intelligence tool existing, and even the organization and the related intelligence culture had started to shape up quite nicely, thanks to Mark's and his team's active service attitude and frequent personal contacts with the MI users. Mark was proud of the MI program, and he could congratulate his team for largely achieving the "success indicators" that he had set one and a half years earlier. Hence he was also happy to be giving this conference presentation.

TOWARDS WORLD CLASS LEVELS

Mark would end his presentation with a notion about the planned next steps for his MI program. He was aware of the risk of excessive self-satisfaction at the stage of having the fundamentals in place, and he was determined to continue to work on the MI program towards where the best companies in the world would be. True, all the pieces were now quite well together in their MI program, yet he agreed with the management team that the next big thing would be to leverage that "MI infrastructure" for still greater impact:

- MI team earning the role as management's trusted advisors

- MI embedded in all important business decisions

- Active co-creation of insight at all levels of the organization

To achieve the next goals and indeed to first break them into concrete development activities, Mark intended to once again refer to the World Class MI Roadmap, assessing the current stage of his company and determining the signposts that would indicate that progress was taking place on the way towards a greater impact MI program.

SUMMARY

There are four key set up activities in the intelligence program implementation:

- Intelligence needs analysis and action planning; i.e. defining the scope and process of the intelligence program

- Intelligence product design and resource activation; i.e. defining the intelligence deliverables and the organization producing and using them

- Intelligence tool development; i.e. implementing the necessary tools (technology and techniques) for intelligence use

- Intelligence program roll-out, internal marketing, and process maintenance; i.e. moving from set up to a maintenance mode and working to create a lasting intelligence culture

The World Class MI Development Framework is useful for setting the initial goals and ambition level for the intelligence program. Once the set up work has been completed and the intelligence program is up and running, it makes sense for the ambitious head of MI to return to the Roadmap, conducting an assessment of the achievements so far and setting goals for further MI development.

16 How to Develop an Existing Market Intelligence Program for Greater Impact

A few months had passed since Mark's conference presentation. It had been well received especially among those who were in a similar situation as Mark himself was when starting his MI development efforts. Mark had even been contacted afterwards by a couple of peers in other companies that wanted to share views with him about particular situations and how to tackle them. Mark was happy to share his thinking – one of his goals in participating in the conference had been to expand his network outside his own company, and his presentation had served well to that end.

Speaking of networking, in the conference Mark had also come across the opportunity to join a group of companies conducting facilitated benchmarking around their intelligence programs. The primary goal of the benchmarking project was to share best practices and help each other in their shared aspiration to not get stuck with an "average MI program" status, but to move forward and take their Market Intelligence programs towards the highest global standards. In practice, the participants in the benchmarking project wanted to increase the impact, the very value of their Market Intelligence programs to the organization.

BENCHMARKING MARKET INTELLIGENCE FOR GLOBAL BEST PRACTICES

Mark felt he could use some external advice on how he himself could go from here, pursuing the goal of "impact"; hence he joined the benchmarking group. Equally important as the substantial content of the workshops though would be the social aspect that was bound to generate shared inspiration among the participants, Mark thought. Even though he himself was leading a team of analysts and he was indeed a networked person overall, he felt he simply wanted to share experiences with other MI heads who faced the exact same challenges as he did. He was sure the others, too, would be nodding at this point.

Illustrated in Figure 16.1 is the situation that the participating companies in the benchmarking group were facing: each had an MI program existing by now, some had even had theirs for a decade.

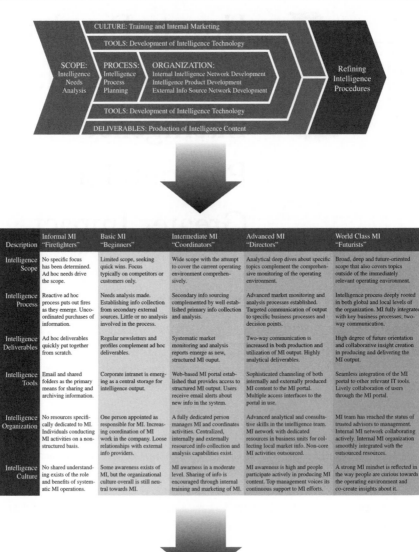

Description	Informal MI "Firefighters"	Basic MI "Beginners"	Intermediate MI "Coordinators"	Advanced MI "Directors"	World Class MI "Futurists"
Intelligence Scope	No specific focus has been determined. Ad hoc needs drive the scope.	Limited scope, seeking quick wins. Focus typically on competitors or customers only.	Wide scope with the attempt to cover the current operating environment comprehensively.	Analytical deep dives about specific topics complement the comprehensive monitoring of the operating environment.	Broad, deep and future-oriented scope that also covers topics outside of the immediately relevant operating environment.
Intelligence Process	Reactive ad hoc process puts out fires as they emerge. Uncoordinated purchases of information.	Needs analysis made. Establishing info collection from secondary external sources. Little or no analysis involved in the process.	Secondary info sourcing complemented by well established primary info collection and analysis.	Advanced market monitoring and analysis processes established. Targeted communication of output to specific business processes and decision points.	Intelligence process deeply rooted in both global and local levels of the organization. MI fully integrated with key business processes; two-way communication.
Intelligence Deliverables	Ad hoc deliverables quickly put together from scratch.	Regular newsletters and profiles complement ad hoc deliverables.	Systematic market monitoring and analysis reports emerge as new, structured MI ouput.	Two-way communication is increased in both production and utilization of MI output. Highly analytical deliverables.	High degree of future orientation and collaborative insight creation in producing and delivering the MI output.
Intelligence Tools	Email and shared folders as the primary means for sharing and archiving information.	Corporate intranet is emerging as a central storage for intelligence output.	Web-based MI portal established that provides access to structured MI output. Users receive email alerts about new info in the system.	Sophisticated channeling of both internally and externally produced MI content to the MI portal. Multiple access interfaces to the portal in use.	Seamless integration of the MI portal to other relevant IT tools. Lively collaboration of users through the MI portal.
Intelligence Organization	No resources specifically dedicated to MI. Individuals conducting MI activities on a non-structured basis.	One person appointed as responsible for MI. Increasing coordination of MI work in the company. Loose relationships with external info providers.	A fully dedicated person manages MI and coordinates activities. Centralized, internally and externally resourced info collection and analysis capabilities exist.	Advanced analytical and consultative skills in the intelligence team. MI network with dedicated resources in business units for collecting local market info. Non-core MI activities outsourced.	MI team has reached the status of trusted advisors to management. Internal MI network collaborating actively. Internal MI organization smoothly integrated with the outsourced resources.
Intelligence Culture	No shared understanding exists of the role and benefits of systematic MI operations.	Some awareness exists of MI, but the organizational culture overall is still neutral towards MI.	MI awarness in a moderate level. Sharing of info is encouraged through internal training and marketing of MI.	MI awareness is high and people participate actively in producing MI content. Top management voices its continuous support to MI efforts.	A strong MI mindset is reflected in the way people are curious towards the operating environment and co-create insights about it.

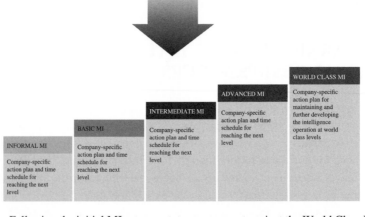

Figure 16.1   Following the initial MI setup, a status assessment against the World Class MI Roadmap will yield a company-specific plan on how to move towards world class levels in MI

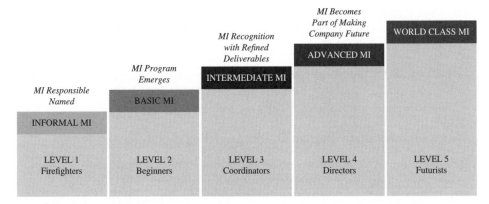

Figure 16.2 The development efforts required to reach the next level of overall MI program status are specific to each company and need to be determined based on a customized assessment.

However, measured against the six KSFs in the World Class MI Roadmap, each company also had gaps to close. Now the question for them was how to take their MI programs forward.

The required MI development efforts would necessarily be specific to each company (Figure 16.2), and the very purpose of the benchmarking project was to conduct an assessment of each organization's challenges and jointly develop a plan forward, while sharing fruitful ideas in the process. As well, through the benchmarking project the group intended to avoid re-inventing the wheel or making mistakes that someone had already learned from.

Case: Statoil Develops a Strategic Corporate Intelligence Program in Five Years

This case will highlight the development of Statoil's intelligence program on a timeline. It will also outline the "10 commandments of intelligence" at Statoil as described by Anders Marvik, head of corporate intelligence.

2006 – The Initiation of Statoil's Intelligence Program

Up until 2006, intelligence assignments at Statoil had been handled as occasional ad hoc projects with the support of management consulting companies. Following the decision to establish a full blown intelligence program in-house, the vice president of business development in the company appointed Anders Marvik to set up the intelligence program.

2007 – Developing a Team for Intelligence

Three months later, it had become evident that more resources were needed, and two more people were recruited for the job. The intelligence deliverables were rather basic

(Continued)

at this point and consisted of general news feeds that were complemented by and ad hoc research and analysis projects.

By 2007 the Statoil and Norsk Hydro merger had resulted in the strategy team merging with the business development team. The headcount total was now 12 persons, of which eight were working on intelligence projects and four were focusing on the strategy process.

2008 – The Intelligence Program Evolves: Launching the Intelligence Website

By 2008, it was apparent that the intelligence program at Statoil should be rolled out to serve many more people in the organization than the small group in business development and strategic planning. Statoil's "Sharing is Power" philosophy was applied in making the news monitoring and analytical reports available to a large group of people.

2009 – Expanding the Scope of the Intelligence Program

Building up a team of intelligence people with multiple backgrounds and experiences was a KSF that enabled the increase in in-depth focusing on a variety of topics. A strict recruiting policy was enforced to keep up the high standards, and Statoil hired the best brains with a variety of backgrounds and arranged extensive on the job training for the new recruits.

2011 – Intelligence Goes into Corporate Strategy

In 2011, competitive intelligence (CI) is placed in the corporate strategy unit at Statoil and it consists of 15 intelligence people and five others managing the strategy process. In addition, a pool of 15–20 researchers is available to work on Statoil's intelligence projects as an out-sourced resource. The MI team now regularly supports 500 key decision-makers; however, in total 2,500 people in the organization have access to the intelligence website. The top 500 decision-makers are the CEO and the executive committee, top 100 managers, and divisional managers. The deliverables include external news reports, flash reports, M&A analysis, strategic reviews, deep dive analysis, personal presentations, and CEO briefings.

Statoil's CI Success List: The 10 Commandments

Anders Marvik highlights ten KSFs that have been instrumental on the road to success:

1. **Top management sponsor**

    You never get to the CEO without that. Support is needed for resources, contact generation, process interaction, and protection. Competing intelligence units were created and our CI people got internal job offers. Top management support is needed in order to resolve these issues. This support is also needed when you bring bad news to the table.

2. **Diversified CI team**

    Having people from different countries, industries, and companies is a necessity. The questions we come across at corporate strategy are so diverse that we need a broad competence pool to tap into.

3. **Strong internal and external networks**

    Outsource low and consult high is our device. We outsource fact finding and infor-
    mation gathering so that the CI team can focus on insight and conclusions. In order
    to hedge our bets, we discuss our findings with management consultants and invest-
    ment bankers in order to get feedback on our ideas and also to get alternative per-
    spectives. Being close to these contacts is essential. We need to be in the industry
    hub, i.e. London. This is even more important than being close to top management
    who are located in Norway.

4. **Resources needed**

    You need to face it that resources are needed and that it is an investment to develop an
    in-house CI capability. But we are still much less expensive than having a management
    consulting firm on a retainer basis. We can deliver more for much less. I have seen the
    bill for management consultants on a retainer basis and the fee can be very, very high.

5. **Professional peer-reviewed presentations**

    Ensure that your presentations look just like presentations from management consult-
    ants or investment bankers. Content is still king, but you need to ensure that all your
    deliverables look good on any platform whether it is email or the mobile phone. You
    can only develop trust over time by delivering top notch presentations. You need to
    be able to do bottom up analysis and present your own opinion, not just opinions of
    others. If you apply the copy cat strategy in the long run, you will be out of business
    after a while. We have conducted presentation training but the most important trick
    is really that we peer review all our reports. This is of great benefit both to senior and
    junior team participants. For very important reports we also do an external review
    with the help of strategy or industry consulting firms.

6. **Grounded conclusions**

    Back up your conclusions with facts and proper analysis. Sooner or later someone
    will ask for this.

7. **Embedding MI in the strategy process**

    Being part of the strategy team has been important for us in order to get access to
    top decision-makers and being able to integrate our work into the strategy process.

8. **Analysis needs to be done close to the business**

    You need to be close to the business in order to be able to do appropriate analysis.
    We are working tightly with business development and work a lot with M&A issues.
    If you are not close to the business you cannot ask the right questions let alone
    answer them.

    (Continued)

9.   **Sharing is power**

We have an open intelligence culture, we share our portal with 2,500 users and we have 500 prioritized management users.

10.   **Right employee profiles**

I believe that intelligence is an art form and it takes one to two years to become good at it. What I look for is: multitasking capability, strive for change, curiosity, reading and understanding wide topics, spotting trends, liking a chaotic environment, mastering the art of asking questions. Creative business thinking is also critical. We have routines for profiling personalities and all new applicants must also do several tests in order to assess their skills. I have identified the right profiles and our HR unit are conducting the tests. In fact, we have been using the GIA MI Roadmap framework in order to understand which skills we need for each of the levels from "Firefighters" to "Futurists".

Intelligence Vision

"The last thing is really that you need a CI vision in order to establish what you need and how you are going to develop your program. We use the GIA roadmap for this. You need to define what success looks like for an intelligence program in the oil industry."

"It took us five years to get these pieces together", says Marvik. "It was indeed hard work, but we are now very satisfied with the situation we have today."

ASSESSING THE STATUS OF MARKET INTELLIGENCE

To Mark's pleasure, the benchmarking group was now about to gather together for the second time. In the initial meeting a few weeks ago, the agenda had been about getting to know each other and seeking the common ground, i.e. the common pain points to address in the upcoming MI benchmarking workshops. The final decisions about participating in the project had been made based on the first meeting, and Mark was happy that every company had decided to continue. Mark thought this was probably because not every company had exactly similar experiences, hence they could genuinely learn from each other.

The second workshop went straight to the point in that the participants were supposed to assess their own company's MI status against the World Class MI Roadmap. The exercise was outlined by one of the participating companies first presenting their MI case for inspiration to the others. After the brief presentation, the group took a while to familiarize themselves in silence with the assessment questions related to each of the six KSFs.

The Assessment Questionnaire

Rating scale: how strongly would you agree or disagree with the following statements? (5 = strongly agree, 4 = somewhat agree, 3 = neither agree nor disagree, 2 = somewhat disagree, 1 = strongly disagree).

Intelligence Scope

In our organization, the purpose of Market Intelligence is clearly defined.

Market Intelligence is well-aligned with the strategic goals of our organization.

1. All relevant divisions and units of our organization are benefiting from Market Intelligence.

2. All relevant people in our organization are benefiting from Market Intelligence.

3. Our Market Intelligence covers all important topics in our business environment.

4. Our Market Intelligence analyzes our business environment on a very deep level.

5. In our organization, Market Intelligence is future-oriented.

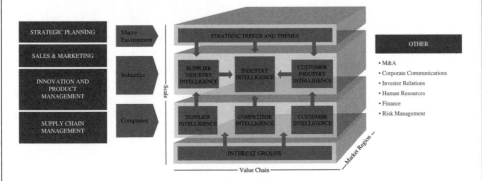

Figure 16.3 Intelligence scope

Intelligence Process

1. Our Market Intelligence people are doing a great job at analyzing the information needs of the end users in our organization.

2. Our Market Intelligence people are doing a great job at finding valuable information from publicly available sources.

(Continued)

3.   Our Market Intelligence people are doing a great job at interviewing experts inside and outside our organization.

4.   Our Market Intelligence people are doing a great job at analyzing information.

5.   Our Market Intelligence people are doing a great job at giving recommendations and advice to our decision-makers.

6.   Our Market Intelligence people are actively asking for feedback.

7.   Overall, our Market Intelligence program is tightly integrated with the decision-making processes in our organization.

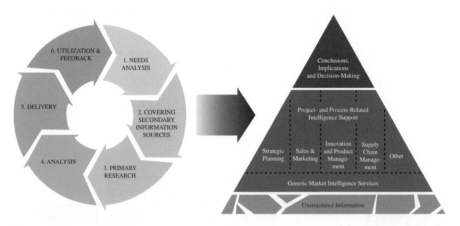

Figure 16.4   Intelligence process

Intelligence Deliverables

1.   Our Market Intelligence people are doing a great job at providing self-service access to Market Intelligence sources, deliverables, and tools.

2.   Our Market Intelligence people are doing a great job at monitoring our business environment and delivering regular updates about competitors and market developments.

3.   Our Market Intelligence people are doing a great job at conducting small research assignments on short notice.

4.   Our Market Intelligence people are doing a great job at conducting large strategic analysis projects on an ad hoc basis.

5.   In our organization, people are receiving regular and highly relevant market signals (e.g. news about markets and competitors).

6.   In our organization, people have access to up-to-date and relevant company profiles, product profiles, or market profiles.

7.   The analysis reports that are provided by our Market Intelligence are insightful and useful in decision-making.

8.   Our Market Intelligence people are doing a great job at providing interactive presentations and briefings.

9.   Our Market Intelligence people are doing a great job running workshops in which intelligence is created together.

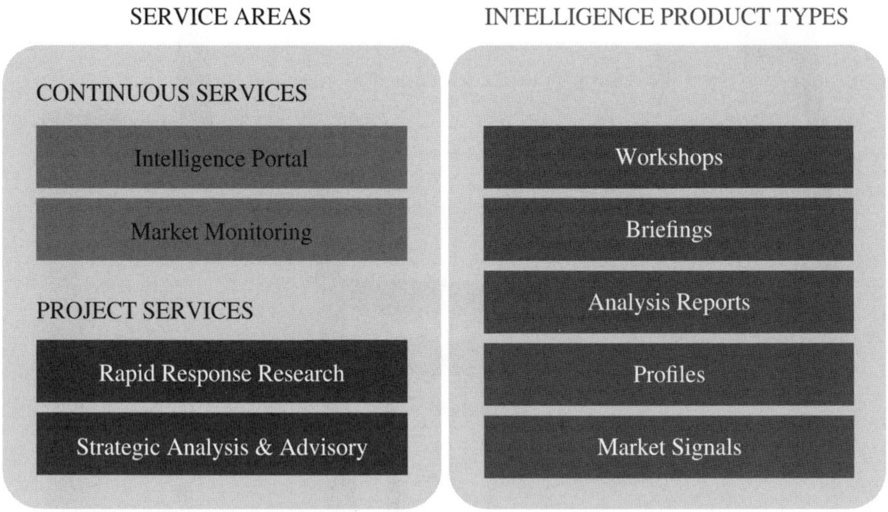

SERVICE AREAS   INTELLIGENCE PRODUCT TYPES

CONTINUOUS SERVICES

Intelligence Portal

Market Monitoring

PROJECT SERVICES

Rapid Response Research

Strategic Analysis & Advisory

Workshops

Briefings

Analysis Reports

Profiles

Market Signals

Figure 16.5   Intelligence deliverables

Intelligence Tools

1.   The Market Intelligence tools in our organization enable me to share information proactively.

2.   The Market Intelligence tools in our organization enable me to provide comments and to participate in discussions.

3.   The Market Intelligence tools in our organization enable me to find colleagues that have specific expertise.

4.   The Market Intelligence tools in our organization are tightly integrated with other information systems.

5.   The Market Intelligence tools in our organization enable me to subscribe to email alerts about topics important to me.

(Continued)

6. The Market Intelligence tools in our organization enable me to easily search for information I need.

7. The Market Intelligence tools in our organization enable me to visualize and analyze information.

Figure 16.6   Intelligence tools

Intelligence Organization

1. Our Market Intelligence people are very competent.

2. Our Market Intelligence team has the resources and the budget it needs to do a great job.

3. Our Market Intelligence is well-managed and has good leadership.

4. The top management in our organization sees our senior Market Intelligence experts as trusted advisors.

5. In addition to dedicated Market Intelligence people, our organization has a network of people who are actively contributing to producing intelligence.

6.   Our Market Intelligence team has access to the best available information sources.

7.   Our Market Intelligence actively makes use of experts from outside our organization.

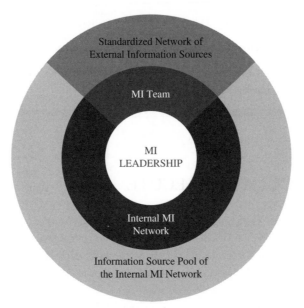

Figure 16.7   Intelligence organization

Intelligence Culture

1.   The top management of our organization actively shows its commitment to Market Intelligence.

2.   Our Market Intelligence deliverables have a brand of their own, e.g. a name, logo, or similar, that makes them easy to identify.

Figure 16.8   Intelligence Culture

(Continued)

> 3. Market Intelligence is very well-known throughout our organization.
>
> 4. Decision-makers in our organization see Market Intelligence as a necessary function or program.
>
> 5. We have an organization culture where information is actively shared.
>
> 6. Our top management uses Market Intelligence when making decisions.
>
> 7. Market Intelligence users in our organization actively offer their contributions and assistance to Market Intelligence.

LEARN, PLAN – AND EXECUTE

Mark noticed that almost every single statement in the questionnaire could be subject to lengthy sharing of thoughts, even debate. It would have been easy to get carried away with the assignment, but the facilitators reminded them to only briefly think about each of the KSFs and subsequently choose one that they would be working on in smaller groups to make use of the face time.

Mark had concluded that his company was doing quite OK with regards to the scope, process, deliverables, and organization, but there was room for improvement particularly on the tools and culture fronts. Hence Mark joined the "tools team" with Anne who had just implemented a sophisticated intelligence software product and would be happy to discuss her experiences from the project. Each group was to later present their findings and insights to the entire group, that way sharing ideas on each of the KSFs.

Towards the end of the day, Mark thought he would have plenty of ingredients to work with in preparing his own MI plan for the next two years. How the benchmarking project would continue, i.e. what particular topics would be on the agenda of the following meeting in three to four months' time, would be decided in consensus among the participants. However, judging by the amount of lively discussion, Mark thought there would be no shortage of topics. Additional ones would definitely be obtained from the Market Intelligence trends presentation that would conclude the workshop day.

Beneficial and inspiring as the workshop was, Mark also knew that the real acid test to its usefulness would not be how sophisticated the MI plans were that the participants would produce as a result, but how they would manage to execute them. Mark expected to hear experiences about that in the next workshop: the participants had challenged each other to provide concrete examples in the next meeting about new ideas that they had implemented in the meantime.

Case: Making the Leap from Data-crunchers to Market Intelligence Consultants and Trusted Advisors at Cisco Systems

"The market intelligence function at Cisco used to be viewed as simply a source of data. We have changed the perception of the function by changing our own behavior. We are not simply data-crunchers, but we ask people how they will use the market intelligence and for what purpose. We suggest what other information may be useful and proactively make recommendations", says Joost Drieman, director of market and business intelligence European markets, Cisco Systems Inc.

"In practice, I believe that to cultivate an intelligence culture means to first evaluate how we, as market intelligence experts, are doing in our roles. Often, it all boils down to one thing: consultancy skills", concludes Drieman. "What we did at Cisco was to first identify the change needed: a) improving the MI process, b) creating better relationships with MI users, and c) becoming trusted advisors to top management."

"We then conducted a five-day offsite training program in order to improve our internal consultative skills", Drieman says. "The topics we studied and trained ranged from how to engage top management in discussions, how to negotiate and argue in a positive way, the art of asking questions, differences between research/analysis projects, and consultative projects with management. The results were very good and the newly sharpened skills of the team were applicable immediately."

SUMMARY

- Provided that resources will not be a major bottleneck, an intelligence program can typically be brought to "Intermediate" levels on the World Class MI Roadmap in a relatively short timeframe, say one to two years.

- Reaching levels 4 and 5 on the MI Roadmap will require significantly more effort, as is the case with so many ambitions: to become average is quite easy, to really make a difference is not.

- While the characteristics of a World Class MI program can be outlined, and they indeed have been in this book, textbook instructions cannot be given about making a plan to take an MI program all the way to the "Futurist" levels. All companies are inherently different and so are their MI challenges, especially after the initial MI set up phase. Hence the best way to work towards world class levels in MI is to pose smart questions to self, learn from others, prepare a customized MI roadmap for one's own company – and to execute it methodically.

17 Demonstrating the Impact of Market Intelligence

"So now, if we decide to invest our time and money in an improved intelligence program, how can we be sure it yields benefits in excess of what the costs are?"

"Right", the MI director thinks. "The return on investment question. How can I demonstrate the impact that I expect MI to have? How do I convince my bosses that I can help generate that impact? Do I know what it takes in the first place?"

Market Intelligence (MI) professionals have been struggling to answer questions related to the expected value and impact of the MI investment for just about as long as the profession has existed. The struggle is inherently there: MI is just one function out of many that have an impact on the company's performance. It cannot be meaningfully isolated to accommodate for traditional return on investment (ROI) calculations.

And yet, questions about the expected, tangible benefits of MI almost always come up when a company is considering investments in market information. An investment by definition means that the future returns are expected to exceed the cost up front. Hence even if calculating the ROI on MI in exact terms for a specific company would be impossible, the question remains: on what grounds should we put some of our time and money into an improved MI capability?

This chapter approaches the value and impact of MI from three perspectives:

1. **Usage of MI in decision-making.** Whether a company is *ready* to adopt MI as a decision-making tool is not often the question under discussion when considering MI investments. However, it will be as important for the eventual value and impact of MI as the quality of the MI activity itself.

2. **Calculating the financial worth of MI.** Calculating the exact financial worth of MI investments at program or company level is virtually impossible. However, financial value can be calculated for specific projects and initiatives where MI plays a major role. Also, recent research shows that, on average, companies with world class MI have performed significantly better in the stock market than the average stock listed companies, indicating that high quality MI is linked to better overall company performance.

3. **The "soft" contributions of MI to company performance**. Companies with well-organized MI are able to make better grounded decisions faster than those without systematic MI. Decision-makers who have good experiences from MI will also help to further spread the culture of backing up decisions with shared insights. Executives and professionals save time from low value-adding data searches, and can rather concentrate on making educated decisions and generating new ideas based on insights.

FIRST THINGS FIRST: MARKET INTELLIGENCE IS ONLY IMPACTFUL WHEN IT IS USED

The starting point for most MI investment initiatives is an information needs analysis among decision-makers, i.e. the users of MI. Typically, decision-makers are quick to point out trends, market players, and geographical areas that the company should understand better. The wider the perceived gaps in market understanding, the more obvious the need for further MI investment is.

Indeed, many MI investment decisions have been made to just fill out the gaps in knowledge without paying too much attention to specific financial calculations. This is typical especially when financial resources are relatively easy to obtain.

Filling in gaps in market knowledge goes far beyond acquiring information, however. MI may be of high quality but what if it's not used? The traditional discussion about the worth of MI should be viewed from the perspective of the desired end result, i.e. educated decision-making, rather than from the point of view of the immediate MI deliverables: tools, reports, or market monitoring. MI should not exist for its own good.

Despite the conventional discussion about the merits of MI being frequently limited to assessing the direct value of MI tools and deliverables, some executives intuitively recognize the real question: whether their organization is ready to take on the challenge of "becoming smarter" and incorporating MI into the business activity. They will know that this is a process that often requires organizational transformation and, hence, time and leadership effort. They might question the MI director's ability to lead that change, and they might also question whether there is space on their own agendas to make room for the discussion that the MI deliverables will necessarily have to provoke in order to generate impact.

FOR MAXIMUM MARKET INTELLIGENCE IMPACT, EITHER AIM HIGH OR DO NOT START AT ALL

In essence, the eventual value of an MI investment is both an MI infrastructure (the tools, resources, and deliverables) question and a leadership question. The MI infrastructure is a necessary prerequisite for business impact; however, if not used, it becomes irrelevant with the exception of its price tag: an MI infrastructure will have its costs anyway. If its deliverables are not used, the return on the MI investment is necessarily negative. Hence the decision to invest in MI infrastructure should always go with the decision to invest time and leadership effort into using the program's output.

Viewed in the framework of GIA's World Class MI Roadmap, making the most of the investment in MI comes down to setting the long-term ambition level at levels 4 or 5 ("Director" and "Futurist", respectively). For maximum returns and impact, one should never settle with levels 3 ("Coordinator") or below. Why? Because advancing from a "Beginner" to a "Coordinator" (from level 1 to level 3), i.e. creating an "MI infrastructure" will necessarily consume financial resources in one form or other. Without a parallel investment on the "soft" side, i.e. gradually solidifying the MI network and fostering intelligence co-creation and systematic sharing of insights, the return on the financial MI investment may even remain on the negative side, i.e. only the costs will materialize and not the benefits. On the other hand, working towards making MI a natural part of the organization's everyday routines will help the organization make educated decisions at all levels and greatly improve the probability of success in the future.

When looking to demonstrate the impact of MI, companies should measure not the impact of MI infrastructure as such but the impact of all the activity that leverages that infrastructure. Eventually this is a leadership challenge, and it alone gives enough reason to treat any larger MI investments as a topic for the executive management to discuss and commit to.

Considering especially the investment required to adopt the MI deliverables and make them part of the company's routine processes, enough time should also be allowed for the eventual impact of MI to materialize. In a large organization, one year tends to be a short time when people also work with a number of other priorities and development initiatives than those related to MI.

For ambitious intelligence professionals, all of the above means that they will need to convince their internal stakeholders not only about the worth of the MI resources and infrastructure in the first place, but also about their own ability to do their share in facilitating the utilization of MI. Finally, however, MI's role in decision-making is that of advisor's: MI is responsible for giving high quality support to decision-making. Whether the eventual decisions are wise and correct, are the decision-makers' responsibility.

RETURN ON MARKET INTELLIGENCE INVESTMENT – THE CASE FOR AND AGAINST FINANCIAL CALCULATIONS

CHALLENGES WITH MEASURING FINANCIAL ROI FOR MARKET INTELLIGENCE

In the discussion so far we've stressed that the impact of MI as a program in the long run will require both financial and leadership investment. Neither of the two will yield high results without the other. Oftentimes in reality, however, the discussion about the value and benefits of MI really centers on the financial part, which is natural. No MI program will take off without any financial investment, and when money comes in to play so do the calculations of whether it will be spent or not. What do we expect the financial MI investment to produce on the bottom line in the future?

Traditionally, calculating the return on the financial investment in MI at a program or company level is problematic for at least three reasons:

1.   The revenues or benefits may be dependent on many other variables than MI, such as the overall market and economic conditions, new advertising programs by the company itself or competition, new regulatory developments, and so forth.

2.   MI is either used in decisions or it is not, and once a decision is made one cannot go back and see what would have happened if another one had been made.

3.   Many of the benefits of MI are typically deferred and qualitative, and so don't lend themselves to short-term, quantitatively-oriented return measures.

Hence, measuring exact, quantitative returns for MI at the entire corporate program's level is mostly artificial and even pointless.

LINKING WORLD CLASS MARKET INTELLIGENCE AND STOCK MARKET PERFORMANCE

Even though measuring financial ROI for an individual company's MI program as a whole is problematic, the Global MI Survey 2013 by GIA yielded a ground-breaking result. On average, those companies that run world class MI programs (11% of the 1,207 surveyed respondents), significantly beat the average of the most common stock market indices: where the world's major stock market indices gained, on average, 7% in 2012, the average share price increase among the companies with world class MI was 16.2% during 2012. Furthermore, the growth in profits during the same time period reached 10.3% for the companies with world class MI, while the average for Fortune 500 companies was only −0.55%.[1]

Since correlation does not mean causality, these findings alone do not mean that the sizable difference in stock market performance and profitability by companies with world class MI could be attributed to MI specifically. Nor does the result mean that any particular company that reaches world class levels in MI would automatically beat the stock market indices in return.

---

[1] *GIA research based on the Global MI survey 2013 (n = 1,207) and public company information, shows that global stock market indices grew an average of 7.0% in 2012. During the same year, the average share price increase for companies with world class market intelligence was 16.2%, which is a positive difference of 9.2 percentage points, or 131% faster growth. The market indices used in the research were: FTSEurofirst 300, S&P 500 Index, Nikkei 225 Tokyo, Dow Jones industrial average, Nasdaq Composite. Growth was calculated from 1 January 2012 to 31 December 2012 (or first and last trading day when applicable).*

However, the fact that high quality MI strongly correlates with superior share price performance should not come as a surprise: at world class levels, MI is inseparably embedded in the company's high performance culture. One may even ask whether there can exist many high performing companies in today's business world that do *not* run high quality MI programs.

Again, we come back to the combination of high quality MI output and the leadership investment that are both required in order for the company to maximize the returns on its MI investment. The stock market example suggests that, on average, companies where both the financial and the leadership investment in MI are in balance and produce world class results grew twice as fast as global stock markets. Remarkable in this context is to also note that, on average, companies with world class MI did not spend more money on their MI activity than an average company in the Global MI Survey 2013.

PROJECT SPECIFIC SUCCESS STORIES: WHERE CALCULATING CONCRETE FINANCIAL VALUE MAKES SENSE

We have discussed already that measuring the financial worth of an individual company's MI program is no exact science, since attributing successes or failures to the quality of MI program specifically is problematic. At the same time, on an aggregate level, high quality MI programs have been shown to link with stock market performance.

Growing business

Under the regular MI activity there are sometimes specific projects and initiatives where MI plays a particularly significant role. Here, some companies have identified opportunities to very tangibly demonstrate the value of high quality MI work. The MI director will do well to recognize these sort of opportunities to first maximize the impact of MI, and then prove the worth of the MI investment through subsequently building the success stories into promotional tools.

If, for instance, a large investment or a major sales opportunity has been secured thanks to MI efforts, it pays to make the achievement visible internally. Oftentimes, there will be individuals and functions in the organization that have not even realized that MI support could be available to them as well, and success stories may breed more of the same in the future.

Optimizing regular cost base

Most large companies are purchasing information in various formats and by many functions to begin with. What is often lacking is central coordination of purchases, or even the knowledge of who is buying what and where. It often pays financially to go through all the information sources that are being used in the company, to search for synergies and overlaps. At the same time as optimizing cost, information gaps that are shared among several interest groups can be filled.

Naturally, searching for synergies and removing duplicate costs is more than a technical exercise. The central MI director should treat people's budgets and independent decision power as potentially delicate topics and use consideration when suggesting changes to them based on the "common good". Especially in companies where businesses are relatively independent, it may make sense to do the cost optimization exercise within businesses, and only seek synergies where the similarities of information needs are the most apparent.

Case: Value of Competitor Monitoring to Product Launch Decision

A consumer products company was planning to launch a new product. The main competitor was anticipated to launch a similar product as well. The company was monitoring their main competitor on a daily basis, collecting intelligence from the media, press releases, investor reports, and so on. The market monitoring costs the company about USD 100,000 per year. The daily monitoring provided indications that the competitor was about to launch their product earlier than expected. As a result, the company decided to launch their own product ahead of schedule, and was able to get to the market two weeks ahead of the competitor. The management of the company estimated they were able to capture an extra USD 20 million of revenue during those two weeks.

Case: The Value of Multi-Country Research Project for a Divestment Decision

A large multinational company was making a decision to sell one of its product lines and needed MI to help in deriving a valuation for the business. This required detailed information about market size and competitive landscape. The company invested USD 500,000 in collecting data from 27 countries and created a highly analytical summary report. The MI project improved the company's bargaining power and the unit was successfully sold for a price that the top management estimated was millions of dollars higher than it would have been without the MI project.

Case: The Impact of Value Chain Analysis for Market Entry

An internationalizing company wanted to expand their business for one product into a new customer segment in a new industry. An MI project costing USD 75,000 was initiated to analyze the value chain of the industry from the point of view of market entry. The analysis included identification of key players, distribution of margins and decision-making power within the value chain, and recommendations for entry points and entry strategy into the industry. The company successfully entered the market based on the intelligence, and the management estimated they were able to enter the market substantially faster and with quicker results than without the intelligence projects, resulting in USD 5 million more revenue than targeted for the first year.

Avoiding incremental costs

The financial worth of MI can also be viewed from the perspective of avoiding other, potentially much higher, costs. For instance, pharmaceuticals companies that invest huge amounts of R&D resources into developing new drugs are typically keen to keep up to date with what their competition is doing. Accurate MI can easily save the company millions, for example, if a competitor's drug development program is detected early and the conclusion is made that it's pointless to continue investing in the company's own resources on that specific area.

THE LONG-TERM, QUALITATIVE BENEFITS OF MARKET INTELLIGENCE

BETTER AND FASTER DECISIONS

More than anything, MI is a tool for making educated decisions as opposed to merely doing guess-work. Although "decision-making" is a slippery concept and tough to measure accurately, the six Global MI Surveys conducted by GIA between 2005 and 2013 have consistently reported that respondents in companies with systematic MI perceive their decision-making as being more efficient than those in companies without MI. The difference in decision-making efficiency is still more pronounced in companies with world class MI (Figure 17.1).

What does it mean that decision-making is "efficient"? First, it's timely, i.e. making decisions is not significantly delayed due to missing information. Second, the eventual decisions are based on

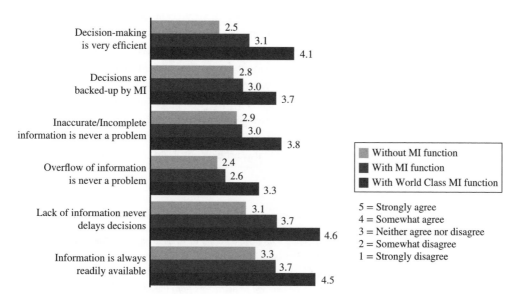

Figure 17.1   MI and the efficiency of decision-making
Source: Global market Intelligence Survey 2013, GIA.

researched facts. Third, decision-making is not significantly slowed down by unnecessary or misleading "noise" information getting in the way. While MI is not always flawless (surprises do happen and not all research uncovers all the right things), backing up decisions with facts greatly increases the probability of success in the long run.

INTERNAL CUSTOMER SATISFACTION

An MI program has internal customers that it serves; ideally a segmented customer base whose MI needs have been clearly defined and addressed. One of the obvious Key Performance Indicators (KPIs), and hence a measure of impact, for the MI activities is internal customer satisfaction. Measuring customer satisfaction is best linked with the overall performance evaluation of the MI director and the MI team. People's satisfaction with the MI program should be measured at least once every year; however, it also makes sense to conduct more targeted feedback surveys: with regular MI deliverables such as quarterly business area reviews, a quick poll could be linked to each delivery of the report. Major ad hoc studies such as research to back up an investment decision should always come with a feedback loop: the project should not only be presented and discussed, but the MI team should also make sure they will get their specific feedback in one format or other.

The MI software tools should also make it easy for people to express their views on MI topics spontaneously: one can calculate, for instance, the numbers of thumbs-up, comments on articles, or just plain visits to a software system as an indication of customer satisfaction with the company's MI activities.

The Net Promoter Score (NPS)[2] system has become a very common tool for companies to measure their external customer satisfaction. Increasingly, the NPS system is also being used for tracking the performance of internal functions, MI being one example. NPS is particularly suitable for the purposes of MI, since basing the assessment on the respondent's inclination to *promote* the MI deliverables gives a good indication of where the MI as a program is headed. One of the most important success factors of MI is the size and activity level of the internal network using and producing MI. Since the network will become stronger through people being encouraged to share their good experiences with what the program delivers, just the NPS measurement process itself may be a good internal marketing vehicle, and that way help contribute to the quality of the output of MI in the future.

---

[2] *In the NPS system, customers are asked to evaluate on a scale from 0 to 10 as to how likely they would be to promote the company's products and services to a colleague or a friend. Ratings between 0 and 6 make the customers "detractors", ratings 7–8 "passively satisfied", while only the ratings 9 and 10 make a respondent a "promoter". The NPS score is calculated by subtracting the percentage of detractors from the percentage of promoters. In the calculation, passively satisfied respondents are worth zero. NPS was originally developed by Satmetrix, Bain & Co., and Fred Reichheld.*

Finally, one must bear in mind that internal customer satisfaction does not always mean that the eventual MI deliverables are actually being used. Hence some of the customer satisfaction questions should ideally be geared towards measuring the tangible benefits of MI, not just the perceived benefits.

TIME SAVINGS

Several GIA surveys since 2005 have indicated that in companies that have a systematic MI program in place, decision-makers perceive that they save, on average, approximately one and a half hours per week from the frustrating search for business information. The time savings result from the MI users having constant access to timely and accurate business information that is relevant to them personally.

Technically, it will be easy to calculate a financial value for this saving based on an average hourly wage of a white-collar worker in the company. If we use a very conservative hourly average wage of USD 50 in a company where there are 300 active MI users, including top management, we end up saving the company USD 22,500 on a weekly basis, close to USD 100,000 per month, and more than a million dollars on an annual basis. Another way to look at the value of time savings is opportunity cost: if decision-makers *do not* spend their time drawing conclusions based on insightful MI, but rather wonder about where to find data, just how much is the cost of the business potentially forgone?

Despite the undeniable value of the time saved by highly paid experts and executives, the softer benefits may still outweigh the direct time savings of a well-managed MI program: the sheer fact of always knowing where to go to and whom to ask when in need of information seems to rank high among executives that seek to use their time wisely. *How* time is used often matters more than how *much* time is used. If an emerging MI topic calls for close attention, as might well happen when executives receive interesting enough market signals, the hours spent on the topic may exceed those that were originally saved thanks to the systematic MI program. Obviously, executives won't mind if the emerging topic represents a significant new business opportunity, or a potential competitive threat.

IDEA GENERATION AND KNOWLEDGE SHARING

Perhaps the most intangible impact that an MI program has on a company is the sharing of knowledge and ideas within the organization. While intangible, and hence impossible to measure accurately, shared knowledge and ideas may in the long run be one of the most powerful contributors to the company's success. The global competition already revolves around who is the fastest one to learn and renew: who can first bring innovative products to the market and reap the commercial benefits before the product is commoditized and its margins eroded.

At the end of the day, companies do not share knowledge and ideas but people do. Even though innovativeness requires far more than the MI program alone, MI can greatly contribute to the generation of new ideas. First, MI contributes to people's knowledge about the solutions currently existing and emerging in the marketplace. Second, MI may also support creativity by bringing in useful insights about adjacent industries. Many new ideas are actually old ones but introduced in a new context. Finally, MI often provides a platform for sharing thoughts on various topics inside the organization.

Systematic idea generation and knowledge sharing rarely happens automatically, but will require a lot of facilitation and structured workshopping. This is typically the area where companies lag behind, and it brings us back to the discussion in the first section of this chapter about the impact of an MI program as a whole. The greatest impact of MI is achieved in companies that invest not only in MI infrastructure, but also in the human work around it: leadership commitment, facilitated discussion, and dynamic co-creation of insights.

SUMMARY

This chapter approaches the value and impact of MI from three perspectives:

- Usage of MI in decision-making

- Financial ROI calculations for MI

- The "soft" contributions of MI to company performance

    o   MI is only impactful when used in decision-making. In the context of the GIA World Class MI Roadmap, this means that companies should either set the ambition level high in MI program development from the beginning or not start at all. This is because the first steps (from "Beginner" to "Coordinator") will involve financial costs anyway, yet without a parallel investment in adopting MI in the company's processes, that way bringing the company towards world class levels in MI, the company risks that only the costs will materialize while benefits will lag behind.

    o   Traditionally, calculating financial ROI on MI is difficult for three reasons:

        ◆   The revenues or benefits may be dependent on many other variables than MI.

        ◆   MI is either used in decisions or it is not, and once a decision is made one cannot go back and see what would have happened the other way.

        ◆   Many of the benefits of MI are typically deferred and qualitative in nature.

        Therefore, calculating an exact ROI for an MI program or a company is virtually impossible. However, ROI can sometimes be calculated relatively meaningfully for specific MI projects or initiatives such as large investments or sales opportunities.

o   A recent finding in the Global MI Survey 2013 by GIA indicated that on aver-
       age, companies with world class MI (11% of the surveyed 1,207 respondents)
       yielded 16.2% share price returns during 2012 while during the same time
       period, major stock market indices yielded an average of 7%. While these
       figures do not indicate the performance and ROI on MI for an individual
       company, they suggest that there is overall a positive relationship between
       extraordinary MI quality and extraordinary stock market performance.

o   The "soft" contributions of MI to company performance are varied: compa-
       nies with well organized MI are able to make better grounded decisions faster
       than those without systematic MI. Decision-makers who have good MI expe-
       riences will also help to further spread the culture of backing up decisions with
       shared insights. Executives and professionals save time from low value-adding
       data searches, and can rather concentrate on making educated decisions and
       generating new ideas based on insights.

18 Trends in Market Intelligence

Market Intelligence (MI) by its very definition is about looking into the future and providing actionable insights. However, what does the future hold in store for MI itself as a discipline and profession? In this chapter, we are looking into the anticipated developments of MI over the next few years, organized around the six Key Success Factors (KSFs) of MI in the World Class MI Development Roadmap.

The findings presented in the chapter are based on a global survey conducted by Global Intelligence Alliance (GIA) about MI trends specifically. A total 146 respondents of whom 83% were intelligence professionals and 17% end users, answered 19 questions, both closed and open ended ones.

The scale of the results presented in the exhibits runs from −2 (strongly disagree/decrease significantly) to +2 (strongly agree/increase significantly).

INTELLIGENCE SCOPE

The emerging growth markets such as China, Asia Pacific, Latin America, the Middle East, and Eastern Europe are rapidly becoming part of the geographic scope of most companies' intelligence programs. The primary focus in these areas is gradually shifting from looking at investment opportunities and market entry strategies to continuously keeping the areas on the radar screen. Many Western companies already have an established presence in the growth markets, and they now need to stay on top of the local market dynamics both on an everyday basis and looking into the future (Figure 18.1). As a result, processing and translating local language business information will most likely consume more resources than before.

From a value chain perspective, customers, end consumers, and competitors will continue to be the primary focus of the intelligence efforts for most surveyed companies; customers and end users since they drive the business whether in the mature markets or emerging ones, and competition since it typically influences the pricing and differentiation strategies (Figure 18.2). Suppliers and distributors, in turn, tend to be heavily on the radar of organizations in industries undergoing rapid changes in the value chain, i.e. M&A activity, partnerships and joint ventures on the supplier side, or, for instance, shifts in manufacturing technology or distribution strategies.

Which areas in the business environment will be under the heaviest change and therefore have the most significant impact on MI efforts?

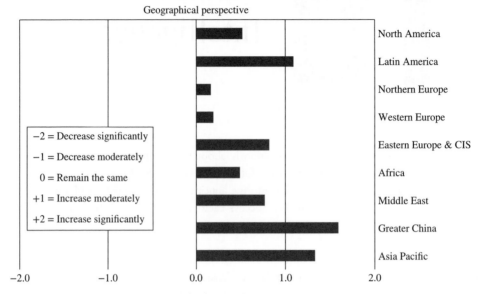

Figure 18.1   Anticipated changes in the regional scope of the intelligence program

Which areas in the business environment will be under the heaviest change and therefore have the most significant impact on MI efforts?

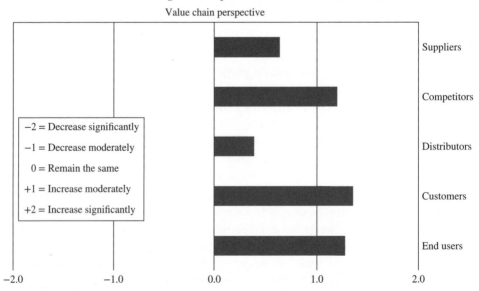

Figure 18.2   The dominant focus of MI efforts continues to be on the front end of the value chain

The scope of the intelligence efforts is initially determined by the needs analysis for the MI program that should be revisited once in a while even if the company is not expanding to new geographic areas, or its value chain remains stable. Intelligence program user groups are also part of the scope of the activity, and the existing intelligence infrastructure can be leveraged to serve additional corporate functions and activities, of which risk management is an emerging example.

RISK MANAGEMENT EMERGING AS AN APPLICATION AREA OF MARKET INTELLIGENCE

With the Sarbanes-Oxley Act in force since 2002 and the more recent major failures in corporate risk management, it is becoming increasingly important for especially public companies to comply with strict risk control measures both financially and qualitatively. From the MI perspective, this means that, for instance, sizable strategic investment decisions should be backed up with sound research and analysis, not only to ensure business success in the first place, but also to avoid the management being held liable afterwards for bad decisions made based on improper or missing information.

MI can bring an external point of view to the risk management discussion that is typically internally focused: on top of internal business risks, management should consider risks originating from the customer base, competitive dynamics, macroeconomic factors, political environment, or technological shifts.

INTELLIGENCE PROCESS

The survey results suggest that social media applications will be used increasingly for collecting and sharing information for MI purposes. Three perspectives were specifically brought up in the survey:

- **Information collection and analysis around individuals.** By monitoring the activities in social media of some key people at customer, competitor, and supplier organizations, it will be possible to identify projects, new competence areas, travel plans, business relationships, and open positions that combined tell a lot about the company's strategy and initiatives.

- **Internal use of features from social media applications.** Competitor and customer wikis will be created in order to enhance the internal knowledge about them. Blogs will be used in order to provide internal context and alternative perspectives to relevant business signals, and crowd forecasting will emerge as a parallel tool to traditional forecasting methods.

- **Cultural shift triggered by social media.** As people get used to both networking virtually and communicating on the go through smartphones and pocket computers, it should become easier to engage different parts of the organization in the daily intelligence efforts.

The survey results give strong support to co-creation as an emerging trend also in the corporate world, i.e. intelligence deliverables are created jointly by MI professionals and various decision-makers and stakeholders. In practice, MI professionals will need to increasingly give briefings and presentations and facilitate workshops such as scenario planning, war gaming, and others arranged around strategic topics.

From the MI perspective, the co-creation trend means two things:

- Decision-makers, i.e. the end users of the intelligence deliverables, will engage more tightly in the process of actually producing the insights. This is typically rewarding for the intelligence professionals who will get to see the strategic decision-making process that will leverage the intelligence efforts.

- However, to claim their position as the management's trusted advisors, intelligence professionals must truly understand the company's business fundamentals and the management's mindset, and incorporate this understanding in their deliverables in an analytical and thought-provoking manner. In practice, co-creating intelligence deliverables with management does not mean less work for the intelligence professionals, but more.

The survey results in Figure 18.3 suggest that ideally in the future the intelligence team needs to spend their time on taking the intelligence deliverables to a high analytical level, after which it is time for the management to get involved and reach the final conclusions jointly with the intelligence team. Not surprisingly, the analysis process as a whole is not something that many companies

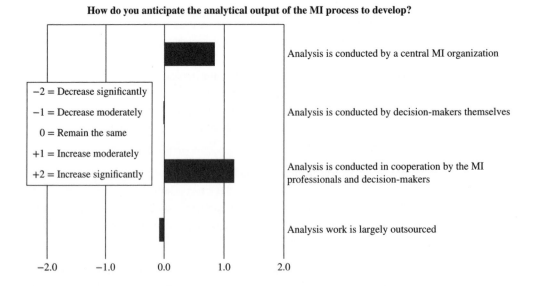

Figure 18.3   Anticipated developments in the analysis process

would see being outsourced; neither would management spend much time on turning information into analyses. Outsourcing other parts of the intelligence process than analysis will, on the other hand, be considered in the interest of liberating time from the in-house resources to concentrate on working close to the management and decision-making.

STANDARDIZATION OF THE MARKET INTELLIGENCE PROCESS THROUGHOUT THE ORGANIZATION

Typically in large organizations, intelligence efforts first emerge in regional units, without any significant central coordination that would ensure uniform research approaches, analysis methods, or presentation templates. Many companies have realized, however, that building a solid world class intelligence program that is recognized company-wide requires a headquarters-centric approach to ensure that the local units have a common platform to base their own efforts on. By at least partly standardizing the presentation templates, analysis frameworks, and sourcing of data, companies will achieve cost savings, avoid doing double work, facilitate cross-functional cooperation, and maximize the benefits of the intelligence program for the entire organization.

DECISION-POINT INTELLIGENCE

One of the frequently mentioned topics in the survey – and indeed in any MI-related discussions lately – is the integration of MI into decision-making and corporate business processes. Considering the popularity of the topic, it is surprising how few companies to date can honestly say that their decision-point intelligence is in good shape, i.e. that all strategic decisions have been backed up with timely and well prepared analyses. Two conclusions can be drawn:

- Intelligence teams still need to work further on proactively understanding the business fundamentals and growth drivers of the company – and the related decision-making processes.

- Decision-makers, in turn, need to understand that the intelligence teams will need continuous visibility not only to the concrete assignments that are requested from them, but to the decision-points in the background from which the intelligence needs are derived.

INTELLIGENCE DELIVERABLES

In general, MI deliverables will become increasingly sophisticated as time goes on. The survey results suggest that MI products in the future will feature an increased level of analysis and insight, online availability, and still greater future-orientation. The sophistication of the intelligence deliverables ties in

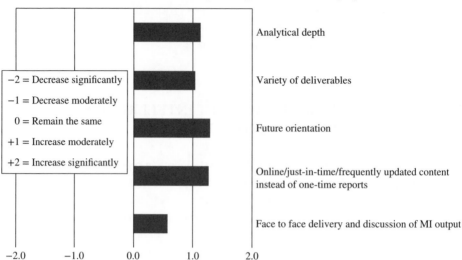

Figure 18.4   The anticipated development in MI deliverables

with the overall stage of development of the intelligence program; combining experience with tools and resources it is possible to concentrate on increasingly analytical and future-oriented intelligence output, such as analytical deep-dives, scenario analysis, and war gaming workshops, while in the early stages there's typically more emphasis on rather basic deliverables (Figure 18.4).

The survey respondents do not seem to put as much emphasis on the face to face delivery and discussion about the intelligence deliverables as on the technical qualities such as analytical depth and future orientation. This is somewhat surprising considering the earlier discussed trend of increased co-creation and interaction between decision-makers and intelligence professionals. The results can perhaps be interpreted from a timeline perspective: the need to develop the technical qualities of the deliverables is still more immediate for many companies than the face to face delivery that only comes as the next step.

Figure 18.5 highlights areas where the respondents expected the intelligence deliverables to develop the most over the coming years. Additional trends and developments that were raised in the survey through the questions and open comments included:

- **Increasingly visualized intelligence deliverables.** Using graphs, dashboards, and score cards to visualize the analytical output of the MI process as opposed to delivering results in plain text and figures format. This trend again ties in with resourcing the intelligence function adequately: producing insightful visuals requires time, highly analytical thinking, and a solid understanding of the company's business fundamentals.

- **Measuring the impact of the MI deliverables.** Related to the increased investment in the intelligence program, companies are becoming increasingly aware of the

How do you see the end user value of the following intelligence deliverables developing?

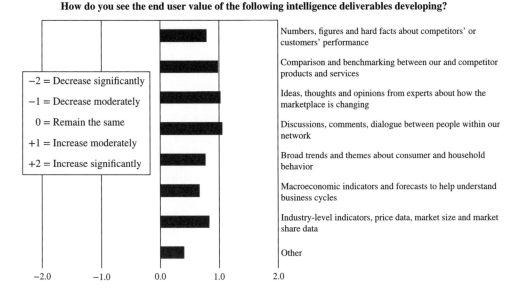

Numbers, figures and hard facts about competitors' or customers' performance

Comparison and benchmarking between our and competitor products and services

−2 = Decrease significantly

−1 = Decrease moderately

0 = Remain the same

+1 = Increase moderately

+2 = Increase significantly

Ideas, thoughts and opinions from experts about how the marketplace is changing

Discussions, comments, dialogue between people within our network

Broad trends and themes about consumer and household behavior

Macroeconomic indicators and forecasts to help understand business cycles

Industry-level indicators, price data, market size and market share data

Other

Figure 18.5   Value of MI deliverables

necessity of keeping track of the benefits. In the future, the survey respondents expected to see more of measures such as communicated success stories, direct feedback requests, and usage statistics of certain intelligence deliverables.

- **Adding the early warning and opportunity perspective to existing MI deliverables.** Interpreting market signals and analyses from the perspective of both negative and positive risks for the company will increase the strategic value of the intelligence deliverables. The early warning and opportunity perspective will also provide a framework for assessing the relative importance of different developments in the operational environment of the company.

- **Personalized delivery.** While it is not meaningful for the intelligence team to even aim at personally delivering all intelligence output, much of the greatest strategic value is typically created not alone by either decision-makers or intelligence professionals, but in groups of both. Therefore as the intelligence deliverables develop towards increased sophistication, the survey respondents expect to see more and more briefings, workshops, and informal discussions as the delivery format of strategic level intelligence output.

- **Decision-point intelligence.** Referring to the already discussed topic of the linkage between intelligence programs and business processes, we need to once again stress that decisions drive intelligence efforts. Therefore the intelligence deliverables will need to be built around the decision points that the intelligence input is needed for. This is not possible without an open dialogue and through needs analysis conducted jointly by the intelligence team and the decision-makers themselves.

INTELLIGENCE TOOLS

As Figure 18.6 illustrates, the top four trends that surfaced from the survey results regarding the respondents' preferences of receiving information in the future were:

- RSS feeds to individual desktop

- information feeds from Google or other free information sources to the desktop

- using smartphones for MI purposes

- using video materials (through e.g. YouTube) for MI purposes

At the same time, delivering information in paper format or through radio and television was expected to further decrease in volume.

The survey also looked into the technologies that the respondents expected to be in MI use in the future (Figure 18.7). In addition to smartphones, crowd forecasting tools, Microsoft SharePoint, and social media platforms were mentioned as technologies that will shape the way intelligence is being produced and communicated in the future.

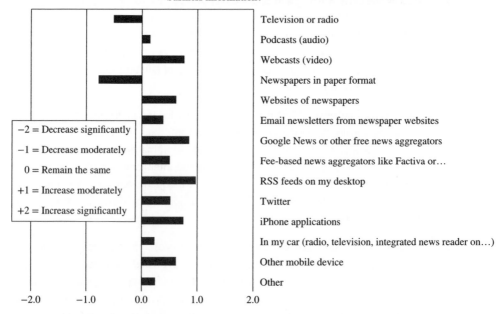

How do you expect your own preferences to develop over the next 5 years regarding receiving business information?

Figure 18.6   Development of MI-related IT tools

How do you expect new technologies to change the way business information is shared in your organization over the next 5 years?

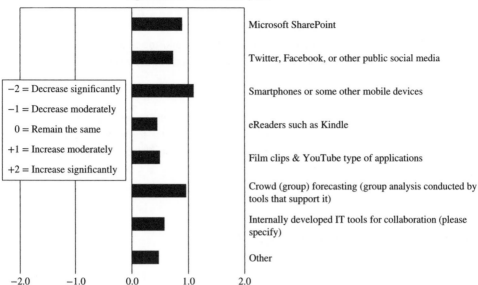

Figure 18.7   Technologies that will have an impact on MI activities

Several tools and technologies also provoked commentary in the survey:

- Collaborative tools: wikis, blogs, and crowd forecasting

The internal use of wikis around, for instance, competitors, customers, or key markets will increase. The technology of course only provides the platform; however, with people growing increasingly used to being part of virtual communities, the survey respondents expected the internal wikis to be adopted rather quickly. Crowd forecasting tools are also emerging rapidly, as people have started to see their value in quickly facilitating the co-creation of insights to relevant business topics. Finally, blogs are not a new phenomenon, but their use for MI purposes is still in its infancy. The potential future impact of blogs is huge, however, as people in general tend to be more interested in provocative viewpoints and opinions than plain newspieces and neutral business analyses.

- Artificial intelligence and desktop text mining tools

While the technical tools to aid automated analysis have been under discussion for a long time already, there are few signs yet of any tangible developments in the area. The interest is there, however, especially as the intelligence teams are looking forward to drive their own work towards drawing analytical conclusions and discussing them with management rather than spending time on the early phases of analyzing data.

- Geographical Information Systems (GIS) tools for providing geo-demographical and competitor data

The GIS applications to provide geo-demographic data about customers (and competitors) have gained ground rapidly over the last few years, and their value as an MI tool has subsequently increased. Further growth was expected in the survey results as well.

- Integration of different technical tools

With most companies already looking at several separate systems that all cater to intelligence needs (CRM systems, MI/CI software, intranets, social media platforms, etc.), increasingly many are also seeing the necessity to integrate these tools, at the very least by arranging for a single point access to all systems.

INTELLIGENCE ORGANIZATION

Based on the survey results, there's growth to be expected in MI investment following the initial impact of the economic downturn in 2008 (Figure 18.8). However, it is good to

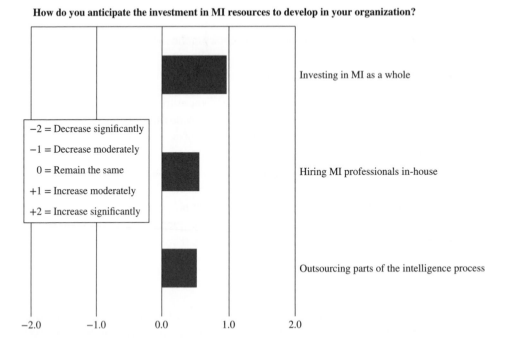

Figure 18.8   Development of MI investment

remember that many companies did *not* downsize their intelligence programs in the first place, as there has been an urgent need for companies to quickly identify new business opportunities to fill in the revenue gaps generated by the recession. As for the split of resources, the survey results suggest that there's a balance between hiring professionals in-house and outsourcing parts of the process.

Interestingly, many respondents expected the degree of centralization to increase in the intelligence organization, while at the same time the open comments suggested the opposite; i.e. that the level of decentralization would increase.

The polarization of the responses can perhaps be explained by the increasing maturity of the intelligence programs in many responding companies. On one hand, centrally coordinating, branding, and facilitating the intelligence program gained a lot of support – not least since this typically also means the program has top management's strong support. On the other hand, as the intelligence program becomes increasingly embedded in the organization, local and unit-specific intelligence activities also become more systematic, which in turn speaks of decentralization of the intelligence program. As a conclusion, both the centralization and decentralization trends can simultaneously take the corporate intelligence program towards increased sophistication.

INCREASINGLY INDEPENDENT CORPORATE LEVEL MARKET INTELLIGENCE TEAMS

Some respondents to the survey indicated that in the future, MI units might become more independent, being no longer organized under a specific function such as business development, marketing, or strategic planning. This development will likely make the intelligence teams increasingly neutral stakeholders in the organization, enabling them to give independent support to different business processes, which should serve the entire company's interests.

OUTSOURCING OF BASIC MARKET INTELLIGENCE ACTIVITIES TO INCREASE

The survey respondents expected to see outsourcing activities around the following activities:

- Collecting information from external sources

Monitoring news, blogs, websites, and analysis reports will typically be outsourced. Increasingly, companies are also looking to outsource the management of their entire information source portfolio in the interest of optimizing subscription costs.

- Structuring information

While IT tools already provide some help in structuring the regular flow of informa-tion, much of the work still needs to be done manually, and companies expect this part, too, to be a potential outsourcing area in the future. Examples of outsourced deliverables may be company or industry profiles, regular sales leads reports, or monthly industry briefings.

- IT tools for MI

Despite the initial interest of many companies in tweaking existing corporate IT tools to also serve MI purposes, the survey results suggest many have realized that developing and maintaining such in-house tools is so resource-consuming that the company's internal resources are best used elsewhere. Hence IT tools were viewed as one of the typical areas where outsourcing would be considered.

- MI process set up

Especially companies with little previous knowledge about the intelligence processes and tools typically consider using external help in setting up the intelligence program. With the increasing maturity of the profession, however, it is also typical for a company to hire an experienced MI executive from another company to build up the capability, once the mandate has been given by the management.

- Additional viewpoints and methodologies from outside of the own company

Some of the respondents to the survey also saw value in engaging external consultants in the high level analytical work. These companies considered that outsourcing would bring in additional analytical viewpoints and specific methodological skills such as scenario planning or war gaming.

INTELLIGENCE CULTURE

The importance of executive commitment and active internal marketing of the intelligence program were also reflected in the survey results, suggesting that the above will continue to be the key success drivers for the intelligence program also in the future (Figure 18.9).

An intelligence culture, like culture in general, is much about social cohesion, common beliefs, and common behavior. The fundamentals such as management's support and marketing efforts will continue to drive the intelligence culture, but an interesting addition will be brought by not the social media tools themselves, but by people growing familiar with expos-ing their thoughts and views to large virtual audiences. The survey results indicate that this trend might bring significant changes to the cultural side of corporate intelligence activities, going forward.

Please rate the most useful tools in developing a corporate (MI) culture

Executive commitment

MI Training for new employees

MI Training for all employees

−2 = Decrease significantly

−1 = Decrease moderately

0 = Remain the same

+1 = Increase moderately

+2 = Increase significantly

Marketing of the MI activities within the company

Making MI deliverables recognizably differentiated by logo, name, report structure, etc.

Making people accountable for MI efforts in their personal assessments

Providing incentives such as prizes or social recognition

Demonstrating the value of the MI output to its users on an everyday basis

−2.0   −1.0   0.0   1.0   2.0

Figure 18.9   Tools for developing the intelligence culture in the future

SUMMARY

This chapter highlights some of the most significant global trends in MI that will continue to shape corporate MI programs and their influence on decision-making over the years to come.

Intelligence scope

- Customers, end users and competitors as the change drivers

- Emerging markets presenting the biggest opportunities and hence driving the intelligence efforts

Intelligence process

- Intelligence co-creation

- Decision-point intelligence (MI integrated to major business processes)

- Social media tools becoming part of the intelligence process

Intelligence deliverables

- Increasingly sophisticated intelligence deliverables
- Increased degree of future orientation
- More emphasis on providing conclusions, provocative arguments, and executive briefings on strategic topics

Intelligence organization

- Centralization and decentralization trends in parallel; both representing progress
- Intelligence networks and expert teams (fixed and virtual teams)
- Outsourcing of non-core activities

Intelligence tools

- RSS feeds to desktop, free news aggregation, and video webcasts
- Mobile devices will be used increasingly as tools for sharing intelligence
- Graphical approaches and dashboards ensure a high degree of visualization

Intelligence culture

- Executive commitment
- Demonstrating the value of MI on an everyday basis
- Internal branding of MI, training of users
- Social media paving the way for increased virtual collaboration

Index

ABB automation technologies   12–15
acceptance, Intelligence Culture   134, 135, 139
account management   175–86
  needs   177, 178–80
  process needs   178
  support   183
acquisitions see mergers & acquisitions
action plan, world class MI programs   224
ad hoc projects   10, 30, 90, 95
  B2B/B2C contrast   44–5
  EWOS   171-2
  world class MI programs   224
advisory services   92, 120, 128–9, 239
advocacy, Intelligence Culture   139
aerospace company case   212–13
African region   34
ammonium bi-fluoride assessment case   84–5
analysis
  inaccurate/incomplete information   26
  industry analysis   182, 225
  intelligence portals   104
  Intelligence Process   78–9, 255, 256–7
  Intelligence Scope   70, 72
  macroeconomic analysis   169, 211
  market attractiveness   169-70
  market monitoring   145
  market size and share   181–2
  oil company case   166-7
  outsourcing   264
  PESTEL analysis   166
  product life cycle stages   197–8
  reports   93
  retail company case   183–4
  software selection   108–9
  Statoil case   231
  teams   120
  see also cost benefit analysis; industry analysis; needs
    analysis; scenario analysis; strategic analysis
annual strategy clocks   158, 159–60
apparel company case   3
approved vendor listing (AVL), purchasing   204, 205
artificial intelligence   112, 261
Asia Pacific region   34–5, 253
assessment case, ammonium bi-fluoride   84–5
Assessment Questionnaire   233–8
assistance, Intelligence Culture   134, 135
AVL (approved vendor listing), purchasing   204, 205
awareness
  Intelligence Culture   134–5, 138–9
  organizational-wide   143–56

B2B companies see business-to-business
    companies
B2C companies see business-to-consumer
    companies
"Beginners"
  description   57
  Key Success Factors   55
  World Class MI Roadmap   219, 243
benchmarking   33, 184, 205, 208, 210–11, 227–32, 238
benefits see Market Intelligence, benefits
Best Buy case   96–8
best-in-class
  procurement   210
  purchasing   208
best practices   136–7, 227–32
Beurschgens, Andrew   162–5
BI see Business Intelligence
blogs   153, 255, 261
boards of directors see top management
bottlenecks removal   81–2
bottom line, IT company   17
branding   97, 131–4, 138–9
briefing packs, Orange UK case   164
briefings   93–4
Britton, Philip   96–8
Brooijmans, Jan   71
budgets, MI   32–3, 34–8
  B2B/B2C contrast   46
  bottleneck removal   81
  industry comparison   49
  world class   40–1, 43, 224
business cycle study, chemical industry   84
Business Intelligence (BI)
  ABB automation technologies   12–13
  Lubrizol Corporation case   63
  Orange UK case   162–4
  tools   103
  Vopak liquid storage company   57, 59–61
  see also Market Intelligence
business-to-business (B2B) companies
  account management   183
  B2C differences   46–8
  Global Market Intelligence surveys   21, 30, 43–8
  marketing and sales   177, 183
  sales leads monitoring   184–5
business-to-consumer (B2C) companies
  B2B differences   46–8
  Global Market Intelligence surveys   21, 30, 43–8
  marketing and sales   177
buying functions see purchasing

car tire manufacturer case   189
centralization   41–2, 48, 109, 125, 263
change, global organizations   6–8
channel intelligence, Cisco Systems case   73
chemical industry case   84
chief executive officers (CEOs)
    head of MI relationship   27, 28
    Intelligence Culture   132, 134, 136–7
China/Chinese companies   6, 184, 253
CI see competitive intelligence
Cintas case   123–5, 156
CIS (Commonwealth of Independent States)
        case   84–5
Cisco Systems case   73–5, 239
co-creation
    Intelligence Culture   135
    Intelligence Deliverables   88, 89, 94
    Intelligence Process   256
    Intelligence Tools   109, 111–12
    workshops   171
coatings and paints company case   112
collaboration
    social media and   152–4
    software selection   108, 111–12
    tools   261
collecting intelligence   101–13, 185, 255, 263
commercialized innovations   190, 193
Commonwealth of Independent States (CIS)
        case   84–5
company strategy see corporate strategy; strategy
competition
    understanding   175–80
    value chain   253
competitive action, Cintas case   156
competitive intelligence (CI)
    car tire manufacturer case   189
    Cisco Systems case   73
    Statoil case   230
    see also Market Intelligence
competitive landscape, company taxonomy   151–2
competitive technical intelligence (CTI)   189
competitiveness
    decision-makers   3–8
    MI definition   9
competitor analysis
    innovation/product life cycle management   198
    Orange UK case   164
    retail company case   183–4
competitor monitoring, product launching   246
competitor reaction analysis   164
concept phase, innovation/product life cycle
        management   194
conferences see management conferences
consultation   70, 120, 239
content management features, software   107
content, market monitoring   150–2

context, market monitoring   150–2
continuous development
    Intelligence Culture   137–9
    Intelligence Deliverables   94–5
    Intelligence Organization   127–9
    Intelligence Process   83–5
    Intelligence Scope   72–3
    Intelligence Tools   111–12
    Vopak liquid storage company   60–1
continuous market monitoring   10
    customer processes   186
    innovation/product life cycle management   199
    purchasing   210
    strategic sourcing   212
continuous services   90–1, 144–5
"Coordinators"
    description   57
    Key Success Factors   55, 56
    World Class MI Roadmap   219, 243
corporate function, Intelligence Scope   65
corporate-level market intelligence teams   263
corporate strategy
    needs analysis   67
    Statoil case   229–32
corporate-wide scope, MI professionals   31–2
cost base optimization   245–6
cost–benefit analysis
    Intelligence Scope   117
    Key Intelligence Topics   69
cost-efficiency, IT departments   104–5
cost savings   15–17, 209, 247
country risk analyses, logistics   211
crowd forecasting   109, 255, 260, 261
CTI (competitive technical intelligence)   189
culture see Intelligence Culture
customer processes
    Intelligence Deliverables to support   180–6
    MI needs   176–80
    support tools for   186
customers
    Cisco Systems case   73
    profiles   183
    satisfaction   248–9
    understanding   175–80
    value chain   68, 253
cyclical intelligence process   77–79, 81–2

data
    Cisco Systems case   239
    Global Market Intelligence survey   2013   22–4
    insight and   8–17
    Intelligence Process   77–86
data sourcing
    market monitoring   149
    software   107
    world class MI programs   225

databases 122, 145
DCs see distribution centers
decentralization 41–2, 109, 125, 263
  see also outsourcing
decision-makers/decision-making
  challenges 3–8
  co-creation trend 256
  efficiency 26–7, 39–40, 247–8
  impact of MI 241–6, 244
  "information disconnect" 9
  information needs 80
  insight/information requirements 8
  Intelligence Process 77, 83, 257
  market signals delivery 153
  MI programs 11–12
  strategic planning 157–8, 161
decision-point intelligence 79–80, 94, 257, 259
  concept phase 194
  development phase 195
  idea generation 194
  launch phase 195
  post-launch phase 196
  product life cycle management 193
deliverables
  B2B/B2C contrast 45
  MI teams 30
  see also Intelligence Deliverables
delivery format, Intelligence Process 79
desktop text mining tools 261
development phase, innovation/product life cycle
    management 194–5
diesel engines market case 170
"Directors"
  description 57
  Key Success Factors 55
  World Class MI Roadmap 219, 243
directors of companies' needs 176
discussion forums, monitoring 157
disseminating intelligence 101–13
dissemination features, software 107–9
distribution centers (DCs), aerospace company
    case 212–13
diversified teams 230
divestment 14–15, 246
divisional strategy, Luvata case 159
Drieman, Joost 73–5
dry ice purchasing case 203
DSM Open Innovation case 199–201
Dunkin' Brands case 136–7

Early Warning and Opportunity System
    (EWOS) 146–7, 154–5, 158, 161–2,
    171–2, 259
Eastern Europe, Intelligence Scope 253
ecological aspects see PESTEL analysis
economic aspects see PESTEL analysis

efficiency
  decision-making 26–7, 39–40, 247–8
  time/cost savings 15–17
emerging economies 6–7, 253
  see also China/Chinese companies
end users, value chain 253
energy company case 143
engagement of organization, Intelligence
    Culture 131–40
enterprise resource planning systems 209
environment intelligence, Cisco Systems case 73
Europe see Eastern Europe; Western Europe
EWOS see Early Warning and Opportunity
    System
executive-level champions 128
expertise database, intelligence portals 122
external information sources 109
  outsourcing 126, 263
  portfolio 115
  standardized network of 119–21
  strategic planning 167
external networks 128, 231

face to face delivery 258
feedback
  innovation/product life cycle management 200–1
  Intelligence Process 79
  internal customer satisfaction 248
field signals, IT services company case 154
financial crisis, 2008 7
financial services company case 131
financial worth of MI 241, 243–7, 249
  see also return on investment
"Firefighters"
  description 57
  Intelligence Scope 66
  Key Success Factors 55
  World Class MI Roadmap 219
flu vaccine manufacturers case 184
focus areas, Intelligence Scope 63–76
forecasting
  Intelligence Scope 71
  strategic planning 166
  strategic sourcing 212
  see also crowd forecasting
forums see discussion forums
front end sales 13
  see also sales
future orientation
  Intelligence Scope 70–3
  timing of actions and 147–8
Future Watch process 158, 161–2, 166–9
"Futurists"
  description 57
  Key Success Factors 55
  World Class MI Roadmap 219, 243

gaming industry analysis case 182
geographical dimension
   Global Market Intelligence survey
      2013 23
   Key Intelligence Topics 69
   mergers & acquisitions analysis 170-1
   see also regional distribution
Geographical Information Systems (GIS) 262
geographical positioning tools 112
GIA see Global Intelligence Alliance
GIS (Geographical Information Systems) 262
Global Intelligence Alliance (GIA) 10
   benchmarking service 33
   Intelligence Plaza® 106
   trends survey 253
Global Market Intelligence surveys 10
   2011 findings 24–5, 47–8
   2013 findings 21–49, 244
   conducting survey 22–4
global organizations 1–49
   change 6–8
   operating environment 4–5, 7
   state of MI 2013 24–5
global responsibilities, MI professionals 31–2
group analysis, software selection 109
growth
   decision-makers 3–8
   future orientation as facilitator 73
   impact of MI 245

head of MI
   appointing 118
   CEO relationship 27, 28
   challenges 217
   software selection 109
   see also leadership
health and wellness sector 7
Heineken Portugal case 106
human resources see people
hydrofluoric acid market case 84–5

idea generation 17, 192, 249–50
impact of MI 241–51, 258–9
in-house resources versus outsourcing 125–7
inaccurate/incomplete information 26–7
incremental costs avoidance 247
incremental innovations 191
independence, corporate-level market intelligence
      teams 263
industrial diesel engines market case 170
industries
   comparison 36–8, 49
   Global Market Intelligence survey 2013 23, 29–31,
      34–8, 49
   value chain 5
industry analysis 182, 225
industry surveys, procurement 211

information
   architecture 67–70, 72, 93
   collection around individuals 255
   decision-making requirements 8
   delivery, technology/people relationship 150
   flow, intelligence portals 102
   inaccurate/incomplete 26–7
   "must know"/"nice to know" 143–4
   structuring 263–4
   time/cost savings 15–16
"information disconnect" 9
information overload 143
information sources
   external/internal 109
   intelligence portals 103–4
   needs analysis 80
   outsourcing 126, 263
   secondary 78, 91
   standardized network of 119–21
   strategic planning 167
   team's portfolio 115
information technology (IT)
   case studies 16–17, 154
   customer processes 186
   departments 104–8, 109, 110–11
   industry budgets 36
   outsourcing 126
   software selection 109, 110–11
   trends in tools 264
innovation management, description 191
innovation and product life cycle management 189–202
   benefits of MI 190
   Intelligence Deliverables to support 196–201
   Intelligence Scope 65
   market monitoring 198–201
   MI needs 192–6
innovations
   description 191
   impact of MI 249–50
input features, software 107
insight
   creation 159
   data from 8–17
   decision-making 8
   Intelligence Process 77–86
   IT company 16–17
   Orange UK case 162–3
integration
   intelligence portals 102, 105, 111–12
   market monitoring 148
   strategic planning 159–60
   technical tools 262
intellectual property rights (IPRs) 194, 198
Intelligence Culture 38, 131–40
   Assessment Questionnaire 237–8
   definition 56
   maturity levels 55
   planning optimization 133–7

social media and 255
trends 264–5
Vopak liquid storage company 61
world class 137–9, 219, 221–2
intelligence cycle 77–79, 81–2
Intelligence Deliverables 38, 87–99
actionability best practices 136–7
Assessment Questionnaire 234–5
awareness 135
B2B/B2C contrast 45
branding 138–9
capability optimization 88–94
centralization versus decentralization 125
classification 87
concrete products 92–4
customer process support 180–8
definition 56
innovation/product life cycle management
    support 196–201
market monitoring 149
maturity levels 55
product types 92–4
quality 88
rapid response research/strategic analysis 82
strategic planning 165–75
supply chain management 210–13
target groups 69
trends 257–9
Vopak liquid storage company 60, 61
world class 72, 94–5, 128, 219, 221–2
see also deliverables
Intelligence Organization 38, 115–30
Assessment Questionnaire 236–7
definition 56
evolution of 116
maturity levels 55
planning for optimization 117–27
trends 262–4
world class 127–9, 219, 221–2
Intelligence Plaza® 106
intelligence portals 90–1, 101–2, 144
customer processes 186
expertise database 122
planning/implementing 103–9
world class levels 111–12
Intelligence Process 38, 77–86
Assessment Questionnaire 233–4
definition 56
developing 79–82
market monitoring 149
maturity levels 55
outsourcing 126
standardization 257
trends 255–7, 264
world class 83–5, 219–20
Intelligence Scope 38, 63–76
Assessment Questionnaire 233
bottleneck removal 81

breadth 64, 67–70
centralization versus decentralization 125
cost–benefit analysis 117
definition 56
depth 64, 70
determining scope 66–71
maturity levels 55
trends 253–5
Vopak liquid storage company 59
World Class MI Roadmap 219–20
Intelligence Tools 38, 101–13
Assessment Questionnaire 235–6
definition 56
maturity levels 55
trends 260–2
world class 111–12, 219–20, 222
interest groups
global organizations 5
software tools 108
"internal branding" 133
internal customer satisfaction 248–9
internal information sources 109, 167
internal networks 115, 121–5
recruiting members 122–3
Statoil case 231
world class 128
internal stakeholders
B2B/B2C contrast 44
world class MI function companies 42
interviews, needs analysis 67, 223
inventions 190, 191
inventory management, logistics 208–9
investment, return on, MI 25–6, 36–8, 49,
    67, 241–7
investor relations, Intelligence Scope 65
IPRs see intellectual property rights
issue resolution process, EWOS 172

judgmental analysis forecasting 166
just-in-time delivery systems 208

Key Intelligence Topics (KITs) 67
determining 67–70
market signals 93
scale of 68–9
world class levels 72
Key Performance Indicators (KPIs), internal customer
    satisfaction 248
Key Success Factors (KSFs)
definitions 56
market monitoring 149
outsourcing 126–7
world class MI 38–9, 53–62, 220–2
see also Intelligence Culture; Intelligence Deliverables;
    Intelligence Organization; Intelligence Process;
    Intelligence Scope; Intelligence Tools
KITs see Key Intelligence Topics
knowledge sharing, impact of MI 249–50

Korean flu vaccine manufacturers case   184
KPIs see Key Performance Indicators
Kragten, Ubald   199–201
KSFs see Key Success Factors

large companies   17–18, 33
Latin America   253
launch phase, innovation/product life cycle
      management   195
   see also product launching
leadership   16, 115, 117–18, 242, 245
   see also head of MI
Lean Sigma function   209
learning see organizational learning
legal aspects see PESTEL analysis
leverage, service areas   92–4
logistics   204, 208–9, 211, 212–13
long-term benefits of MI   247–50
Loozen, Rene   57–61
Lubrizol Corporation case   63–4
Luvata case   159–60

M&A see mergers & acquisitions
macroeconomic analysis   169, 211
MAMOS see Market Monitoring System
management
   innovation/product life cycle   189–202
   MI needs   176–7
   MI programs   117–18
   structured schemes   18
   support   181–5
   see also account management; leadership; supply chain
      management; top management
management conferences, Luvata case   159
manufacturing company case   198
market attractiveness analysis   169-70
market dynamics, Intelligence Scope   59
market entry
   mergers & acquisitions analysis   170-1
   value-chain analysis   246
Market Intelligence (MI)
   benefits   3–19, 25–6, 247–50
   decision point mapping   79–80
   definition   9–10
   drivers   3–19
   overview   18–19
   as a profession   21
market monitoring   91, 144–5
   big picture of   148–9
   content/context   150–2
   customer processes   186
   energy company case   143
   innovation/product life cycle management
      198–201
   purchasing   210
   strategic sourcing   212

strategy links   145, 146–54
   summary of types   155
   technology/people relationship   150
Market Monitoring System (MAMOS)   146, 155
market profiles   211
market segmentation   181–2
market share analysis   181–2
market signals   93, 145, 149
   continuous monitoring of   186
   delivery to decision-makers   153
   EWOS   154–5
   see also market monitoring
market simulation workshops   71, 72
market size analysis   181–2, 212
marketing   175–87
   ABB automation technologies   13
   Intelligence Culture   131, 133
   Intelligence Deliverables   89
   needs   176–8
   planning and management   177, 181–5
   process needs   178
   set-ups   27
   support   181–5
   Vopak liquid storage company   61
   see also sales
marketplace complexity   4–8
Marvik, Anders   229–32
maturity index, GIA MI framework   36–41
maturity levels
   trends   263
   World Class MI Roadmap   54–7
meaningful content, market monitoring   151
meaningful insight, Intelligence Process   77–86
measurement challenges
   customer satisfaction   248
   Intelligence Deliverables impact   258–9
   ROI for MI   243–4
medical equipment company case   182
meetings, internal MI network   123, 124
megatrends   5
   Cisco Systems case   73–5
   communicating results   75
   identification/prioritization   74
   impact assessment   74
Merck & Co. case   65–6, 128–9
mergers & acquisitions (M&A)   65, 170–1
MI see Market Intelligence
Microsoft SharePoint   104–6, 110, 112, 260
middle class growth, emerging economies   6–7
Middle East region   34, 253
mobile devices, intelligence portals   104, 109
   see also smartphones
mobile gaming industry analysis case   182
monitoring see market monitoring
multinational company case, divestment   246
"must know" information   143–4

national culture, Intelligence Culture based on   133
needs
    customer processes   176–80
    innovation/product life cycle management
        192–6
    supply chain management   207–210
needs analysis
    impact of MI   242
    importance   80–1
    Intelligence Process   78, 80–1
    Intelligence Scope   64, 67
    world class MI programs   223, 224
Net Promoter Score (NPS) system   248
networks
    Best Buy case   97–8
    building   97–8, 123–5
    Cintas   123–5
    external information sources   119–21
    internal   115, 121–5, 128
    personal information sources   115
    Statoil case   231
    workshops   227
    world class   128
"nice to know" information   143–4
Niederer, Daniel   12–15
North America   34–5
NPS (Net Promoter Score) system   248
Nycomed case   121

offshoring   119
oil company case   166–7
"on demand services"   91–2
    see also ad hoc projects
one-on-one interviews, needs analysis   67, 223
Open Innovation, DSM   199–201
operating environment, global organizations   4–5, 7
Operational Excellence control method   208
operational intelligence
    ABB automation technologies   13
    DSM Open Innovation case   200
opportunities   4, 6, 74
    see also Early Warning and Opportunity System;
        SWOT analysis
optimization
    cost base   245–6
    Intelligence Culture   133–7
    Intelligence Delivery   88–94
    Intelligence Organization   117–27
    market segmentation   182
Orange UK case   162–5
organization see Intelligence Organization
organizational culture   133
organizational learning   17
organizational-level awareness, MI   143–56
organizational-level engagement, Intelligence
        Culture   131–40

organizational-level standardization, Intelligence
        Process   257
organizational set-up see set-ups
Outotec case   153
outsourcing   119
    in-house resources versus   125–7
    Intelligence Process   257
    MI functions   42, 46, 48
    trends   263–4
ownership, MI leadership   117

paints and coatings company case   112
partner screening and analysis   197–8
partnerships, leaders   16
patents   194
peer-reviewed presentations   231
people
    impact generation   115–30
    importance of   18
    Intelligence Deliverables   95
    technology relationship   150
    see also teams
perceived ROI, MI   36–7
personal information source networks   115
personalized delivery   259
PESTEL analysis   166
Pfeffer, Troy   124–5
pharmaceutical company case   203
pilot versions, software   225
planning marketing and sales   177, 181–5
    see also strategic planning
Planning Process   158, 161–2, 169–71
political aspects see PESTEL analysis
portals see intelligence portals
portfolios see product portfolios
POs see purchase orders
post-launch phase, innovation/product life cycle
        management   195–6
potential customer identification case   185
power solutions company case   138–9
presentations, peer-reviewed   231
primary research
    Intelligence Deliverables   91
    Intelligence Process   78
    Intelligence Tools   104
process development   88–9
    see also Intelligence Process
procurement   204, 205–6, 207–8, 210–11
product development   88–90
product launching   246
    see also launch phase
product life cycle
    analytical support for stages   197–8
    description   191
    see also innovation and product life cycle
        management

product management
  description 191
  Intelligence Scope 65
product portfolios 87–99
profiles 93
  customer profiles 183
  market profiles 211
  strategic planning 171
programs
  deliverables' quality 88
  determining scope of 66–71
  development 227–39
  implementing 217–26
  MI as 10–15, 53
  organizing daily work 116–18
  purpose/target groups/focus areas 63–76
  world class 137, 215–66
Project Management Triangle 81
project services 91–2
promotional gear, Intelligence Culture 135
public company risk management 255
"pull" services see "push and pull" services
purchase orders (POs) 204, 206, 208
purchasing 203, 204–5, 207, 210
purpose determination, Intelligence Scope 63–76
"push and pull" services 90–1, 107–8, 144–5, 186

qualitative benefits of MI 247–50
quality factors, Intelligence Deliverables 88
questionnaires 233–8

R&D see research & development
radical innovations 191
random data, Intelligence Process 77–86
Randstad Netherlands case 71
rapid response research 82, 91
regional distribution
  Global Market Intelligence survey 2013
    24, 34–6
  trends 253–4
  see also geographical dimension
reports see analysis, reports
requests for information (RFIs) 207
requests for proposal (RFPs) 203, 206
requests for quotation (RFQs) 206
requisitions, purchasing 204, 208
research & development (R&D) 13, 27
research/researchers
  Intelligence Deliverables 91
  Intelligence Process 78, 82
  Intelligence Tools 104
  MI teams 120, 128–9
  multinational company case 246
resources 27–36
  bottleneck removal 81
  impact generation 115–30
  Statoil case 231

world class MI programs 225
  see also people; teams
respondent data, Global Market Intelligence
    survey 2013 22–4
retail company case 183–4
Rettig ICC case 178–80, 197
return on investment (ROI) 25–6, 241–7
  industry comparison 36–8, 49
  Key Intelligence Topics 67
  measurement challenges 243–4
revenue groups, budgets and 33
RFIs (requests for information) 207
RFPs (requests for proposal) 203, 206
RFQs (requests for quotation) 206
risk analysis, countries 211
risk management 159–60, 255
Roadmap see World Class MI Roadmap
ROI see return on investment
Royal Vopak liquid storage company 57–61
Russia
  ammonium bi-fluoride assessment case 84–5
  hydrofluoric acid market case 84–5
  industrial diesel engines market 170

SaaS see Software as a Service solutions
salaries, MI budgets 33–4
sales 175–87
  ABB automation technologies 13
  needs 176–8
  planning and management 177, 181–5
  set-ups 27
  support 181–5
  world class MI programs 224
  see also marketing
sales-driven companies, future orientation 71
sales leads monitoring 184–5
Sarbanes–Oxley Act 255
scale of topics, Intelligence Scope 68–9
scenario analysis 71, 72, 164, 167–8, 211
SCM see supply chain management
scope of MI professional roles 31–2
  see also Intelligence Scope
secondary information sources 78, 91
security features, software 107
segmentation of market 181–2
self-service access, software 108
senior management see top management
service areas, Intelligence Deliverables 88, 92–4, 95
Service Level Agreements (SLAs) 83
set-ups, MI 27–36
  B2B/B2C contrast 43–6
  outsourcing 126
  trends 264
  world class functions 39–40
share price performance, world class MI links
    244–5
SharePoint, Microsoft 104–6, 110, 112, 260

ship building projects case 185
signals see market signals
Six Sigma 208
size of companies, Global Market Intelligence
    survey 2013 23–4, 33–4
  see also large companies
skill sets, MI teams 119–21
SLAs (Service Level Agreements) 83
smaller companies, Global Market Intelligence
    survey 2013 24
smart delivery, intelligence portals 104
smartphones 260
  see also mobile devices
social aspects see PESTEL analysis
social media 8, 260
  collaboration and 152–4
  intelligence portals 109
  internal use of features 255
  market monitoring 145
"soft" contributions, MI 242, 243, 249
Software as a Service (SaaS) solutions 105, 106
software tools
  promoting 131
  selection 107–12
  world class MI programs 225
  see also intelligence portals
sourcing see data sourcing; strategic sourcing
sponsorship, MI 117, 230
standalone software 105–8
standardization, Intelligence Process 257
statistical analysis, forecasting 166
Statoil case 229–32
steering group appointment 118
stock market performance, world class MI links
    244–5
Stocks, Julian 178–80
storing intelligence 101–13
strategic analysis
  DSM Open Innovation case 200
  intelligence cycle 82
  "on demand services" 92
strategic planning 157–73
  challenges 157–60
  Intelligence Deliverables 165–73
  Lubrizol Corporation case 64
  MI set-ups 27
  themes for decision-makers 161
  topics demanding support 160–5
  world class levels 73
strategic sourcing 206–7, 209–10, 211–12
strategy
  ABB automation technologies 13–14
  implementing/formulating 146, 158
  market monitoring links 145, 146–54
  Statoil case 229–32
  taxonomy of company 151–2
strengths see SWOT analysis

structured management schemes 18
success indicators, world class MI programs 222–3
  see also Key Success Factors
supply chain management (SCM) 203–14
  functions 204–7
  Intelligence Deliverables 210–13
  Intelligence Scope 65
  MI needs 207–10
surveys, needs analysis 67
  see also Global Market Intelligence surveys;
    questionnaires
SWOT analysis, retail company case 183–4
synergies, cost base optimization 245–6

tactical activities, DSM Open Innovation case 200
tagging 151
target groups, Intelligence Scope 63–76
taxonomy of company 69, 151–2
teams 115, 118–19
  ad hoc projects 95
  continuous development 95
  corporate-level teams 263
  diversification 230
  Global Market Intelligence survey 2013 28–30,
    41–2, 48
  ideal skill sets 119–21
  IT company 17
  Merck & Co. case 128–9
  organizing services 90–2
  Statoil case 229–4
  world class MI 41–2, 48, 224
technical tools integration 262
technology
  Intelligence Tools 260–1
  people relationship 150
  strategic planning 166–7
  see also information technology; PESTEL analysis
text mining 112, 261
threats, complex marketplace 4, 6
  see also SWOT analysis
time constraints, bottleneck removal 81
time factors
  future orientation and 147–8
  Intelligence Deliverables 45
time horizon
  EWOS 155
  Intelligence Scope 64, 71
time savings 15–17, 249
tools see Intelligence Tools
top management
  B2B/B2C contrast 44, 46, 48
  Intelligence Culture 132
  Statoil case 230
  Vopak liquid storage company 61
  world class MI 42–3, 224
topics see Key Intelligence Topics
trend analysis, product life cycle 197

trends 5–6, 253–66
  Intelligence Culture 264–5
  Intelligence Deliverables 257–9
  Intelligence Organization 262–4
  Intelligence Process 255–7
  Intelligence Scope 253–5
  Intelligence Tools 260–2
  world class MI companies 41–3
  see also megatrends
trust 120, 128–9, 239

user groups 141–214
  innovation/product life cycle management 189–202
  Intelligence Deliverables 89, 95
  Intelligence Scope 64–6, 72
  marketing/sales/account management 175–87
  organizational-level awareness 143–56
  software selection 109
  strategic planning 157–73
  supply chain management 203–14
  value chain 253
utilization stage, Intelligence Process 79

value-chain analysis 210, 246
value chains
  global organizations 5
  Intelligence Scope 253–4
  Key Intelligence Topics 68
vision, DSM Open Innovation case 199
visualized output, Intelligence Deliverables 258
Vopak liquid storage company 57–61

war games 71, 72, 168
weaknesses see SWOT analysis
websites, Statoil case 230
wellness sector see health and wellness sector

Western Europe, Global Market Intelligence
  survey 2013 34–5
wikis 261
wind turbine manufacturer case 185
workshops 94
  benchmarking 227, 238
  continuous development 72
  future orientation 71
  needs analysis 67
  procurement 211
  strategic planning 160, 164, 167–8, 171
  world class MI programs 223
world class companies/programs 38–43
  attributes 39–40
  developing 215–66
  implementing 217–26
  key findings 48
  stock market performance links 244–5
  trends in 41–3
world class levels
  Intelligence Culture 137–9
  Intelligence Deliverables 94–5
  Intelligence Organization 127–9
  Intelligence Process 83–5
  Intelligence Scope 72–5
  Intelligence Tools 111–12
  working towards 226, 228
World Class MI Roadmap 51–140, 218–22
  benchmarking 228
  Intelligence Deliverables 87–99
  Intelligence Organization 115–28
  Intelligence Process 77–86
  Intelligence Scope 63–76
  Intelligence Tools 101–13
  investment reasons 243
  Key Success Factors 53–62